ASIA

To San Francisco and New York

Tokyo

elhi
Katmandu
our   Agra   Tiger Tops   Calcutta   Hong Kong
Jaipur

AROUND
THE
WORLD
AND OTHER
PLACES

Ilka Chase

AROUND THE WORLD AND OTHER PLACES

Photographs by
Norton Brown

DOUBLEDAY & COMPANY, INC. GARDEN CITY, NEW YORK 1970

AROUND
THE
WORLD
AND OTHER
PLACES

Chapter 1 NORTH AFRICA

I do not quibble over the premise that dog is man's best friend.
At times it proves falacious but man being a species in need of
friends does well to overlook minor lapses. After all, an occasional
nip, a missing heel . . . who complains when they are stacked
up against soulful eyes, wagging tails, and the receptive intelligence which if admonished to stay in the car leaps nimbly
from the window and heads straight for the oncoming traffic?

As friends yes, warts and all, but as travel agents? It is here
that reason begins to sway. Yet that has been my experience:
our dogs are in the travel business. Possibly unwittingly but
effectively nonetheless.

They hung out their shingle on a bright autumnal day when
we were engaged in nothing more untoward than a casual stroll
over broad neighboring lawns, down a meandering driveway,
past a low house at the water's edge and on beyond to a semi-
wild stretch of beach.

As we approached the house three small dogs darted out.
At that moment they were total strangers. I have since learned
their names. A minute Yorkshire terrier, Twiggy, two minuter
poodles Cindy and Pumpkin. I like small dogs within reason.
Belinda Berry Brown, our black dachshund, belongs in the small
dog category but one must acknowledge that several small dogs

together sound like nothing so much as the cacophony of Allen's Alley in the great days of radio when that peerless commentator on the human scene Mr. Fred Allen was at his zenith.

Anyway, with the confrontation on the sunlit lawn of the three householders and Belinda and Thor our Weimaraner, all hell broke loose. So much so that presently the lady of the house emerged.

"How do you do," I said hurriedly. "I'm sorry to disturb you. Please think nothing of it. Belinda's perfectly friendly and Thor's the most gentle creature who breathes." This last was true. Belinda's friendship is an off-again on-again affair.

"Oh," said the lady, "so the big fellow belongs to you. He's a beautiful dog but I *have* been a little nervous sometimes when he's come over because of the small ones."

"Never fear. He wouldn't hurt a fly."

"I'm glad. I don't mind him eating their food or when he takes their toys and drinks their water, it's just that he *is* big."

It's a little difficult to know what to say when confronted with the statement that a being one dearly loves is an ipso-facto, de-jure, and bona-fide thief. Unfortunately I knew that Madam spoke the truth. It's been going on for a long time and has over the years cost a not inconsiderable sum making good on filched stuffed rabbits, monkeys, rubber balls, and on one memorable occasion a whole baked ham from a stranger's windowsill. Later on there was the matter of a standing rib roast stolen from the present lady but that's another story.

Despite the donnybrook she seemed amiable. Pointing in the direction of a couple of distant houses, she asked if I lived in one of them. "No," I said, pointing in my turn, "we live over there."

"Oh," she said, "then you must be Ilka Chase." I allowed this was the case. "Won't you come in?" Threading our way through the carpet of milling canines we entered the house. I learned that my hostess's name was Jablonski. "Wanda Ja-blonski." She spoke of my writing and occasional television appearances and I asked what she did. "I'm in oil," she said. Having noticed several pictures and bright posters on the wall I thought to myself, Well, it's an odd way of putting it but I suppose she paints.

She does not. When Miss Jablonski says oil she isn't referring to pigments on a palette. She means that gorgeous gooey black stuff in the earth which the Rockefellers and several Texans, Oklahomans, and Saudi Arabians among others have found so deliciously compatible.

She knows a great deal about it and is the editor-publisher of a paper called *Petroleum Intelligence Weekly.* With a small New York staff and assistants and associates in many countries she disperses information that is as accurate as diligent research and trained reporting can make it. Since she sometimes states facts that those concerned would sometimes prefer to have remain unknown she is not necessarily beloved by her subscribers but viscous potentates around the globe read *P.I.W.* with the same dedication the entertainment world brings to *Variety.*

In the course of that first and many subsequent meetings we became friends as well as neighbors and early in our friendship we told her of the plans we were working out with Pan American Airways to fly with them around the world. "And," I added, "this time we hope to get to the Middle East. We had intended going in 1967 after we left East Africa but at that moment the Arab-Israeli war broke out so all bets were off."

"The Middle East!" She was enthusiastic. "That's great. You must go to Saudi Arabia. I'll arrange it."

Up until that moment Saudi Arabia had not entered my husband's or my mind, let alone our conversation, but as has been so truly stated, there is a first time for everything.

"Fortunately," continued the oil queen, "Suliman Olayan is in New York. He's an Arab, an extraordinary fellow. I'll have you meet him and he can arrange everything."

In due course this occurred and we did go to Saudi Arabia, one of the other places mentioned in the title of this book, and it all came about through our dogs meeting Wanda's dogs, which is why I say they served as travel agents.

My first encounter with Mr. Olayan occurred over cocktails in Miss Jablonski's apartment where I learned that Arabs, when in a foreign country, courteously abide by its customs even though this may be against their religion. Mr. Olayan, lifting his glass, expressed himself charmed that we were thinking of a visit to his native land and as good luck would have it Sheikh Kamal Adham, King Faisal's brother-in-law was in New York. They were friends. Would we care to dine and meet him? We would indeed.

A few evenings later Wanda, Norton and I found ourselves in a hotel suite in the company of our host Mr. Olayan businessman extraordinary; a most amiable and efficient lieutenant of his, Mr. Emil Bishuty, and the brother of the Queen of Saudi Arabia, Sheikh Kamal Adham. Sheikh Adham is a remarkably personable man. I should imagine in his fifties with blue eyes, short wavy gray hair, a clear smooth skin and over his tall frame a gentle layer of upholstery testifying to the good and successful life.

As it happened a large part of the conversation turned on health and Wanda said later, "Norton, it's great you're a doctor, you can't help but be a smash hit in Saudi Arabia. All Arabs are hypochondriacs. They adore talking about their symptoms."

Fortunately King Faisal and I, at different periods, had had similar internal disturbances. The king remained in ignorance of this fascinating fact but as far as his subjects whom we met that evening were concerned it created a bond and we were invited to come to Saudi Arabia. An audience with his majesty was implied. Jidda was suggested as our point of arrival but we would be welcome to visit any other part of the peninsula we might be interested in seeing. On learning there was an area known as the Hofuf Oasis I said I wanted to go there. Hofuf in Arabia and Katmandu in Nepal—who would not want to see places with such enticing names?

Thanks to another knowledgeable lady, Ruth Sheldon Knowles, author of *The Greatest Gamblers,* a book about the oil industry and a friend of Wanda Jablonski, I had a preview of the moon-like area surrounding Hofuf, the south eastern section of the country known as the Empty Quarter—or Rub al-Kahli. Through her intercession Mr. David Finnie of the Mobil Oil Company in New York arranged to show us an extraordinary film, *Arabian Sands,* based on a book by Wilfred Thesiger, the gaunt Englishman who spent many years in the desert. On one of his expeditions he nearly lost his life in pursuit of a means to rid the country of the destructive locust plagues. The photography in the film was beautiful and the vast desert had an eerie and desolate allure.

Most of our other preparations for the journey were more prosaic and consisted of long hours in conference with Pan American personnel and now and then our picturesque old native guide, the American Express Company.

When the airline had booked us as far as Katmandu a glance at the map showed that to go forward was very little if any longer than to go back. We would be able to return to our beloved Hong Kong, drop in on Tokyo, and land in San Francisco with a whole extra day at our disposal courtesy of the international date line.

When I proposed this little scheme to our good friend Jane Kilbourne head of the Womens Division of Pan Am she looked me in the eye and said, "You're crazy."

"Why?"

"I never heard of such a thing and I'm in the business. That's a terrible trip. I mean *long.* It'll kill you." She was nearly right, but for the wrong reason. It was the victuals that occasionally did me in rather than the travel per se although at times that was rough. But what I say is, If you're going to go, *go.*

To anyone starting out to spend two and a half months traveling around the world, an invaluable aid is Pan Am's World Guide,
Travel Facts About One Hundred Nineteen Countries. It's a chunky
book to carry by air but the editors obviously don't expect you
to gobble all one hundred nineteen in one bite. Just bone up
on the places you're going to and make a few notes. It deals
with currency, climate, hotels, shops . . . informative and helpful.

My own advice, which I seldom follow although I know it
to be sound, is not to do a lot of shopping when planning a
protracted trip. Packing is ruinous to clothes and you do much
better to take what you already have and save your money
for foreign exotica. Be strong! Say to yourself things like, This
will be new in Katmandu. How can this harass the people of
Paris? My suit will be at home in Rome. Clothes of this kidney
will go well in Sydney. Saves a lot of money.

I only semi-heeded this sage counsel and the new clothes I
bought were disastrous in the sense that for the first half of the
trip they were wildly wrong for the climates in which we found
ourselves. North Africa in early spring . . . all that desert . . .
I thought it would be hot. Ha!

When we left New York the city was just recovering from
the effects of a crippling blizzard and although we did not get
snow neither did we get much surcease from the cold throughout
the whole first half of our journey.

We set out early on a crisp morning in February. Having
flown to Europe many times at night and suffered fatigue for
anywhere from twenty-four to forty-eight hours as a result we
had decided this time to fly by day.

Before boarding I asked the man at the Pan Am counter
whether breakfast would be served. He consulted his chart.
"Continental breakfast, hot lunch." It sounded like meat loaf.
In reality it meant caviar and hors d'oeuvres, onion soup, a
choice of six entrées, vegetables, cheese, fruit, pastry, wine,
champagne, coffee, and liqueurs.

I would suggest to the airlines that they announce their culinary plans at takeoff so passengers may pace themselves.

Despite knowing the world is round it is surprising how quickly night encroaches when one is flying eastward. The brilliant sunshine of 9 A.M. faded so swiftly I thought we were flying through a storm. We were not. "The bright day is done, and we are for the dark."

Halfway across the Atlantic the captain announced that there was a good chance we would be landing at Le Bourget instead of Orly as we might be late and 11:30 P.M. is the deadline for planes flying over Paris. Actually we came in ahead of time but it was Le Bourget nonetheless.

We took a cab to the Orly Hilton—in the event the airline pays—and the bright wood fire blazing in the hearth in the lobby was a cheering sight. Our room was large and there were flowers from the management. How nice. We ordered a couple of drinks and two chicken sandwiches. Not nice. Pressed chicken and stale bread. We had wondered if we would feel cheated, being that close to Paris and not going there, but our supposition that an airport being so impersonal never has the flavor of the city it serves proved correct. The wretched midnight snack confirmed it.

Nor is a night at an airport cheap. The inedible sandwiches and a couple of drinks, our room and two continental breakfasts came to forty-five dollars. We were shaken but staying at the hotel if one must make an early morning flight is more convenient than driving all the way into the city and out again and depending, obviously, on the city hotel probably costs about the same. Glancing at the bill I was happy to have lifted a DO NOT DISTURB sign and a shoe-polishing cloth although seeing me do it my dear husband had murmured, "Let us filch what we can in this harsh world." Those items are *meant* to be filched.

While waiting for our flight to Tangier we were diverted by a quartet of hippies who were to be our traveling companions.

One boy was lean with a somewhat pitted face and frizzy black hair. He wore a suit of violet corduroy, a shirt printed with violet and green flowers and a short cape tossed back over one shoulder. He was carrying a copy of *Playboy*. His bird had skinny shanks encased in black tights, a dress covering her skeletal frame which was more mini sweater than skirt, masses of heavy beads, a leather coat, and an orange felt hat pulled down over her lion's mane hair. I was surprised by the absence of a guitar.

These strolling players were accompanied by a more conventionally dressed couple. The girl in fact seemed almost mousy but she had a sweet little face and gazed lovingly upon her lad. One had to admit they were more colorful than the drab chunky Russian woman with a wart on the tip of her nose who sat across the aisle from us.

The flight was about an hour and a half and in Tangier the day was bright and cloudy, windy and chilly. Driving away from the airport we passed immense carpets of iris growing wild in the fields. Our destination was El Minzah Hotel in the heart of town. It is old-fashioned but comfortable and our roomy accommodations overlooked the bay. We had been met at the airport by a representative of the American Express, Abdullah, who announced that our guide, Hadji, would be appearing at two o'clock. He arrived punctually, a tall pleasant-faced man of advancing years wearing a fez and djellabah, the long woolen robe, the universal dress of the Arabian male, although it is made of different fabrics and goes by different names from one country to the next.

Three Arabian words we learned immediately. Four counting Insha' allah which means God willing—the three were medina, casbah and souk. Medina means town. Casbah is fort and souk is shop. Most of the souks are located in the old medinas and the casbah may or may not be in the same neighborhood. The medina of Tangier is picturesque and although comparatively small it set the pattern for all the others we would see afterward.

Narrow alleys wind between tiny shops that are for the most

part no more than three-sided stalls. The medinas are noisy. One is jostled by the crowds forcing their way along the alleys like a river between narrow banks and invigorated by the sights and sounds and pungent smells. Like their men the women too were robed, and in their gray or brown djellabahs they looked like ambulatory sacks. There were many veils, mostly black worn just over the mouth or over the nose as well so that often only the eyes were visible peering out between the veil and the head covering that was drawn down over the brow.

The flower souks bloomed with iris and freesia, jonquils, carnations, and lilies. In the food souks bags were bursting with every sort of grain; with beans and rice and what I took to be curry. Some was curry but some was henna for hair and fingertips and the charcoal-colored powder was kohl for the eyelids. I bought a little and a slim ivory stick with which to stroke it on but my ability at self-adornment has been weakened by the more easily applied pastes and tubes of the cosmetic manufacturers at home. With the kohl I succeeded only in smearing myself so badly around the eyes that when the wonder of me burst upon him Norton exclaimed, "Good God who gave you the shiner?"

The vegetables, greens and tomatoes and oranges and the small native tangerines were delicious. A bin of glistening olives tempted me and I wanted to buy a bag but when I asked the price the merchant asked Hadji if we were tourists. When he said we were the man smiled. "If the lady wants some olives I am happy to give them to her," and he did, wrapping them in a cornucopia of gray blue paper. I was touched by so unaccustomed and generous a gesture but presently the oil began to leak through and we had to throw them away before they ruined our clothes. There were many tailor shops all of which seemed well supplied with apprentices, small boys who stood a few feet from the tailors holding taut in their hands and weaving back and forth the coarse threads the men used for sewing.

Hadji told us that parents sent them to work rather than to school because if they went to school before they were seven the parents would have to pay the tuition. After the age of seven the state pays but education appears not to be compulsory or if it is the truant officers are lax for school-age children worked or played or ran at large in the streets wherever we went.

It sounds hard-hearted but it is wiser to ignore winsome urchins who sidle up to you murmuring, "Good morning, lady, how you do?" Once acknowledged they harass you for the next half hour trying to lead you to places where you have already been or to souks you have no desire to patronize. Hadji led us to one we *were* interested in. More a conventional shop and considerably more sumptuous than others we had seen it sold carpets and leather goods and brass. We were served the cloyingly sweet mint tea which is the passion and national drink of Morocco and, hoping to overcome any slight to the proprietor which my not drinking it might entail, I said I would buy a brass tray. All Morocco glitters with them and they are authentic. When the merchant gave it a whack it was indeed as sounding brass. I didn't hear any tinkling cymbals although under pressure he probably could have produced those too but the sound of brass like that of crystal is not to be faked.

The price of the tray was five dollars. Remembering our friend, Dr. Charles Poindexter, who has a house in Marrakech and who had dined with us in New York shortly before our departure, I laughed airily and said, "I'll give you a dollar fifty."

"Thirty percent of the asking price, that's what you must offer," Charles had said. "Haggle a bit." I am deplorable at haggling. "Then if you really want the article come up to fifty or sixty percent." I tried horsing around as per instructions.

"Three fifty."

"Five dollars," said the man.

"All right. Five dollars." I retrieved face by adding firmly, "But that must include shipping."

"Shipping included."

In one souk an old Arab had fallen asleep between his sacks of grain. When I lifted my camera to take his picture there were shouts of anger and a furious flailing of arms from two young men in a neighboring butcher stall. We knew that many Arabs do not want their pictures taken and had the merchant been a woman I would not have done it but I thought that a quick snap of a sleeping man would not do him irreparable damage.

Hadji was not of this opinion. "Someone takes my picture, they might throw it away, it would get dirty and be trampled on." This he felt would be insulting, injurious to his person.

"But you have traveled, Hadji. You must have had to have a passport photo?"

"That is different. It never leaves me." He pulled out his wallet and showed it to us. We knew he had traveled because he told us he had been to Mecca and been cleansed and that was why he was called Hadji. He had made the hadj or pilgrimage. In the old days he would have worn an orange turban as a sign. His wife had gone too and they were both, he assured us, extremely honest. "Now when I take my clients into a shop the mark-up is very small." He sighed. Before the hadj perhaps he had been a merry rogue getting a rakeoff on the profits derived from tourists.

"In the old days I used to smoke and drink and take clients to night clubs. No more."

Life sounded a little Spartan. "But wasn't it more fun the other way Hadji?"

"More fun, yes. More better this way."

Hadji is very sure of the after life. I am not. Should it turn out that I am wrong and there is an individual consciousness in another world subsequent to this one I shall, perforce, accept it. I shall also be *very* surprised.

Tea, preferable to the excessively sweet beverage beloved of Arabs, is to be found at Porte a pleasant tearoom in the Rue Goya. A less pleasing spot is the Café de Paris up the street a way from Hotel El Minzah. It is the roost of transvestites and flint-eyed harpies who sit at the small round tables icily appraising any newcomers to the community.

They appraised us as we returned to the hotel where as I was trying to type up some notes my dear husband distracted me by behaving like the juggler of Notre Dame displaying his little tricks before the Virgin.

"I have a stop watch should you need it." He holds it out.

"Thank you, honey, that's very thoughtful. I have one too but I didn't bring it as I couldn't imagine any use for it on this trip."

Tap tap tap on the typewriter. A moment of silence on the part of my prestidigitator as he paws through his treasures.

"I brought my good flashlight too. See." Demonstration. I am dazzled by its brilliance.

"Let's hope that somewhere along the way the electricity will go off" I say cooperatively and return to my typewriter.

"I've got my compass too." Don't I know! He is never without it. Tappety tap tap.

"And my thermometer. Would you like to know what the temperature of this room is?"

"I'd be fascinated."

"It's seventy."

"Bully for it." I cover the typewriter. I know when I'm licked.

In any event it was nearly time to leave for the restaurant in the casbah that had been recommended to us as a colorful place to dine. We were driven to an alley where we got out and groped our way through the dimness until we came to a flight of stairs leading up to the Marhaba Palace. The restaurant itself was a large square high-ceilinged room surrounded by scalloped archways supported on slender columns inlaid with black and white marble. There was a great deal of green and white tiling and elaborate carved plaster of intricate design with borders of Arabian script. It was romantic and quite possibly authentic but perhaps because we feared to appear naïve we considered it a little labored, something laid on for the tourist trade which that night consisted of Dr. and Mrs. Brown.

The person who had recommended it was Abdullah of the American Express and he had said truly enough that it would be quiet. It was not, however, silent, for seated on a low square platform in the middle of the room four men in green and blue silk robes strummed musical instruments. We sat on a cushioned banquette along the wall eating from low tables. I'm afraid we gave way to some unseemly laughter induced by so much grandeur lavished upon only us but the food when it came was good and certainly ample.

A thick soup, lamb en brochette and for the first time Pastilla a light flaky pastry enclosing finely minced chicken. It was the best we had in North Africa. Elsewhere pastry and filling were so sweet we thought they had brought the dessert by mistake but that is the Arab palate. Following the Pastilla the Couscous arrived. I had been looking forward to Couscous mistakenly believing it to be composed of rice. It is not. It is made of semolina a grain I find incompatible. The dessert was apple sauce, a simple dish I have fancied since childhood. (Apple sauce, plain cup custard, and rice pudding. When well made they are delicious. My mother was not noted for her culinary skill. Editing American, British, and French *Vogue* for many years took most of her time but when she turned her hand to it she was the rice-pudding Queen. Rich smooth creamy, delicately browned on top—I have never tasted its equal.)

As we were finishing our meal a young man got up from the platform came down in front of us and started to dance. He was a skinny little creature with a wreath on his head, a swirling skirt and a green garland around his nonproductive loins. He engaged in wild hula gyrations while Norton and I struggled to keep straight faces. "I think," I said, "that you are supposed to leap up maddened and seduce him before my very eyes." The doctor made a coarse noise.

It was past eleven, in Tangier the shank of the evening, so

we decided to visit Michel's Bar and extend the greetings sent
him by Dr. Poindexter in New York. We asked for coffee but
anything that innocuous was not served. "You're early in any
case," said Michel. "Come in around four A.M. We'll have come
to life."

We thanked him and on the advice of our cab driver went to
a bleak little bar where the coffee was good. A television set up
in a corner poured out a flood of rock and an unveiled woman,
we could not tell whether she was Moroccan, Spanish, Egyptian,
or what, belted out tuneless songs. She was joined by three
men whom she didn't seem to care for and indeed her expression
was one of mistrust of the whole enterprise. We decided she was
a better critic than she was an artist and having finished our
coffee repaired to the Koutubia Palace, a night club with seating
arrangements similar to those of the Marhaba Palace—banquettes
and low tables but this time the place was jammed. The clientele
was mostly American and no Arab was to be seen with the exception of the the orchestra and the artists when they finally
appeared about half-past twelve.

These ladies were extraordinary. We were doubly dazzled by
them having been told we would be witnessing a male ballet.
Transvestism is very big in many Arab countries. For the first
dance or two we were absolutely bug-eyed. How *could* they be
men? So small boned, so slender, so supple? As it turned out
they weren't. Stag night would come next week.

Never before had we seen such pectoral, abdominal, and pelvic
activity. Such bumping, grinding, twirling, whirling, and side slipping. They did it on foot, they did it on buttocks and they did
it flat on their backs on the floor. I assumed the performance
was designed to rouse every man in the room to erotic frenzy
and although we witnessed no untoward actions, possibly it did.
However, I should think such goings on more likely to induce
total impotence. Some cooperation from the supine partner is desirable but lowering oneself onto anything that animated might
well arouse sheer panic in the male rather than anything else.

Where would he aim? How could he land? With all that wild toing and froing might not something snap?

When it was over, shaken by exhibitions of skill beyond our ken we were too exhausted to return to Michel's and staggered back to the hotel instead.

The next day presented a sharp contrast. The morning was sparkling and driving out to Cap Spartel, a pleasant excursion from town, we passed fields glinting white and gold, orange and blue like lovely mille fleurs tapestries. In one field two camels rested with their legs folded under them. Their keeper invited me to mount one. Once aboard a person may be toplofty and serene but holding on as the beast unfolds to its full height and afterward creaks down is no small feat. Also my technique was rusty. I had not mounted a camel since 1962 when we were in Egypt. I never have been much of an equestrienne and I am still less a camelarienne.

Once disembarked from my ship of the desert we went on to Cap Spartel that little northwest fillip of the continent of Africa. The famed lighthouse was built in 1864 and from a cliff above it one has a marvelous sweeping view of the Mediterranean and the Atlantic Ocean. The magnificent beach is rarely used for swimming however even in hot weather for the tides and currents are treacherous. A boy and two donkeys admired the spectacle with us and it was peaceful and beautiful except for the mindless caterwauling of a radio from a nearby café.

Less than a mile from the Cape are the Caves of Hercules, where presumably the Greek hero sojourned after setting up his two pillars in the Strait of Gibraltar to show the western limits of his journey. He was involved in one of those formidable labors, this one stealing the cattle of Geryon. Actually the Arab name for Morocco, El Maghreb el Aqsa, means the Far West.

One of the caves is a large dark romantic grotto with a great jagged opening from which one watches the waves come rushing in, hurl themselves upon the rocks and retreat hissing and foaming, the jets of spume rising, curving, and falling in never-ending repetition. As caves go this one is about perfect for it boasts a fresh-water well so that mushrooms, speleologists, or partisans hiding from the enemy could survive there for an indefinite period.

What normally transpires within the subterranean cavern is more practical than poetic. For centuries millstones have been quarried and shaped there and carried out to be sold all over the countryside.

Returning to the city we strolled along the Avenue d'Espagne, a broad boulevard curving above the harbor. It is lined with shops on one side and on the other veiled women perch along the balustrade like birds along a telephone wire.

We also walked through the palace of the former Sultan. Built by the Portuguese in 1440 it was inhabited until 1880 but other than a decorative courtyard it is of little interest except for one baffling fact. Nearly all the buildings we saw were designed for a hot climate: thick walls faced with marble and countless archways opening onto patios and courtyards. In the hottest summer months they must be cool and inviting but northern Morocco has four seasons, not so clearly differentiated as ours perhaps yet our experience was that their springtime is not only chilly, it can be downright cold. True, there were palm trees and flowers in February and the marvel was that they weren't pinched by frost.

The chambers of the palaces, the courts of the mosques, are glacial and the greatest blessing north Moroccans can enjoy, regardless of what they feel they owe to Allah, is steam heat. I am sure it is available in great quantities behind the dazzling white walls of a villa the inhabitants point to with respect since it is the property of the oh so rich American lady, Miss Barbara Hutton.

Adjoining the palace is a large bright restaurant with walls of glass overlooking the sea recently erected for the tourist trade and we went there to drink hot coffee and warm ourselves up. By now Hadji and we were on friendly terms and he was curious about us.

"Where you live?"

"New York."

"Manhattan?"

"Yes."

"Many Italians live there."

"That's right."

"Radio City in the middle."

"Of the Italians?"

He looked at me a moment then a grin started slowly spreading into a wide guffaw. What a splendid joke! Ah, those Americans, true wits!

We lunched at the hotel where the food was good and I spent part of the afternoon hemming washcloths. I am aware this hardly sounds like something you travel to Morocco to do but it was necessary. Like a fool I had forgotten the bitter lesson learned every time we go abroad. There are no washcloths in Europe. There are none in Africa either. Even clean sophisticated rich people do not use them and how they manage I do not know. A sponge has virtues but not when it comes to your ears. Just try it! In lieu of ready-made cloths I bought some small sleazy Turkish towels—they were all the souks afforded—cut them into quarters and hemmed them.

It was a real pleasure to leave my lowly chore to go and call upon the Hubrechts. We had met Peggy Hubrecht's brother in New York. "You must look up my sister when you get to Tangier," he said. "She and Dan live there." He had written to her and given us a letter. When I telephoned she said, "We have just this minute got back from Marrakech. We've been spending a few days with Boul de Breteuil. I'm dressing as we have to go out at seven-thirty but come along at six-thirty and have a drink."

That sounded pleasant in any event but it was also a fortuitous coincidence. When we got to Marrakech Norton and I would be staying with the Comtesse de Breteuil as paying guests and it would be nice to learn something about her and about the house.

The Hubrechts live on the Vielle Montagne, one of the attractive residential quarters of Tangier. They gave us their address but it was no great help. Our driver was a Spanish-speaking Arab and although I have always understood that the Arabs invented arithmetic the mysteries of the printed number had not seeped down to our man nor the fact that there was a neighborhood called Vielle Montagne.

Our Spanish being sparse Norton and I resorted to pantomime. Montagne was not too hard. Arms and hands upraised and joined together. A mountain, what else? Now for Vielle. We acted like dotards, bent over, exhausted, all but slavering. I shook as one palsied. "Vieux. Antico. *Old* for God's sake." In the end art triumphed. We drew up at the Hubrechts' door with a flourish just as two lissom young English gentlemen were taking their departure.

Peggy Hubrecht is English, her husband Dutch although his manner and speech seemed to us as English as his wife's. Dan Hubrecht was an interesting man. His family had been Dutch sugar planters in Surabaya and he had lived for many years in Indonesia, in fact until Sukarno nationalized the sugar industry. When they were obliged to leave he had served as an adviser for sugar interests in many parts of the world.

Recently he had been feeling very chipper as he had been offered and accepted a fine position with an American-British combine only to learn that very day that due to some sort of collision with the anti-trust laws the deal was off. We hoped sincerely that it would get back on the tracks again and possibly it has.

Like Norton, Dan Hubrecht is left-handed and like him a gadgeteer. He had a catalogue from England and every device in it was designed for south paws. My loved one was entranced and further diverted when he was shown a drawing, the back view of a nude. The modeling was good and I thought the caliber of the sketch as well as the subject matter was its attraction but no. Dan found it intriguing because the artist was left-handed as was indicated by the way the fine lines forming the shadows were sketched. A right-handed artist would have had them going from upper right to lower left. These were reversed. By such simple pleasures are bonds of friendship forged.

In fact we were all so congenial that the Hubrechts insisted we go on with them to the cocktail party that was being given by young Mr. Hopkins who lived in Tangier although he was a member of the distinguished Pembroke family of England. David Herbert was there, an old friend of Cecil Beaton, photographer and scenic designer de luxe who is an old friend of mine. Also there were two American couples—a Mr. and Mrs. McGowan from Atlanta, Georgia, and New Orleans and friends of theirs. They were amused when they saw Norton and me. "Oh," they said, "we have just this minute returned from East Africa. We were on safari with Jane and Digby Tatham Warter and your book has the place of honor on the living-room table." The Tatham Warters are the couple I wrote about in *The Varied Airs of Spring,* a book that deals largely with our own photographic safari the last time we were in East Africa.

Around nine-thirty we left the party to dine at Lilly's Parade Bar. The bar is barlike and reverberates to the basso profundo voice of its owner. She made us comfortable and introduced us to Adolpho de Velasco, a young Spaniard who is making a name for himself in designing caftans. He was attired in tight black pants and a black turtle-neck sweater with a gold chain and medallion around his neck. *Muy elegante.* Among his clientele he already numbered the Duchess of Windsor so we felt we had not far to go.

One of the outs about travel is that the moment you have established an amiable relationship nine times out of ten it is promptly broken off. This was the case with our nice Hubrechts. The next day we left Tangier on our way to Fes. It was a chilly morning, 68° by Dr. Brown's thermometer and the sky was overcast. Our driver was Amidou. He was in his forties, not bad looking and with teeth of varying hue: gold, beige, brown, black, even one or two white. He had never gone to school—"School in head," he said, but had learned French working in French factories and English working for the United States Army. His lack of education would not have mattered so much but he was stupid and we suspected a little deaf as well. Still he had virtues. He could drive, he was agreeable and although his French and English were execrable they straddled Arabic, no mean advantage from our point of view.

The road was excellent and the traffic with the exception of an occasional truck virtually nil.

We drove through the provincial hillside towns of Tetuan and Chechaouen and through a fertile valley where three Berber women in dresses of lime green and flowered pink obligingly posed with me for their pictures.

The Berbers are one of the ancient races of the world and their home is the land along the south shore of the Mediterranean from Egypt to Morocco. Unlike the nomad Arabs with whom they share the enormous territory they are farmers and townspeople. Many of them are brunette but blonds among them are not unusual—we saw several blond curly haired children. Their religious beliefs are liberal, the women do not go veiled and the clothes they wear are clear and brilliant, splashing the countryside with color. Passing them along the road with the car radio playing flamenco music was like an ambulatory fiesta.

Around half-past five in the afternoon we arrived in Fes, one of the four capitals of Morocco the others being Marrakech, Meknès and Rabat. Today that is the accepted spelling but it used to be Fez and was the original home of the red felt flower pots worn by all Islam with the exception of Turkey where they were banned by Kemal Ataturk. When Norton and I visited the village of Gloggnitz in Austria in 1959 we were surprised to learn it is now the world manufacturing center for that particular millinery.

Although the town gave the headgear its name the word fez means pickax. According to legend Prince Idris second decided when only a lad of fifteen to establish his capital on the banks of the River Sebou. Wishing to give an example to the workmen he himself set to with a will helping to build the walls. Touched by his youthful zeal the patriotic workers took up a collection and presented their sovereign with a gold and silver fez. According to another source while digging the foundations they came upon a 60-pound fez in the earth and *that* gave the city its name. When Idris died in 828 his capital was already well established.

Arriving there more than eleven hundred years later Dr. and Mrs. Brown drove to the Hotel Palais Jamai where an absolutely delirious confusion over the matter of rooms was under way. The reception desk was small and set in a tiny vestibule and around it milled outraged clients struggling to get the accommodations they had reserved and which had been for the most part already paid for. We joined the clamor. We showed our voucher. "Yes, yes," said the distraught clerk, "I know you've paid, I have your names down . . . right here, you may see . . . but only for the nineteenth. Not the seventeenth and eighteenth."

The clerk summons an assistant clerk and extricating ourselves from the melee we follow him as he shows us what is available. What is available are six ignoble holes. Tiny little rooms on the lower garden with no light, no place to set a bag and token baths.

We rout out Amidou. "Amidou, tell them we wish to see the boss." The boss arrives, the most amiable of men as hopelessly confused as his staff but he at least has the power to act. At this point I turn a bit starchy. "I write travel books," I say. "They are read by *thousands* . . ."

"Hundreds of thousands" says the doctor. Why stint?

"Yes! Hundreds of thousands, and supposing I say this is a crummy hotel? No human *soul* will come."

The death knell chimes in. "No human soul, ever." The manager accepts this gambit in the spirit in which it is offered and gives us a conspiratorial wink. "My best room," he says, "is still left. It was the vizier's room when the hotel was a palace. It shall be yours. It is reserved but the other people shall go elsewhere."

Delighted by the success of our blackmail we smile warmly but Allah looks after his own. The clerk pipes up. "The other people," he says, "have just arrived. They are already in the room."

Ah well, then the next best which as a matter of fact was rather picturesque—pretty tiles—not uncomfortable and with an adequate bath. Our windows overlooked the garden courtyard which was charming and at night I lay awake listening to the sounds so typical of the Arab world: the splash of fountains, the chants of the muezzin calling the faithful to prayer.

That first evening we had barely got up the luggage when a completely strange young Arab in a djellabah appeared at our door. He was, he said, a friend of Arthur Reid, the same Mr. Reid who was the brother of Peggy Hubrecht in Tangier. "Mr. Reid wrote me a letter about you." He hauled up his djellabah and fished around in a pocket until he located both the letter and his calling card. Those djellabahs have their virtues but getting around underneath them requires practice and the explorer's spirit. Mr. Reid in writing to his friend was candid in his assessment of our charms but he had warmed to us enough to want us to have a good time in Morocco and we appreciated the trouble he had taken.

The young man presented his card. We read his name and the title *technicien. Technicien* of what we did not know. After, what I hope was courteous shoehorn work, we finally eased him from our room but he promised to come back the next evening at seven.

We found at dinner what we were to find so frequently; the food was dreary but the service good and the surroundings atmospheric. The Palais Jamai was building a new wing of one hundred rooms and will probably be as complete a motel as is its neighbor Les Merinides which perching on a hillside has a fine view of the city and the Atlas Mountains. We lunched there one day and thought it sterile. It had good baths but the food was no better than that of the Jamai. They have a swimming pool and the Jamai was putting one in too.

All Morocco seems to feel that tourism is going to boom and I shouldn't wonder if it does. It's going on all over the world, why should Morocco be slighted? On the other hand the famed sunshine that one associates with arid and semi-desert country can be largely mythical. People in Morocco will tell you that, during World War I, Marshal Louis Lyautey was the first to observe that Morocco was a cold country with a hot sun. The marshal was perceptive.

Of all the medinas we wandered through that of Fes we considered the best. Happily it still reeks of local color and is quite as good as any foreign quarter built on a sound stage in Hollywood's great days. Its cobblestoned labyrinthine alleyways cover an area twenty-one kilometers square and a visitor would need several days before he could venture to find his way unguided to this or that souk that might have caught his fancy.

We were jostled by throngs of djellabah clad Arabs, by women in the long sacklike garments they affect out of doors and by darting children. We were forced against the walls by donkeys their paniers laden with spices and olives and an occasional bleating victim for we were approaching the Feast of the Lamb when thousands of the animals are slaughtered for feasting and celebration.

On leaving the hotel in the morning Amidou had turned us over to Abdel a young man who was we gathered the souk specialist. The first one we approached in the medina was the outdoor olive market. This was wholesale and huge mounds of glistening globules, brown and green, black and gold were piled on flat round trays on the ground. Here too donkeys picked their way and then trotted off, their masters seated on their backs between baskets bulging with the day's stock.

Each guild was grouped in its own district. The rug and blanket merchants, the spice men—rice, semolina, dried peas and beans and a variety of dried mint leaves for tea. Their area was pungent as was that of the carpenters, fragrant with the scent of cedar wood. In one tiny alley were nothing but great bobbins wound with brilliantly colored silk thread and thrown over wooden pegs were the long silken ropes, orange and rose and blue that Arab women twist skillfully over their shoulders and across their backs and that serve to hold their long full sleeves out of their way when they are working.

As in Tangier we were blinded by the glitter of brass trays and jewelry and ornaments that look like silver but are made from an alloy of copper and tin.

The rug souk was handsome, a high covered courtyard piled to the top with rugs and blankets and leather goods. The billfolds and change purses are useful and well made and the babouches, the slippers of supple kid skin, are comfortable. The heavier ones are not. They look as if they would be but the doctor got a pair and discarded them after a couple of days, said they cut into his instep. Actually, I think he bought them to help move the inventory for there seemed to be so many thousands of pairs all over Morocco we wondered how they were ever disposed of.

There are mosques in the medina and although non-Muslims may look into the courtyard and take pictures they are not allowed to enter. We *were* allowed to wander into the Medersa Attarin. Dating from the fourteenth century it was at one time a university. The student rooms overlooked the courtyard and beside the pool instructors conducted their classes. It is beautifully decorated, the upper walls covered with designs of intricately carved plaster the lower inset with green and blue tiles, divided by bands of flourishing Arab penmanship.

Here Abdel chose to indoctrinate us into the Muslim religion and to tell us what one must do to be a true follower of Mohammed.

There are five primary duties and they are known as the five pillars of faith.

1. The profession of faith which consists of frequent repetitions of the basic formula; La ilaha illa Allah. It looks and sounds like a palindrome but it means There is no God but God, to which sometimes is added: Mohammed is the messenger of God.

2. Prayer five times a day. Devout Muslims faithfully perform

their ablutions washing their noses, ears, mouth, hands, and feet before bowing down and facing Mecca. Friday rather than Sunday is their holy day.

3. Observing Ramadan by fasting beginning with first light when a white tread may be distinguished from a black and continuing until sundown.

4. Zakah or obligatory alms. This a religious tax paid to the government as well as voluntary and personal gifts to the needy.

5. The pilgrimage to Mecca, the hadj. This, however, is set apart from the other four pillars of faith because a Muslim is required to make the journey only if he is financially able to do so. Those who don't are still the children of Allah but those who do are especially holy and are guaranteed everlasting life in Paradise to which our Tangier Hadji was eagerly looking forward.

While I was finding Abdel's seminar interesting I was also freezing to death despite my two sweaters. Such sun as had appeared that morning did not penetrate into the cold and beautiful courtyard. "Come along, Abdel," we said. "Let's go." Abdel was willing. From his comments we gathered that though he wished to be a good Muslim he found the whole procedure rather trying. On our way out he led us through a section of the medina that we found deadly dull. It was completely modern with cement pavements and souks with iron shutters. "The French," he informed us, "burnt the old part in 1956 because Moroccan partisans were hiding there."

Our chief project for the afternoon was to send a cable. Several months before leaving New York, we had conceived the notion that since we were going to be in India and Nepal would it not be fascinating to visit Sikkim? We decided it would be but were alerted to the fact that one must be invited or sponsored in order to obtain a visa from the Indian government.

As it so happened we had friends and acquaintances who knew Hope Cooke, the American girl who married the ruler of Sikkim, the Chogyal and became the Gyalmo or Highness. They wrote to her, I wrote to her, they sent recommendations, made inquiries and in Fes we received a cable saying that one of our interceders, Sheila Johnson, had received a letter from Her Highness and that she, Sheila, suggested we cable at once to the Gyalmo giving her our passport numbers and some other information.

On the strength of this communication we went to the post office.

Dear friend, if you do not absolutely have to send a cable in English from Fes, Morocco, to the Queen of Sikkim my advice is don't do it. Your afternoon will be shot and at the end you will be exsanguinated.

First of all we have the language barrier to cope with. Then there is the etiquette of salutation, next a matter of history, then comes geography. The first hurdle was not too great as thanks to a couple of years of French schooling in my youth I can still maneuver in that language.

The address read, the Gyalmo, the Palace, Gantok, Sikkim, Eastern Himalayas via India. Yes, I know. Code addresses are more practical but in Sikkim they don't have them. The postal clerk reads what I had written and looks up. "There's no name here."

"That's right. There doesn't have to be."

"How will they know who it's for?"

"They'll know. Gyalmo means queen. There's only one." My next remark is a mistake. "She's an American." I say it rather proudly.

"American?"

"Uh huh."

He obviously doesn't believe me. "How did that happen?"

"Well they met each other, I *think* it was in India, they fell in love and got married."

"American!" He shrugs and all but taps his brow. He reads the address again. Gyalmo. The Palace, Gangtok, Sikkim. Sikkim!

We have hit the nub, the kernel, the nitty gritty. In fact the quiddity. "And this place, this Sikkim. Where is that?"

"It's up there, north of India." I draw a map in the air. "You know Nepal? It's right next door."

"But it has to go first to India?"

"That's right."

"Then Nepal?"

"No no, never mind Nepal. It's just that it's *near* there." Why had I been such a fool as to mention it? I was only showing off. "India is what is important." He stares at me. That bit about the queen being an American, that had been pretty strong but *this!* He is frankly incredulous.

"And the Indians? *They're* going to know where Sikkim is?"

"Insha' Allah, they will know."

My man bursts out laughing and gives me a wink that says louder than words "Who are you kidding?" However, laboriously he copies down the message which consists mostly of numbers, our passport and India exit visa numbers and laboriously totes up the cost. "Send it delayed," I say. He retotes. Cost, nine American dollars. We pay and totter from the post office.

At seven-thirty, not having heard a word from our mysterious Arab caller of the day before who had assured us he would be there at seven, we decided it would be safe to go downstairs but as we headed for the bar he popped up complete with female companion. I understood it was his wife, Norton's impression was fiancée. She was shaped like an olive with pale olive coloring and she was extremely intelligent. We asked them to join us for a drink but they would take only coffee. We learned that what he was technician of was agriculture, traveling around the country improving agricultural techniques. They spoke no English but we managed in French and understood that she had a secretarial position in the government. They were eager to come to the States chiefly to see *"les grattes ciel."*

"But now," I said, "we call them high rises and we're pretty sick of them although they keep going on and on and up and up."

They had understood from Arthur Reid's letter that we were going to spend another day in Fes which had been our original intention but we had changed our minds deciding we would push on to Rabat and arrive a day earlier in Marrakech. They seemed disappointed by this and said they would have liked us to come to their house. I murmured an aside to Norton, "What did I tell you? Wife." We should have enjoyed visiting them as when traveling it is infinitely more rewarding to meet native residents rather than other tourists.

We talked about the medina, old Fes and how much we had enjoyed the souks. "From our point of view they're marvelously picturesque. But it's too bad," I added, "about the French setting fire to the medina in 1956."

Mr. Azzedine—we had learned his name—looked surprised.

"That's not true. They didn't burn it deliberately. The whole thing was an accident and the French were just as sorry it had happened as everybody else."

The next morning as we were leaving we imparted this bit of information to Abdel who was hanging around the Palais Jamai, I imagine waiting for more tourists. He was indignant. "If an Arab told you that," he said angrily, "it was an Arab who liked the French." The lot of a would-be historian is hard.

We left Fes under a rainbow passing by the old cemetery. Amidou explained that whitewashed tombstones meant the deceased had a family who cared for his grave. Those that were natural stone color indicated the last of the line. I suppose the system made it handy for the municipality who could make way for newcomers without having to contend with irate relatives.

Arabs streamed past us, nearly every one with a lamb or ram acquired for the approaching celebration. They were draped around their necks like the Good Shepherd who, unbeknownst to the poor creature, was about to turn into Judas. They rode in baskets on the backs of donkeys or they hobbled along on their front feet, their rear legs held up by their owners. I was unable to find out whether or not it was a celebration unique to Islam or whether it shared with Judaism the legend of Abraham and his son and the ram who happened to be so conveniently at hand when God spoke from the heavens saying he would settle for *it* rather than the sacrifice of Isaac. The father, his son and God were all pleased. The emotions of the ram are not recorded.

We were heading for Meknès and passed orange groves, almond groves in flower and vineyards veiled by teeming rain. One would think that in Moslem countries the cultivation of the grape would cause some sort of dichotomy but wherever we went the wine industry was flourishing.

We traveled through beautiful open rolling country to the tiny hillside town of Moulay Idris. It is a holy city and contains the tomb of the founder of the Idris dynasty, the lad who built Fes. Foreigners are allowed to enter between sunrise and sunset but may not spend the night. We felt the prohibition to be no loss for the rain continued to fall in sheets and the hilly cobbled streets while picturesque were slippery and muddy and we were getting very very wet. We stood for a few minutes watching the bakers who work in caves. People make their own dough, knead it into round flat loaves and bring it to the bakers who pop it into and out of their ovens with long handled wooden shovels. Amidou brought two large green candles banded with gold, "For the Feast of the Lamb" and we pushed on to Volubilis.

Founded in the second century B.C., Volubilis was originally a Carthaginian city but needless to say the Romans came along and annexed it and held it until about A.D. 285 when they drifted away.

Considered the most important Roman ruin in Morocco, the city covers an extensive area and is in a remarkably good state of preservation. Arches, columns, foundations, and some fine mosaics but it is worrisome to see these last so exposed to climatic vissitudes of pouring rain or baking sun. The Moroccans should take a hint from the Sicilians who at Piazza Armerina have sheltered the dazzling mosaics of a great villa of the first century under a spacious plastic structure through which travelers pass looking down on the lovely entertaining pictures from slightly elevated cat walks. We would have greatly appreciated a little shelter at Volubilis for we were drenched.

Fortunately succor was not too far away. Amidou who was knowledgeable about restaurants guided us to an excellent one, l'Hacienda, outside of Meknès. After lunching on mushroom omelet, sautéed veal kidneys, boiled potatoes, and a delicious chilled dry rosé sopor interfered with my taking note of the fertile countryside through which we were passing.

For reasons which I fail to understand we seem to have ignored Meknès and it was our misfortune for it is rich in history and judging from photographs there is some quite extraordinary plaster and tile work which is well worth seeing. Sometimes a city, like a piece of luggage, gets lost in the scramble of the trip.

We did not miss Rabat or its Tour Hassan Hotel which is not uncomfortable but the rooms are cramped and lacking in style. The one entertaining feature is the bell boys who wear full red plus fours, short red jackets, fezzes and white stockings and white pointed babouches. We dined one evening in the hotel's Giffa, or banquet room, but thought the Moroccan food only fair and the seating arrangements not well engineered. One sits on either divans or backless poufs, knees hitting low tables, food some distance from mouth.

We did however unearth two very good restaurants. The Cassabella, not far from the hotel—but the route is circuitous—served an excellent luncheon and a nice wine called appropriately enough Vin du Pays.

L'Oasis was what its name implies and our dinner was outstanding, especially the fish and a delicate crisp pastilla, not sweet and stuffed with spinach and egg. There too the wine was delicious and we thought the price altogether fair.

Driving around Rabat we felt that, like Addis Ababa it is at present more an area than a city but it is the administrative capital of the country and I felt sorry for the diplomatic corps. Life cannot be very gay.

Amidou who had a passion for large hotels drove us out to the Hilton and could not understand why we did not wish to leave the car and go in to look at the lobby. The Hilton is stranded in the middle of nowhere but has obviously been built with an eye to urban expansion and one fine day perhaps the location will turn out to be the local Times Square.

It is unfortunate that given open space to work with there seems to be no plan to create a well organized, cohesive and attractive center. Lots are apparently to go to the highest bidders who with the greed and lack of taste that characterize the construction industry will erect such individual horrors as they choose.

There is one broad boulevard with attractive shops and palm trees and indeed there are trees and gardens and colorful flower markets throughout the city so it comes as a surprise to find that King Hassan's palace faces a huge bare square with no blade of grass or shadow of leaves. This it was explained was done deliberately to have room for the crowds who congregate, chiefly on Friday, to see the King as he rides in his coach from the palace to the mosque to attend religious services. According to those who have seen it it is a brilliant and colorful ceremony with drums and trumpets, guards in crimson and spirited horses.

Within the walls there are extensive gardens, two of them open to the public. They are long and narrow and curious in that they are mirror images, both exactly alike, the same vines curtaining the walls reflected in the same pools.

As we were leaving we heard a lion roar which induced in me instant rage as I was certain he was kept in a miserable cage by a callous and indifferent monarch but I could not check the private royal zoo and there is no SPCA.

King Hassan II who came to the throne in 1961 seems reasonably popular. He has one wife, three daughters and a son and when we were there was engaged in enhancing a splendid mosque-tomb for his father the late King Mohammed V.

Since there was not a great deal to see our guide filled the time by repeating everything twice but when we went to the mosque which resembles a giant white wedding cake with a green peaked roof so awed was he by this manifestation of filial respect that he told us everything three times over.

Somewhat surprisingly there are a good many golf courses in Morocco, the King being both an ardent fan and an indefatigable player. An amusing piece on him appeared in the *International Herald Tribune,* an interview with the famous pro, Claude Harmon. King Hassan had met the master when he played at Winged Foot in Mamaroneck in New York and he had twice summoned him to Morocco. He gave the interview on his return to the States.

The King it appears has a bad slice and it was the task of Mr. Harmon to correct it. "I was afraid if he kept on slicing he might have me put against the wall and shot," he said, "but on the golf course the King is really a very mild fellow."

From the point of view of the instructor, however, the honor of teaching royalty was mixed. "He usually plays with a couple of generals or some of his palace guard," Harmon continued. "He runs the country from the golf course. There are people around with brief cases under their arms. The King will hit a ball and then reach over and sign some paper or other. He'll hit another ball and then go into conference on the state of the treasury."

When Mr. Harmon expostulated with him, "Your Majesty you *can't* play golf like that. Not even Arnold Palmer could score with so many interruptions," the King regarded him stonily and said, "I must run my country." He spends about five hours a day doing it on the golf course.

We ourselves do not greatly care for golf and found greater interest in visiting Chellah, the ancient and original city which later became Rabat. A rosy crenelated wall encircles an area of blowing grasses and wild flowers and the ruins are gradually being revealed as work proceeds with the excavations.

The Rabat museum has a few nice pieces, among them a horse

and a human head from Volubilis and the souks are good, especially those selling rugs. Hanging on the wall was a very large one with a white ground, geometric designs of dark blue and black and a tawny yellow binding. A little farther along a blaze of crimson was flung over the cobblestones as a merchant exhibited his wares to an interested American couple.

More modest purchases were amusing little animals, horses and peacocks and crickets, quite modern in feeling, made of iron and metal. I bought several as they cost only dirhams. (Like the French franc, which they are not too keen on accepting, the Moroccan dirham is worth twenty cents.) I found these treasures not in the medina but in a little souk at the entrance to an outdoor café built on a kind of parapet. One looks through its blue painted arches across the sandy river bed to the companion town of Salé, in the Middle Ages the abode of pirates and the greatest African port on the Atlantic.

The morning we left Rabat for Marrakech was cold and overcast but we were bowling along a fine open road on the way to Casablanca when the car slowed and then rolled to a dead stop. "What on earth's the matter?" I asked. Norton's tone was resigned. "I suspect we're out of gas." This was indeed the case, our alert Amidou having forgotten to refuel. We were annoyed with him for his carelessness but his own reaction was bitter. He was convinced the tank had emptied itself out of sheer malice.

After some moments, having fished a green plastic bottle from the trunk, he succeeded in flagging down a car that would take him back toward Rabat and a filling station. We settled down to wait but in about twenty minutes, sooner than we dared hope, he was back, the bottle full of precious plasma. He filled the tank and we were off again secure now except for uncertainty about oil, water, the battery and tires.

The country between Rabat and Casablanca is fertile, flat and uninteresting. In Mohammedia we stopped for coffee at the Hotel Miramar. It was an attractive spot with a beach, casino, swimming pool, tennis, and an eighteen-hole golf course nearby. A

room with a balcony overlooking the water is thirty-five dollars
a day for two with full pension. The only drawback is that one
would be pretty well confined to the hotel as the environment
is not appealing—flat and a good many factories.

Business obviously is another matter but if one is traveling
for pleasure there would seem small point in going to Casablanca,
a big modern commercial city lacking charm. Given the route we
were traveling we had no choice but to go through it and also it
was lunchtime and we were fortunate in that thanks to Amidou
we found a very good restaurant, the Calluand.

We were traveling on Friday and as we drove we passed long
strings of horses and camels on their way to Settat for Saturday
and Sunday were market days and trade was brisk.

We approached Marrakech in the late afternoon.

It is curious that even if one thinks one has no preconceived
vision of a place one may on seeing it exclaim, "But this isn't
at all what I expected!" I don't know what I had expected of
Marrakech but I was surprised to find it so large and so open.

It is a spacious city of over a quarter of a million people lying
in a vast plain extending from the sea to the Atlas Mountains.
There is, thank God, no "downtown" commercial section. With
the exception of its famed Koutoubia tower built at the end of
the twelfth century it is low. Low and rosy brown. More than
twelve miles of pink walls enclose pinkish brown houses and
thousands of palm trees. In the European section, Marrakech-
Gueliz, the boulevards are wide and most are shaded by palm
and orange trees. When we were there the town was en fête,
sprouting triumphal arches and glowing with strings of electric
light for a double celebration: The Feast of the Lamb and three
days later the anniversary of the King's accession to the throne.
The red banners of Morocco with the five pointed interlaced
green star fluttered against the sky. We made a brief tour of the
city without getting out of the car and then drove to the Villa
Taylor where we were to stay.

We followed the curving driveway through what appeared to

be a small jungle, the four-acre garden, and drew up before the largest front door I have ever seen. It was a huge gleaming panel of heavy wood carved in a lattice-like design and with enormous hinges.

We rang the bell, waited, and presently the giant portal began to move. As we were to learn it moved very very slowly because of its weight. It finally swung wide enough to reveal two maids, Minna and Radouche. Together with Lahouine the cook, Madame herself, and a visiting laundress they did the work of the big house.

We stepped into the front hall and then into the patio which in sunny weather was delightful but on that day was cold and somber. It was surrounded by an arcade, a graceful architectural feature but one which effectively cut out light so that even when the sun did shine all the rooms were tenebrous. Presently our hostess the Comtesse de Breteuil appeared. She was slim and blonde with sharp features and bright blue eyes and she was dressed in admirably cut slacks, a jacket and hat. I noticed that everything was wool. The Comtesse knew her climate. She was sorry to have held us up she said, but she had been in the garden. We were shown the bedrooms which opened onto the patio and urged to take two since they were unoccupied. "You can sleep in one and the doctor can have the other for his clothes." We appreciated her practicality. Love is very beautiful but so is closet space and affection is more likely to endure when the loved one's shoes and pants are not crowding out the lovers' dresses and coats.

The beds were low, the rooms elaborately carved and painted, the lighting dim and the baths sumptuous. If you like sunken tubs. Many people consider them the ultimate luxury but I see them as death traps. To begin with you have to kneel on the floor to turn on the water. You have to descend a short flight of steps to get into them and this is a slippery business, breaking a leg is child's play. When in them you are eye level with the floor giving you a strange submerged feeling and the chore of cleaning them out whether for mistress or maid is pure hell.

Also at the villa the space between toilet and tub is infinitesimal, the narrowest of little cat walks and a railing installed for protective purposes is about three inches high so one may topple headlong with the greatest of ease. Other than that the baths are poetic.

Tea was brought and Minna, the older of the two maids, helped me unpack. A small pile of mail was awaiting us and to my delight one letter was from the Gyalmo of Sikkim. I opened it and started reading aloud to Norton. Paragraph one: We are invited to Sikkim. Elation. Paragraph two: "We ourselves won't be here as we shall be in England for the holidays of our older children." These were the children of the Chogyal by his former wife. Deflation. *Way* down. *Now* what to do? Would there be much point in going if their Highnesses were not there? True, the Gyalmo added that people at the palace would look after us but it was still an anticlimax and I was neatly hoist on my own petard. In the letter I had written asking if it would be possible for my husband and me to visit her and the Chogyal in Sikkim I had been eloquent in my praise of a strange and fascinating land. It would be a little awkward to write back, "Never mind the land, if you and his Highness aren't going to be there we don't want to come."

"Well," said Norton—in such circumstances he is the Brain— "I think the thing to do is for you to write and accept the invitation. Who knows? As the time gets nearer they *might* change their plans. It's happened before. Better to be prepared instead of sorry we'd said no when maybe we could have gone."

That seemed sound. What did we have to lose? I accordingly wrote asking for further details of procedure and being most meticulous in giving our itinerary and addresses so that Her Highness might send a reply to any number of places at her own convenience.

We then turned our attention to our present surroundings. It so happened that our friend Lewis Galantiere, banker and gentleman of letters, was spending the winter in Marrakech. We phoned him and learned that another friend, Dr. Justin Greene, was flying down from Switzerland. Lewis was planning to take the train to Casablanca to meet him. "Don't do that," said Dr. Brown effusively, "our driver Amidou is going back there. Take the car we came down in." Mr. Galentiere was delighted. I thought of Amidou. "How do you know he *wants* to drive right back to Casablanca? Just because he lives there doesn't mean anything. Maybe he has a whole little harem going here in Marrakech." Dr. Brown was indifferent to Amidou's sexual requirements.

Whatever his secret wishes Amidou agreed to leave the next day taking our friend with him but before we parted he handed me a large flat notebook asking that we write a reference and a few remarks about how much we had liked him. I glanced through the pages. Several other Americans had extolled his virtues enthusiastically, one couple in particular lauding him as a very fine gentleman. I contented myself with saying that he was obliging, helpful, and knowledgeable about good restaurants. I could write in honesty that he was an experienced driver and I glossed over the lapse with the gasoline. I handed him the book.

"There you are Amidou," I said, "thank you very much. We've had a good trip and I'm sure when other tourists read what we've all written they'll be eager to engage you."

It was when he looked down at the page and looked up at me with a pleasant blank expression that I realized he couldn't read. And not only English. He had brought along a sheaf of forms from the garage printed in French and he pointed to the places where Norton should sign but he could not read.

Our first evening at the villa we went into the drawing room around seven-thirty. Steam heat made it comfortable but there was no wood-burning fireplace. Such a hot country as everyone knows! The room was long and narrow with couches, easy chairs, a large radio, and a low platform at one end where a desk was placed. The walls were partially tiled and above the tiling were plaster and wood intricately carved and painted in a close formal floral design as was the remarkable high, hipped ceiling, one of the most notable ceilings I have ever seen in a private house.

Small pyramids of shining marble eggs caught the glow of the lamp light and during our stay we would often see Boul sitting on the floor beside the coffee table polishing them in her cupped hands or with a soft chamois cloth.

Soon other guests began arriving until we were eleven in all: English, American and one Russian, the vigorous and imposing Madame Ira Belline a niece of Stravinsky's and a long-time inhabitant of Marrakech. She wore a sweeping caftan and her head was wrapped in a turban.

About a quarter to nine the dining-room doors were thrown open and dinner was announced. The table was huge. So wide it was almost impossible to talk across it but my right and left hand neighbors were companionable. One of them kept staring at me intently and then said, "Please don't think me rude but years ago I used to go a lot to see Ilka Chase in the theatre and movies. It's extraordinary how much you look like her. I hope you don't mind. I always admired her."

"Not at all," I said, "I was a fan myself." I could keep this up for about a minute before I burst out laughing. When I revealed the dazzling secret my companion was overwhelmed!

Our first meal at the villa was delicious as was every subsequent one we were served. The knowledge and imagination of the hostess plus the skill of her cook produced some of the best meals we have ever eaten. That night we had artichoke bottoms stuffed with béchamel sauce, sprinkled with Gruyère cheese and browned under the broiler. We had squabs stuffed with raisins and almonds and a unique dessert a fanciful arrangement of oranges and mousse, in what appeared to be a brown wire cage which in reality was made of chocolate. The red and white wine was local and palatable but not outstanding and our only gastronomic complaint was that it never changed.

One day at luncheon we had an extraordinarily good fresh

fruit compote and I asked if there was any liqueur in it. Boul
said, "No. The kitchen eats what we eat so as it is against their
religion there is never any alcohol other than the table wine."
Dr. Brown was saddened. He is a man who fancies pork but pork
was against their religion too so pork was not to be.

The maids, Minna and Radouche, waited on table as they did
everything else, discreetly and effectively. They were like birds
with their softly shadowed faces, their brilliant plumage the
turbans they wore and their bright silk dresses of blue and rose
and gold caught at the waist with narrow gold belts. In the evening they covered them with tunics of shining gauze.

In Morocco the employers tu toi their servants which might be
considered patronizing since this familiar mode of address is usually reserved for children and animals. On the other hand the
servants tu toi the employers so it is hard to say who is patronizing whom. Since close friends also address one another that
way friendship would seem the most pleasing and accurate defi-
nition.

Our social life was agreeably launched that evening and we
lunched the next day with two Englishmen, friends of Boul de
Breteuil, Glynn Burnand, and Dicky Bird. The other guests were
two English doctors, a surgeon and his internist wife. That luncheon too was memorable—this time the cook was Swedish—and
we decided that in Marrakech the good life was appreciated.

On our return to the villa Boul took us up to the tower for
the first time. Built by an American woman, Mrs. Moses Taylor,
in the 1920s the house surrounds two flowery patios and with the
exception of the tower is all one story. The patios are tiled. In
one of them nasturtiums float in the basin of a central fountain
and they are shaded by palms, cypress, orange trees, and bougain-
villea.

The villa was originally known as La Saadia and during the
war was inhabited by an American diplomat, Kenneth Pendar.
Boul gave us a brochure he had written about the house and
specifically about the visit paid it in 1943 by President Roosevelt

and Winston Churchill after the Casablanca conference. This was
the conference in the course of which Mr. Churchill and the President dined with the Sultan of Morocco, an occasion of which
the late Mr. Gavin Maxwell wrote slyly in his book, *Lords of the
Atlas*.

"The conference took place at the Hotel d'Anfa outside Casa-
blanca and included President Roosevelt, Elliot Roosevelt, Harry
Hopkins, Winston Churchill, General Noguès, General deGaulle,
General Ribaud, the Sultan of Morocco and his eldest son, Moulay
Hassan. The only two guests who did not enjoy the party were
General Noguès, who rightly feared his early dismissal, and Win-
ston Churchill who suffered acutely from the absence of alcohol
on which President Roosevelt had insisted in deference to the
Sultan's religion. (His programme for the day noted to Harry
Hopkins for information read: 'Dinner. At the White House
(dry, alas!) with the Sultan. After dinner recovery from the
above.')."

Security preparations for the arrival of the two men at the
villa were efficient to say the least. According to Mr. Pendar
"Anti-aircraft guns went into place outside the house . . . Endless telephones went in with bright red boxes called scramblers
to safeguard telephone conversations, a switchboard in a little
porter's room at the right of the entrance, and our own exchange
on the army system. There were telephones in every bedroom,
in the salon, at the door, at the entrance gate, at different places
in the garden, so that the secret servicemen could check the
guards. . . .

"Ramps for President Roosevelt's wheel chair had to be made
and put in place so that he could be wheeled anywhere in the
house and garden and at the same time walk (with railings) in
case he wanted to. They had to be placed carefully and incon-
spicuously so they wouldn't be constant reminders to him and to
everyone else of his infirmity."

No matter how discreet they tried to be with that much activity going on rumors inevitably flew and Mr. Pendar was told

on the best authority that the King of England, Pètain, Stalin, Mussolini *and* the Pope had been seen skulking about Marrakech.

Mr. Churchill had been there before the war and it had won his heart. When staying in the house he asked to be taken up to the tower. It was near sunset and he said to his host, "Don't you believe, Pendar, that it can be arranged for the President to be brought up here?"

The President was eager and since the staircase is too narrow for a chair two aides carried him up the ninety-two steps to the roof from which there is a magnificent view of the entire city and the Atlas Mountains, "their snow capped peaks glittering against the blue cloudless sky," as the guide books say.

"Just as the sun set," Mr. Pendar continues, "the electric light on the top of every mosque tower in Marrakech flashed on to indicate to the faithful the hour of prayer. There was a feeling of suppressed drama in the landscape at this moment, heightened by the beauty of the mountains and the thickening light. The points of electric light on all the mosque towers were like a gong announcing the end of the day. . . . Both Mr. Roosevelt and Mr. Churchill were spellbound by the view but it became perceptibly colder and the whole party started down again." An honest man, Mr. Pendar adds in parentheses, "Marrakech is too hot in the sun even in winter, but at night the water in the fountains sometimes freezes."

At the end of the year Churchill was back at the villa recuperating from a severe illness. He sent a telegram to President Roosevelt: THE VILLA IS PERFECT . . . THE WEATHER IS BRIGHT THOUGH COOL. THE COOK IS A MARVEL. WE GO FOR PICNICS TO THE MOUNTAINS. LAST NIGHT EISENHOWER WAS WITH US . . .

It is comforting to know that in the grim and prolonged ordeal of the war the two leaders had a brief respite from the insupportable load they were carrying.

The Comte de Breteuil who was a newspaperman bought the villa in 1947. He died in 1960 leaving his widow and one son. The house is too large for a woman alone and the upkeep cannot be negligible. On the counsel of friends and following too her own inclination the Comtesse decided on paying guests as an occupation and income, a decision which has turned into a merited success.

She kindly put a room in the tower at my disposal. It was a pretty painted retreat blue and flowery and the only room in the house where the sun could penetrate.

I used to make efforts to work there at least a couple of hours every day but stern endeavor was easily aborted. After all, I would think self-righteously this *is* a holiday, and one afternoon when Boul asked casually if I would like to go with her to the Hotel Mamounia to pick up her cousin I snapped at the chance assuring myself it is enriching to broaden one's contacts.

The gentleman in question was Mr. Davis Allen, a partner in the well-known New York architectural firm of Skidmore, Owings & Merrill. He was interested in carpets for their new offices and in his cousin he had a knowledgeable guide. The souk to which Boul led us was large and the inventory impressive. There were some magnificent carpets and I gathered the firm was prospering because while for many individuals the prices would be lofty our man did not boggle and I do not question that clients paying a first visit to the eminent architects are duly impressed by the floor décor.

The carpet souk lies just off what may accurately be termed the heart of Marrakech. Loosely called a square—actually it is more the shape of an enormous rough triangle—the Grande Place, the Djemma El F'na came into existence about 800 years ago. Its name means Meeting Place of the Dead because the Sultan used to cut off the heads of his enemies and place them on the walls as a warning to other dissenters.

The Place bustles in the morning with people marketing and en route to shopping sprees in the souks but around four in the afternoon it begins to Live!

Despite its name this big area, nearly four acres, seethes with activity and crowds. Every day is carnival. Noise, shouting, enter-

tainment, music, hucksters, hawkers, and con artists. Long-robed
men cluster in circles like thick doughnuts around their preferred
performers. There are blue men from the South—blue because
their skin absorbs the dye from their clothes; Berbers from the
mountains, camel drivers and fellahs, small farmers from the surrounding countryside.

A group of white-clad African dancers stomping and leaping to
pounding drums and shrill stringed instruments draws its fans.
A little farther off jugglers and tumblers compete for and get
an enthusiastic audience.

Catering to other tastes a snake charmer and three mild and
rather tired cobras exercise their appeal. A few feet away white
pigeons, mysteriously foretelling the future by strutting between
pink cotton roses stuck in bottles and picking up brown and yellow grain from the earth, attract the introspective types.

Singers and story tellers have their adherents and a big circle
has formed around four men who are weaving back and forth
in what seems to us a desultory manner singing, or perhaps chant-
ing is a better word, as they saw away on curious fiddles shaped
like horseshoes, a piece of gut stretched across the open end. One
thing that unites all these varied and multiple entrepreneurs is a
sharp eye for a newcomer on the periphery of the group. He is
immediately accosted for his contribution. Most travelers are generous. It is wonderfully colorful entertainment and the best of it is
its authenticity. By far the great majority of spectators are Moroccans who have been drawn to Djemma El F'na for generations
and who will doubtless continue to come as long as the vitality
of the performers lasts.

The maze of souks roofed with straw matting and latticing,
lies to the north of the Place. It exerts a strong fascination as all
of them do and while here and there one finds tempting merchandise we still thought the souks of Fes the best we saw in both
North Africa and the Middle East. I understand those of Damascus are extraordinary and we had wanted to go there but alas

the vicissitudes of politics, so inimical to the average person's natural instincts, made the journey impossible.

In Fes the silken ropes that I bought to serve as belts and that maids used to tie back their long-flowing sleeves had little glinting paillettes sewn into them. In Morocco the colors were good but the ropes were glintless. I mention it because of what happened later in the day.

Boul had organized a cocktail party and the first comers were Ira Belline and her two house guests, Mr. John Hopkins and his friend, who had been hosts of the cocktail party to which the Hubrechts had taken us in Tangier. The carpet-buying Mr. Allen and a Spanish friend arrived with two other chaps one of whom if I understood correctly was an American doing his military service in Turkey. Apparently there is now a choice and one may do service out of the country. He was in codes and ciphers. The other man was a bearded mystic, name uncaught.

Presently the star guest and his troop arrived. The star was Monsieur Yves Saint Laurent world-famous couturier, darling of womankind, who has a house in Marrakech. He was slender and elegant with long blond hair curling on his shoulders. His professional eye lighted at once on my sparkling silken belt. "How pretty that is! Where did you get it?" Watch next season's collection! With a small start of surprise and some amusement we were introduced to his companions. They were our hippie passengers on the flight from Paris to Tangier. We had deplaned there but they had flown on to Marrakech.

Mademoiselle Slim Shanks bore the name of a distinguished old French family and her escort was alliteratively introduced as Fernando the Furrier. He worked for Yves Saint Laurent in Paris. The more subdued couple were pleasant and polite but their function escaped us. The party bubbled along with everyone mounting to the tower to see the great view before departing.

The next day for luncheon there was more social life. Our friend Lewis Galentiere, the successfully retrieved Dr. Justin Greene and a French soldier who had been of inestimable aid to the Americans during the war, General Antoine Bethouart and his wife.

In the afternoon Norton and I were shepherded around by Mr. Rom Landau, an Englishman in his seventies who has lived for more than twenty years in Marrakech. He is a friend of King Hassan and has become a sort of official historian of the city.

He took us to the souks and bargained mightily with the shopkeepers and then to the tombs of the Saadian kings of the sixteenth century. Raised a few inches above the sod, rectangular slabs exquisitely carved pave a courtyard entered through a narrow passage way winding between thick pink walls of the mosque of El Mansour. The tombs of more exalted personages engraved with elegant calligraphy were set under high carved and gilded canopies of stucco upheld on slender columns.

The Medersa or university and students courtyard is a lovely expression of Moorish architecture and design: colored tiles, lacelike plaster bands of delicate calligraphy and ceilings of carved cedar wood.

The Bedi Palace built in the latter part of the sixteenth century was partially destroyed in the seventeenth but its pink walls still stand and today with the great pools in which they are reflected serve as a permanent set for the annual spring festival.

Another spectacle that draws enthusiastic crowds, the Fantasia, takes place in January. This is a mock battle with Berbers mounted on horses and camels swooping at full gallop toward the spectators, their guns blazing into the sky. Many years ago I saw something similar in Paris when the Spahi troops from Algeria staged a performance at the race course. They bore down on the grandstands with wild cries, their rifles splitting the air, their long crimson-lined white cloaks streaming out behind them. They reined in abruptly, their horses rearing in front of the French President. It was wildly thrilling and I was terrified.

At the end of our cultural promenade Mr. Landau took us to his apartment. He lives in the Moorish style and requested that we take off our shoes before entering. He is proud of his carpets and has every right to be. They are handsome. There was one large room furnished in red and white and a blue study. A bath and small kitchen completed the layout. He has couches but sleeps on mats on the floor.

There were many photographs of himself taken with the King and copies of his own books in foreign languages bound appropriately enough in red Moroccan leather. We thanked him for his kind and instructive guidance and took our departure.

From the shopping point of view—excepting perhaps the best and most beautiful of the rugs—Morocco did not seem expensive although we got into a slight tussle with a French woman in a stationers shop who, when we offered her a bill to pay for a little account book I had bought, snapped out, "I am not a bank." She refused our money.

Boul was annoyed by her country woman's behavior. *"Voilà!"* she exclaimed. "Only the French can be that disagreeable. And they wonder why I prefer to speak to Moroccans."

We had been unaware of our offense but on closer examination it seemed to us the bill *was* too large a denomination to offer for so small a purchase and we didn't blame the woman.

Some of the change we had managed to collect I gave to a dwarf who came and sat on the steps of the café terrace where we were having coffee. He seemed pitiably poor and, I do not know for what reason, a Moroccan dwarf seemed to me sadder than an American one. The day was sprinkled with little kindnesses. We had not sassed the French woman back, the dwarf benefited modestly, Norton ministered to the injured toe of the assistant to the laundress and I photographed Boul's pet turtles. They were all right although the ones I prefer are the enormous sea turtles who come ashore only to lay their eggs in the sand.

Feeling we were getting to know the ropes and that it was unfair to expect the Comtesse to be a daily guide as well as hostess, Norton and I took off by ourselves to the Place.

As we were strolling about we were picked up by an urchin as maddening as a fly one can't swat. We kept shooing him away but he was more determined than we so in the end we gave in and accepted him as our guide through the souks although this entailed much retracing of our steps. Morocco is famous for its amber and I wanted to buy a string of chunky beads but the natives are canny in their use of plastic and as my knowledge of amber is negligible I restrained myself. We are up to here in plastic in my native land.

One souk area we had missed and were eager to see was that of the dyers. Our urchin ran interference through thronged passages as we threaded our way between voracious merchants eager for our trade until we wound up in the Street of the Dyers. It was an exhilarating sight. Just at that moment the sun broke through striking fire from the thick loops of crimson, green, blue, and blazing gold silk flung over poles that stretched from roof to roof across the alley.

We gave our little chum the equivalent of .50 in dirhams but he was furious demanding twice the sum. Considering we had done our level best to get rid of him we felt he was receiving fair payment for his valuable time and services. We were to find however that North Africa and Asia are the lands of the outstretched palms and that furthermore just like other businessmen beggars set their own price although since neither goods nor services are involved it is hard to know how they arrive at it.

There are many excursions to be made outside of Marrakech, some ambitious some modest. Norton and I made three of the latter kind and enjoyed them very much. One was a drive into the smiling fresh green valley of Ourika. The round trip is about eighty-three miles and its charm lies in the hilly fertile countryside and the square mud huts of the Berbers. They are cooperative about posing for their pictures and it is nice to have a record of their friendly faces and the sharp brilliant colors in which they clothe themselves.

We went also to Asni. For that junket Tuesday is your day because that is when they hold the big camel and donkey sale and the enormous roadside souk mills with Arabs and cattle churning up mud or dust depending on the season. There were hundreds of stalls and a big tent city off to the side. I was having a fine time hopping about and trying to get pictures but the doctor was seized with one of his occasional attacks of male self-consciousness.

"Come along," he said. "People are looking at us." That scarcely seemed any reason to leave. "Why not?" I said. "We're looking at them," but he was male and mandatory.

Another commodity besides livestock in that mountainous area is amethyst quartz. Heavy rains wash it down from the heights and people pick it from the river beds. If one lived there it might be pretty piled on a windowsill where it would flash and sparkle in the sunlight but it is not an ideal purchase when traveling by air.

Our destination was the Sanglier Qui Fume, a country bistro one arrives at after a good deal of twisting and turning along mountain roads. It has acquired a modest fame and although a rickety rackety nonsense it is not unamusing.

The large, loud, and lusty patron who was born in Paris but who has passed his life in Morocco has also established a small zoo to beguile clients while they are waiting for luncheon to be prepared. He has white pigeons, an eagle with clipped pinions, two boars, monkeys, many dogs and cats, and a tame stork who rattles his bill obligingly when his keeper kneels down and croons to him and cossets him.

We hadn't been there long when a busload of French tourists arrived. Show me a lower middle class Frenchman and I'll show you a lower middle class French woman, a noteworthy combination in much of North Africa.

Luncheon with the exception of a superfluity of olive oil was good and our bottle of Oustelet, the local rosé very pleasant.

For a brief interlude when the sun shone it was really hot and the jovial patron passed around straw hats. They were only on loan but the French tourists were enchanted—men and women snatching them from one another and planting them on their own heads with whoops of delight. We suspected the owner was going to have a tussle retrieving them.

After our hearty lunch, dinner that night at the villa seemed unusually civilized: steamed cauliflower stuffed with cheese and parsley, a stronger more flavorful variety than ours, and for dessert individual grapefruit soufflés.

Another excursion we greatly enjoyed was our trip to Ouarzazate over the mountains and into the desert. Both drive and destination are dramatic. The road stretches long and straight for some time and then the climbing begins. At last the Atlas range emerged from the overcast, the distant peaks clear and glittering against a shining sky. The nearby peaks were stained with curious muted colors: deep red and ochre, gray and greenish yellow. The brown mud villages of the Berbers nestled in curves in the mountain flanks carpeted with bright green grass of spring and below the fluttering golden leaves of the trees women walked in their dresses of strawberry pink and acid yellow.

We stopped for coffee in the hillside village of Taddert and then began the climb. The rushing streams and small swiftly flowing waterfalls were beautiful and we finally approached La Terrace leading to the Col du Tichka. The road is an extraordinary feat of engineering doubling back and forth and round about as it mounts ever higher until it achieves the pass at some 7400 feet. On the desert side of the mountain range was Paradise. Hot sunshine, clear skies, pure air.

We arrived at one o'clock and went to lunch at the Hotel de Sud owned by the Club Mediteranné. The swimming pool sparkled. In the large dining room the table linen was immaculate. The waiters in white caftans and jackets were immaculate. In the washrooms the toilets were filthy.

There are primitive aspects of life that can be enjoyable. When they are not, excuses are sometimes not only easy, they are legitimate. But in a hotel, in other aspects civilized, why should the lavatories be disgusting? Money isn't the excuse. No one is

so poor he can't be toilet trained and in an establishment such
as the Hotel du Sud finances have nothing to do with it. Of finances they have an ample supply. There is an indifference to
sanitation which ill becomes anyone and in a hotelkeeper it is
deplorable.

We spoke of this to Boul on our return. "Yes," she said, "it's
appalling," and she added by way of langniappe, "Sometimes
you know the Arabs use stones instead of paper."

Our luncheon finished, we went to visit the house of El Glaoui
in the Casbah. After the Second World War and until they were
obliged to withdraw from Morocco, the French dealt with and
then betrayed one of the most extraordinary and anachronistic
figures of the modern world. El Glaoui was a Moroccan by defi-
nition but through his veins flowed the mingled blood of Arab,
Berber, and Ethiopian. Part barbarian, part Renaissance prince,
part traitor, for he was a bitter foe of his own people in their
fight for independence against the French. He degenerated in the
end to a sick old man riddled with cancer.

With the return to the throne of the Sultan, Mohamed V, whom
he had done so much to depose his enfeebled constitution broke
and he died in Marrakech on the last day of the year 1956.

To enter the Casbah or "palace" we passed through wooden
gates into a courtyard where men were carrying and stacking
heavy bags of grain. The two-storied house was of adobe brick
with a balcony from which, explained our pungent black guide,
"Ladies of harem could watch entertainment in courtyard below.
See without being seen." Throughout the East great emphasis
was placed on the fact that the ladies could see yet not be seen
as though this were in some way enjoyable. The women must
have been bored to death. With nothing to do but adorn themselves from dawn till dusk why should they not have longed for
so much artistry to be admired by the opposite sex?

The dining room of the harem and the bedroom of the favorite
was still open to visitors. It was still prettily tiled and in relatively

good shape. The rest of the place was closed up and had gone to seed.

On our way home as we were rounding a sharp curve we were brought up short by a group of wild-looking mummers. Their heads were covered with animal skins and the women wore heavy red veils and gold bangles. Our driver jammed on the brakes and the car skidded to a stop. The people leaned in the windows shouting and gesticulating and I admit to a moment of funk. Who were they? What did they want? Laughing our driver reassured us. "Give money, give money. It is just a game." I breathed a sigh of relief. As long as it wasn't "your money or your life." Norton handed out a few dirhams. They grabbed at them, laughed and vanished as abruptly as they had appeared.

On a cool and cloudy day, and which one was not, our Comtesse drove us to see the Menara. This, truth to tell, is of no great interest being the ruins of a small pavilion, a sort of Folly built beside a reflecting pool but the two rooms, one above the other hung with rugs, are rather attractive.

At the foot of the terrace on which it stands, an Arab was showing off his snakes: two small cobras and a couple of unknowns. I find them distasteful but I am not as terrified of snakes as I used to be and when Norton had taken the man's picture he came close to the car in which I was sitting to collect his tip. Two of his pets were draped around his neck but I did not scream. Also, and I am at a loss to explain it, when he returned to where the cobras were coiled up waiting for him there was something almost wistful in the way they turned their heads to greet him.

From Menara we drove through the Agdal, an enormous orchard two miles long and nearly a mile wide, the whole area enclosed by a fifteen-foot wall of pinkish red earth. Most of the trees are olive but there are oranges too and reservoirs the size of lakes, the water to fill them flowing through canals from the mountains. Women and children picking olives from branches that had been beaten down from the trees formed patches of brilliant color against the dappled ground.

Driving around we came to a disintegrating adobe building and climbed the mud stairs made slippery by rain and loosened tiles to get to the roof. The view was worth the effort. Expansive Marrakech lay spread at our feet, nestling in its palm groves surrounded by its rosy walls that glow pink or red depending on the light. We looked down on the thousands of olive and orange trees and lakes of the Agdal. In theory turning around one should gaze upon the majesty of the Atlas Mountains glittering white against a vault of purest blue. I believe some lucky people have seen this spectacle but we did not. We saw thick gray clouds and spattering showers.

It was interesting to learn that in the days of his dubious derring-do when he was riding high all the Agdal belonged to El Glaoui.

Gavin Maxwell's *Lords of the Atlas,* a book featuring this fantastic figure, had brought something less than satisfaction to the Comtesse de Breteuil. Boul had several phrases which were an integral part of her conversation and she used them frequently: *quelle horreur,* charming with many r's, charrrming, *stupide,* and poor darrrling one. I do not know that she would have gone so far as to apply *stupide* or *quelle horreur* to Mr. Maxwell but he was definitely not a poor darrrling one. "He came here to Marrakech, he stayed only three weeks and then he wrote about El Glaoui! What does he know?"

If one reads the book the answer is a very great deal. It is a staggering job of documentation yet Boul's indignation was understandable. Non-writers seldom take into consideration the wealth of information gleanable from research nor the time that may be devoted to it. In *Lords of the Atlas,* Mr. Maxwell states in his forward that his research alone consumed several years. The statement is obviously true.

Furthermore, I never quite buy the reasoning of those who say, and they do so frequently, that they had come to a country, usually one in Asia or Africa, intending to write a book about it. "I could have done it in the first two or three weeks but now I have lived here ten years," or twenty or thirty, "and I know less of the native mind than I did when I arrived."

Such comments make me curious. I am never sure if the speaker is genuinely humble, so overawed by the inconsistencies, subtleties, complexities, or potentialities of the residents that, considering himself unworthy, he abandons the project or if he simply can't write.

It is usually true that the more we learn about a subject the more we appreciate how much we don't know but for better or worse life is a long series of deadlines. There comes a moment when the job must be started, carried through and ended. Whether or not it is finished may be open to dispute but if we're going to do it it's got to be tackled.

On our return to the Villa Taylor we found friends of Boul's who had dropped in for a pre-luncheon drink: Mrs. Pears and her brother Mr. Bevan and an elderly lady, a friend of theirs, Mrs. Pym from Ireland. She was crippled by arthritis but she told us that before her misfortune she had been an expert horsewoman mad for fox hunting. "I adore animals," she added by way of explanation. "Except foxes," I said. "Nonsense, nonsense," she cried. "The fox loves the hunt, gets as much of a thrill as we do. And believe me, setting dogs on them is the most humane way to exterminate them."

Since I could see no reason to exterminate them and certainly not in that fashion, I was pleased that Providence had seen fit to incapacitate Mrs. Pym.

Obviously no farmer wants foxes in the hen house, but nature has a nice sense of balance. Several years ago in our own country community a hunt was organized—this one in cars as there weren't any horses around—and the very small fox population was wiped out. There was a hunt breakfast and champagne and the spirit of Tally-Ho rampant. Next spring every vegetable in everybody's garden was devoured by rabbits.

There was another guest who had been at the house the night before. We told her of our morning's junket and spoke about *Lords of the Atlas* and another book of Gavin Maxwell's, the unique and beautiful *Ring of Bright Water*. The lady knew Mr. Maxwell. "What with one thing and another, those otters among them," she said drily, "his wife had quite a time living with him."

We had been invited to dine with Ira Belline. She and Boul were old and intimate friends and she had generously included us. We set off in the pitch black night along a straight flat road which was nevertheless a nervous strain. Arabs in long earth-colored djellabahs riding their bicycles with no light of any kind and impossible to see in the dark, presented a real hazard. Boul was deft at skirting around them and presently she made a sharp left with as far as we could see no landmark to indicate the spot. We bumped along for a few minutes and arrived at an attractive whitewashed adobe house. The house itself was roomy but the door so low we were obliged to stoop to enter. We were greeted and shown into the living room by Madame Belline's brother, a tall lean man with a small beard. A fire of upright olive logs was burning brightly and wild grasses in a large vase made a lovely pattern against the white walls. Our hostess was handsome in a long pink wool caftan, her head bound in a scarlet turban. She is a painter and some of her pictures were hung around the room, the most recent propped on the mantelpiece. Pictures displayed this way, not hung for all eternity, play a more immediate role in one's life. They are like books and records, accessible, to be used, changed about and enjoyed.

The one I liked best was a figure in a white robe on a white horse with shells casting shadows on the pale sand in the foreground. It was reminiscent of Chirico and Dali, but still had a personal and individual flavor.

With drinks we were given luscious home-grown and home-cured olives and a pregnant maid in a shining golden robe served dinner: rich nourishing spinach soup, chicken, saffron rice, and an unsurpassed orange compote.

Ira Belline was with the Ballet Russe. At one time she held a job in the French couture, now she paints and farms. All that variance seemed in character. To learn that she had also been Barbara Hutton's secretary was unexpected.

The farmhouse seemed to us replete with an engaging old world atmosphere and Ira and her brother live there very contentedly but she told us that two years before they had been for eight days without water and frequently they have no electricity. The charm of the Moroccan countryside is not unadulterated.

We drove home after one of the coziest, most pleasant evenings we were to spend on the entire trip. There are some Outs but there is one great In about the Villa Taylor for it *is* like being a guest in a private house. One meets many delightful people who are friends of Boul's and wherever she goes visiting, those staying in her house are usually invited.

A couple whom Boul knew well and who were by quirky coincidence also patients of Norton's and friends of ours were the writers Edita and Ira Morris. Long time habitués of Marrakech they were there on their usual winter holiday staying at the Hotel Mamounia and we went over one morning to call on them. "You should have been here in January," they said. "January was pure heaven." They had a pleasant room with a balcony overlooking the gardens beloved of Winston Churchill and which he frequently painted. The Morrises were on the third floor, the choice location as otherwise you look into the trees and down onto the swimming pool, but do not have a view of the mountains. They were devoted to the management who, devoted to them, provided them with an extra small room so each could write at the same time without distracting the other. I believe I am correct in saying that the rates are about $20 a day for two, including continental breakfast. Full pension for two comes to about $38. A good many people prefer the former plan as there are several small nice restaurants in Marrakech where it is fun to eat and of course one may always dine at the hotel if in the mood.

The Morrises and Norton and I had a good deal to talk about as we had attended the wedding of their son when for the second time he married a Japanese girl. We had never met the first one but the second was a tiny engaging little creature named Nobuku. A real cherry blossom if ever I saw one but those who know her well claim she is a tough cookie when it comes to drawing a contract. "Cherry blossom, my foot," one friend had said, "a cherry blossom encased hammer when it comes to driving home her points." His eyes shone with admiration.

We took a taxi home and as it was the Day of the Lamb—it had come at last—the driver said, when asked what we owed him, "Pay whatever you wish." It had been a very short drive so we gave him four dirhams, eighty cents. We received no Merci in return. Most natives are disillusioned by Americans. Assuming limitless wealth, having for the most part no conception of what travel costs, they are bitter when the cornucopia does not disgorge never-ending largess. Because it was such a great celebration Radouche and Minna were off for the day but Boul, Norton, and I fared happily on the cold lunch they had left for us, read, wrote, and rested in the afternoon and for cocktails went off to see an old friend of mine, Isabel Bunker, and a friend of hers, Mary Howard.

The two women were traveling together and had rented the house of Dr. Charles Poindexter. They had taken it sight unseen on the rave notices supplied by the owner, a bachelor who saw it with the eyes of love. To Isabel and Mary used not only to housekeeping but to housekeeping with considerable fanfare it was a jewel not without flaw.

Situated in the medina or old part of Marrakech which, in New York, had sounded madly picturesque, they found that the uninhibited night life of the quarter swirled around them and sleep was chancy. Downstairs, besides the living room and kitchen, was one tiny bedroom and bath and a larger apartment upstairs.

They had tossed to see who would get which and Isabel drew the upstairs one. This was fairly commodious but the only means of access was an outside staircase totally unsheltered and as there had been so much rain, going to bed was a moist proposition.

The vaunted maid had been a let down as was the gardener but there was one true pearl in the person of Ahmed who cooked like Brillat-Savarin, drove like an astronaut and kept the wheels of progress turning. Ahmed they loved. The property itself is tiny but it adjoins a mosque so the owner is reasonably safe from intrusion.

Isabel Bunker is the widow of Arthur Bunker and the sister-in-law of Ellsworth, the long-time American Ambassador to Vietnam. When she heard we were going to Katmandu, she said immediately, "But you must go to see Carol Laise, Ellsworth's wife. You know she's our Ambassador in Nepal." We had not known but accepted gratefully Isabel's offer to write to her and to send around a letter to the Villa Taylor which we would present when we got to Nepal.

We left the hospitable ladies and went off to dine at a restaurant called La Petite Auberge which though good, could not match the table set by the Comtesse. A pleasant Frenchman, Monsieur Lemaitre, had joined us and after an enjoyable but calm evening we returned home, went to bed, read for a while and fell asleep.

About half-past two I was awakened by the most terrifying noise I have ever heard. A violent shuddering roar that grew louder and louder. It was like an express train roaring into a tunnel, a dive bomber screaming down from the sky and the whole house was vibrating. It had to be an earthquake but it was incredible that we were in it. I shouted to Norton, "What is it? What is it?" and pawing desperately in the blackness found the switch on the lamp cord. Mercifully, the light went on. My husband is an old California type and at that moment I was ready to kill him. Rousing himself with an effort, he murmured, "It's a earthquake," and turned over on his pillow.

"An earthquake! Well my God, don't just lie there! Do something!"

"What would you suggest?" he shouted back. I know it's hard to shout philosophically but he seemed to be doing it. Even as he spoke, however, the dreadful noise began to diminish and finally faded altogether. "It will probably come again," said the doctor. The words were no sooner out of his mouth than it happened. The ominous rumble acclerating to a roaring wave of sound coming nearer and nearer, impossible to tell from what direction.

I leaped out of bed and this time even the California Calm roused himself. "We should stand in the doorway." I yelled, "I've always heard that's the safest place in an earthquake." We wrenched open the door which I had feared might have jammed just as lights went on in the patio and we saw Boul running toward us.

"What is it?" I asked, "what's happened?"

"It's an earthquake."

"Do you get them often?"

"Never," she cried, "never before."

She was very pale and hastily crossed herself. "I must go and find the cook."

"He can't stop it," Norton muttered, bundling himself into his dressing gown but she was hurrying along the arcade to the cook's room. By this time the roaring had tailed off like the rumbling of distant thunder as a storm moves away. We waited, I with apprehension, but it did not start up again.

Having found the cook in good condition—his loss would have been irreparable, a little color came back to Boul's face. "Thank God this house is strong," she said. That was true. Built of stone and plaster and all on one floor it was a good earthquake shelter. With the exception of the tower. Boul's great fear had been that the tower would crumble but it held firm against the night sky.

Curiously enough only two hours before her young son had called her from his school in California. "He asked me several times, 'Are you all right, Mama? Is everything all right?' Yes,

yes, I assured him. I think God had him call." I thought it was nice of God to have remembered that domestic detail before loosing the powers of darkness in all their fury.

We finally parted when reassured that the quake was really finished. As I was getting back into bed I remembered that Boul had had a glass in her hand which struck me as a good idea. The Spirit of the Andreas Fault moved in relaxed majesty to the mantelpiece where he had staked out a small makeshift bar and the Vodka he poured me warmed my quivering stomach. For a long time afterward the dogs continued barking in the town and when toward dawn we heard the muezzin's voice I assumed he was telling the faithful that Allah was merciful and all was well.

Norton's fear had been that the pool, the huge beautiful swimming pool that Boul had installed at great expense and of which she was so proud might have cracked but that catastrophe had not happened. Except for a severe and universal fright little damage was done in Marrakech, although we learned later that a few of the columns of the patio arcade had cracked and had to be reinforced.

The next morning Radouche brought us a little note from our hostess. This room to room correspondence was customary, the French Arabic *cous-cous* spoken by the staff not being conducive to a meeting of minds of varied nations. Boul had written, "You were wonderful" and for several days afterward when people would be discussing the quake she would gaze at us with tender admiration and say, "They were wonderful." We were not but we were there. In a crisis companionship counts.

Another American couple who came to stay in the villa, Bob and Helen Uhry had undergone the quake in a hotel in Casablanca. Getting out of their room and downstairs was a nervous business but their real concern had been the fear of a tidal wave that so often follows an earthquake. That fortunately did not happen. Morocco as a whole escaped virtually unscathed but Spain and Portugal suffered severely.

While Boul had been at the airport waiting for the Uhrys' plane, a charming couple whom she had invited to dine arrived at her house. They were Hugh and Emi Lou Astor. He was delightful and she was remarkably pretty and very young, I assumed about twenty-four or -five. It turned out she was the mother of five children and her oldest daughter was seventeen. It is ladies like this about whom very mean things are said by other ladies who have not captured the secret of perpetual girlhood.

The social pace we decided was definitely quickening when the next day brought James Michener and his party for pre-luncheon cocktails at the swimming pool. It was our first really hot, sunny day and optimistically the pool was being filled. Mr. Michener's Japanese wife was a charming and extremely intelligent woman.

They were accompanied by a young girl and a Mr. McAvoy, the son of J. P. McAvoy of my theatre days. McAvoy senior used to write comedies and books for musical shows and I remember once standing with him at the back of the house watching a play of his that was closing Saturday. The audience was sparse and the laughter not deafening with the exception of the author's, who unabashedly and wholeheartedly was enjoying his own jokes. He was a dear.

Mr. Michener was very nice and very formally dressed: dark suit, black socks, and black polished shoes with which he beat a tattoo on the coping of the swimming pool. He drank only orange juice and when telling us about a lethal cigar he had smoked, he took out a notebook and read off its ingredients. I thought that a scientific approach. Mr. McAvoy was traveling with the Micheners because he was writing an article for *Reader's Digest* on James Michener writing a book. Perhaps on the equal time theory they would also publish Mr. Michener's reaction to Mr. McAvoy's reactions to Mr. Michener writing a book. It would be like standing between two mirrors seeing those reflections receding into eternity.

The young lady was an American working on a thesis on Spanish literature at the University of Madrid. So far the weather had been too bad for the demonstrations she had anticipated but she was eagerly looking forward to violence in the on-coming spring. "Changes have got to be made," she declared dogmatically. I said I recognized that and could often agree, but that I disliked destruction. Today's young enjoy it but then so did Lenin who was not all that young.

In Marrakech I was deep in a paperback edition of Robert Massie's *Nicholas and Alexandra* and had just read of Lenin's dejection when under the Czar the lot of the peasants began to ameliorate. He feared it would make the revolution unnecessary and he took a grim satisfaction in learning that his son and daughter-in-law had committed suicide because they thought society was improving without extreme measures. A yearning for bloodshed and suffering is surprisingly prevalent. Hence wars, I suppose.

When the Michener party left, we lunched on the terrace and Boul told us that King Hassan and the Pasha of Marrakech had once spent a few nights in her house. She and her sister had slept in the smaller wing that opened on the other patio. She had told His Majesty that she would be honored to have him as a guest but she had stipulated sternly that there were to be no women, in which he concurred.

Around four o'clock the Uhrys and Boul and I—the doctor had begged off—departed for the souks. After wandering around for about an hour making small purchases, we went into a hand-some Moroccan restaurant, a sort of interior covered courtyard with high fluted columns and balconies and boxes like a theatre. We ordered mint tea and it was nearly the end of me. It induced violent and painful upheavals and from then on to a greater or lesser degree I was host to the miseries. Traveler, beware!

The next day, although not for that reason, we left Marrakech. It is an exotic and fascinating place and when the weather is good must be unadulterated joy but apparently the seasons are hard to pin down. In early May we received a letter from Boul saying the weather was not cold but she added, "I think the sun must be on the moon."

We had enjoyed the Villa Taylor and while one cannot say that a sojourn chez la Comtesse is economical the $72 a day for two covers everything, drinks before meals, wine, even laundry and there are many advantages. Instead of being in a hotel one is in a private house presided over by a discriminating and meticulous hostess. The food is delicious and the cocktail hour is adequate if not prolonged. This after all is a French establishment and food quite rightly takes precedence.

Of course, despite paying, the very fact that one *is* in another person's house does impose certain restrictions which do not obtain in a hotel. Punctuality at meals—knowing how good they were, we were usually ahead of time—but also a certain curtailment of guests. In a hotel you may invite friends to lunch or dine with you and that's that. At the villa it is a little more delicate, one asks permission or sometimes the Comtesse will suggest that you might like to bring someone along. If you do, despite the private house atmosphere, you must expect that the meal will be an extra on the bill just as it would be in a hotel.

We departed with a rush and a roar. Helen Uhry asked Norton for a prescription for some pills she wanted and I had to fish around in my brief case, already in the trunk compartment to find his prescription pad. I then thought I had forgotten my glasses and rushed back to our room to search for them. Bedclothes, books, towels tossed madly about as Minna and Radouche search with me. An annoyed shout from the master at the car. Glasses found. Rush out, hop in, car starts to pull away when Boul calls and waves frantically. "Here, here the remedy, you forgot it!" We back up and she thrusts into my hand a small metal tube of tablets she swears by, for calming inner disturbances such as mine brought on by the mint tea. I grab it. *"Merci, merci mille fois, au revoir."* We are off.

The drive to Casablanca was an anticlimax: long straight flat dull, 237 kilometers, two and a half hours. Our reward was the airport luncheon. Excellent but be sure to go upstairs, do not tarry at the snack bar at ground level. The food up there is as far above anything served at Kennedy as Kennedy is far from Casablanca. Our enjoyment was further enhanced by an engaging French family lunching at a nearby table. Mother, father, a little girl six, two small boys four and five. Fortunately there had been a production hiatus for the next offspring was a few-months-old infant. The other children kept jumping up and down and leaving the table to cuddle the baby in his basket on the floor so that he felt very much a participant in the festivities. Those youngsters were trenchermen. When we saw them devouring the hors d'oeuvres which were many and varied we assumed that that one course would stay them. Not at all. Right along with their parents they made their way through the entire spectrum. Hors d'oeuvres, main course, dessert, cheese and fruit. Naturally washed down with a few swallows of good wine.

We had been obliged to drive to Casablanca to get the plane to Tunis, a three-hour flight including a stopover in Algiers. Diary note: *Airborne dinner between A. and T. a mess.*

In Tunis the next morning, just to keep the welkin ringing, we woke to the rain which was to be the pattern of our days. Two or three months before in New York I had met a capable and amusing young woman named Shasha Guiga whose husband was the head of the Tunisian Tourist Bureau. She had been helpful in her suggestions and asked me please to call her on our arrival. I did so from the Hotel Hilton. Avid seekers after local color, we had suggested to her via a telegram from Marrakech that we might go for something a bit more native. She sent a gentle reply: SUGGEST YOU KEEP YOUR RESERVATIONS HOTEL HILTON. It was a good idea. Stereotyped, comfortable, satisfactory service, and no leaks. This considering the weather was a bonus.

A car from Monsieur Guiga's office came to fetch us, bringing a knowledgeable young man with the debonair name of Taoufik Kastalli. Taoufik means victory and his American friends, of whom he had many, called him Victor.

He drove us into the center of town—like all the Hiltons in that part of the world this one was somewhat removed—and we liked the town at once. There is a hustle and bustle about Tunis that one senses immediately, very different from the rest of North Africa. It is small but it is a capital city like Lisbon or Copenhagen or Dublin, and Norton said rightly that it had the same vigor as Barcelona. Physically it is attractive. The population numbers about 500,000 and one's impression is of prosperity, cleanliness, and high keyed color. Most of the buildings are white with bright blue shutters, balconies and grill work, a theme repeated wherever we went.

Tunisia became independent of France in 1956. On the whole, the divorce was amicable, without the bloodshed and bitchery of the French-Algerian debacle and the country today is a republic with a president, Habib Bourguiba.

The merchandise in the shops of the republic is tempting although I made a mistake in buying a woolen burnoose, a straight robe of apricot, coral, and beige stripes with a hood. I fancied myself in it on our beach at home but when I put it on it was like the flaming garment of Medea, it was a maddening hair shirt and I tore it off but not before I had broken out in a scarlet rash from head to toe. This was probably caused by a personal allergy, which nobody else might experience but for what it is worth, I pass the information along as a warning. A bit of stock from the shelves of the same shop that proved more congenial was a narrow horizontal panel woven in blue, green, and white wool, a Tunisian scene with a little mosque and palm trees.

We lunched at the Café de Paris where the food was reasonably good and watched with amusement a couple engrossed in each other; an older man who, we were sure, had money and a young one all smiles, dimples, and curls hanging on his every word, laughing extravagantly at his jokes.

In the course of our stay I had occasion to call a Tunisian business acquaintance at his office. It was after luncheon, during the siesta hour when he had said a telephone call would not disturb him but when he answered I thought his manner abrupt. "That's funny," I said to Norton, "maybe I interrupted him at something."

"A dame," said my husband, adding airily, "or maybe a boy. Isn't that what siestas are for?" He was getting very sophisticated.

On our first afternoon in Tunis we decided we would Grapple with History. Despite the pouring rain we would visit Carthage. All my life I have been vague as to where Carthage was. The north shore of Africa, yes. But where? "On such a night stood Dido with a willow in her hand and waved her love to come again to Carthage." Very beautiful but where was she? I will tell you. In the suburbs where well-off Tunisians and the diplomatic corps have their summer homes some fifteen kilometers northeast of Tunis. Reversing the usual trend of the rural community overcome by creeping asphalt and concrete rot the urban glory of Carthage is today but a memory. Founded in the ninth century B.C. by, so legend has it, Queen Dido, the willow waver, it was destroyed in 146 B.C. by the Roman, Scipio Africanus. He was a thorough man. It took two weeks for the city to burn to the ground and we may assume he watched with gloating satisfaction. Later on the Romans rebuilt Carthage, it flourished anew and was finally destroyed by the Arabs in A.D. 698.

Dido was a Tyrian emigrant. Her father was the Tyrian king, Mutton I. Good solid name. *Her* name was Elissa but she came to be called Dido because it means the fugitive. Authorities claim there is no truth in it but I still like the story of how she bought some property to build a new city. According to the agreement she was to have "as much land as could be contained by the skin of an ox." It was to be a small city. But that Dido, she was a wily one. She cut up the skin into narrow strips and was thus enabled to encircle a whole hill which because of the ruse was named Byrsa and *that* say the authorities accounts for the story. It's a

play on words; Byrsa meaning hide or skin and the Phoenician
bosra or borsa meaning citadel.

I will not go into the history of Carthage and I assume we
all learned as much about the Punic Wars as we care to know in
our schooldays but for the very reason that the city is such an
integral part of one's youth and education when one is in the
neighborhood it exerts a strong pull.

As I say, we drove there in the teeming rain only to learn
that like Philadelphia on Sunday, Carthage is closed on Monday.
However, our alert driver, supplied courtesy of Mr. Guiga and
his tourist office, did a bit of telephoning from a booth at the
gate and they said we could look around.

Norton was pulling himself up from the back seat, one hand
on the upright framing the window when the driver, unaware of
his movement, slammed the door on his fingers. My husband
neither screamed nor fainted, which I thought remarkable as the
pain was excruciating. When the first shock had abated I told
him he was marvelous, a true stoic. He gave a little half laugh.
"Yes," he gasped, "we should have been in Sparta." When able
to take an objective view of his hand he said he was lucky the
car was old and the door a little warped. "Had it been brand
new and fitted," he said, "I'd probably have lost the tips of three
fingers." The poor driver was distraught, "Monsieur, Monsieur,
pardon, oh pardon," but fortunately the results were not lasting.
The doctor's nails turned black but he didn't lose them and in
about four months they were as good as new.

With the exception of a few fragments and capitals, all the
marble of the city's great days has vanished, mostly filched by
beys of Tunis and used to build the Bardo Palace. Some conduits,
foundations and arches of baths that were larger than those of
Caracalla in Rome still remain. I do not know if it was native to
them or if bathing was imposed by the Romans but from the
evidence, the Carthaginians appear to have been a very clean
people.

Cap Gamarth, the small harbor of La Goulette, and the village

1. The travel agents relaxing on their commission

2. The householders: Twiggy, Pumpkin, Cindy

3. Wanda Jaclonski, the oil queen and associates

4.　From north to south: Ilka, camel, outside Tangier

5.　Looking at the sea from within the caves of Hercules

6. Berber child. Morocco

7. Souks and customers in the Medina of Fes

8. "Come with me, Bub." Two men in the Medina, Fes

9. Mosque courtyard. Infidels may look but not enter

10. Courtyard of Medersa where we stood freezing while Abdel indoctrinated us into the Muslim religion

11.   Roman arch at Volubilis

12.   Mosaic floor. Volubilis

13.   La Comtesse. Boule de Breteuil

14.   Patio of the Villa Taylor

15.   Salon of the Villa Taylor looking towards the dining room

16.   Dining room of the Villa Taylor

17. Donkey market on the road to Asni

18. Casbah of El Glaoui. Ouarzazate, Morocco

19.   Good Dr. Brown in the Bardo Museum. Tunis

20.   Dancing dwarfs. Bardo Musuem. Tunis

21.   Masques. Bardo Museum. Tunis

of Sidi-bou-Said, form a triangle which encompassed the area of Carthage at its peak and today Sidi-bou-Said is an engaging spot, Tunisia's answer to Provincetown on Cape Cod.

Situated on a cliff dropping to the sea it is picturesque, old and the architecture is more interesting than Cape Cod. Most of the houses are white with blue shutters and the forms are basic and pure: the cube, the dome, an occasional arch. In the summer artists, writers, and journalists flock to the small villas that straggle up and down the hillside and the streets are so narrow that no cars are allowed to enter. We were told that on one steep staircase that leads up to a popular café the young people cluster so thickly that waiters have all but to kick their way through them when trying to fulfill orders.

A nearby colony is La Marsa where the Guigas have a villa. As far as we could gather they are domiciled all over Tunisia and from personal experience can advise tourists on places most likely to appeal to individual taste.

The restaurant they advised and where we dined that evening, the M'Rabet is worth recommending. To begin with going there is fun because it is in the souk El Traik, the souk of the tailors. However, since we arrived around nine the tailors had departed and the doctor drew a sigh of relief.

We left the cab at the entrance to the medina and walked through narrow twisting alleyways between shuttered shops and in thick gloom since the naked light bulbs that hung at intervals from the vaulted roof served only to intensify the shadows.

On the ground floor of the restaurant were wide platforms covered with mats on which people sat, their backs against the wall, their legs straight out in front of them. This was the chatting and coffee room, the restaurant proper was upstairs.

We had reserved a table, a good idea since the place is popular, and sat down among our co-diners; French, Tunisian and Arab. The food was delicious, especially the briks, extremely delicate and crisp pastries, fluted and fan shaped. They come stuck in wedges of lemon to be eaten with the fingers and are

stuffed with anything your own taste or the cook's imagination
may dictate: eggs, spinach, delicately broiled and chopped calves'
liver—chicken—the variety is endless. The waiter also brought
a small charcoal grill not unlike a habachi and cooked the fish
at the table. The white wine was excellent and we longed to try
the tempting desserts but by that time we had reached capacity.

In the course of the evening the inevitable belly dancer appeared. She had long black hair and wore rather modest gauzy
robes with a crimson bra and low placed jeweled belt but although she was supple and energetic, I felt she lacked the élan,
the joie de vivre, the je ne sais quoi of her sisters in Tangier.
The doctor, however, kept nodding appreciatively and murmuring, "Not bad, not bad."

When we left the restaurant to return to our hotel, bemused
perhaps by the gyrations he had been witnessing, he most uncharacteristically—for he has a great bump of location—took a
wrong turning. I myself felt we were in error but as I am usually
wrong in these matters I did not like to correct the walking compass to whom I am married.

We slogged along through the dank, gloomy alleys, our foot-
steps echoing on the cobblestones and I was beginning to think
we would slog on through the night with neither thread nor
breadcrumbs to guide us out when ahead of us we noticed a
man who although he kept walking, also kept turning his head
to look back at us. Finally he slowed his pace and stopped until
we caught up with him. In French I asked him if we were headed
for the Rue de Casbah and a taxi. We were not. "As soon as I
saw you," he said, "I was sure you were lost." He most obligingly turned and led us back to the paths of righteousness and a
fortuitous taxi. He told us he was a student and was going the
following year to France for exchange group living. He was looking forward to it just as Taoufik had told us he was looking forward to going to America.

Another excellent restaurant, perhaps the best in Tunis, is
the small unpretentious Slah in the Rue Pierre de Coubertin. It

was clean, the food was delicious, the prices reasonable and the atmosphere tranquil yet spirited with a clientele for the most part young and heterosexual.

The next morning we met Driss, Mr. Guiga, husband of Shasha who kindly gave us two handsome illustrated books on Tunisia. We were delighted to have them but when traveling by air heavy gifts no matter how grand are an embarrassment. We tactfully wondered if it would be possible to send them home which subsequently was tactfully done and eventually they arrived tactfully in New York.

I should not say the souks of Tunis are as fascinating as those of Tangier, Fes or Marrakech and although they were almost Scandinavian in their cleanliness, cleanliness is not really a souk virtue. A little local color, a little peasant earthiness—they are preferable. One amusing specialty they do have and which we did not see elsewhere is white wire onion domed birdcages. They come in every size from tiny ones in which one could keep a cricket to great pallazos worthy of eagles. I hope no one would dream of caging an eagle but were it only an overnight stop, he might shack up in one of those comfortably enough.

The best of the other purchases, as they had been in Morocco, were brass, leather goods and rugs. We also bought two little stuffed cloth hands emerging from fat cloth crescents sewn with bangles and stuck with bits of tinsel. One was purple, one crimson. They are kooky baubles supposed to bring you good luck and they are known as the hand of Fatima, the daughter of Mohammed the Prophet.

But if the souks of Tunis are not outstanding, their Bardo Museum is extraordinary. Originally a palace, the building itself is of no great interest but the art objects installed in what was once the harem are remarkable. Their collection of Roman mosaics is one of the finest in the world. The life of Roman Africa is there displayed in all its color and variety. There are circuses and country life lived in charming villas, fishing scenes and farming scenes, a naked lady admiring herself in a mirror

and heads of leopards and swans surrounded by garlands. Here
are riches and the Tunisians know that there are quantities of
mosaics still to be unearthed.

Besides the mosaics the museum contains a marvelous head,
a bearded satyr pockmarked by time, aging virile irrepressible,
a happy hedonist. There are great urns and bas reliefs and a
bust of the Emperor Vespasian looking strikingly like Lyndon
Johnson. Among the most beguiling of the exhibits are animated
figures of Greek dancing dwarfs stolen from a ship that sailed
the seas in 81 B.C. The dwarfs and other articles are known as
the Madhia treasure and it is thought likely that they were part of
the great booty collected by Sulla in Asia Minor after his
victorious campaign against Mithridates. I may add that we
viewed these treasures in a glacial chill and returned to the hotel
to pick up sweaters as much as to pick up my old friend, George
Sebastien, who was living there and who was going to drive with
us to Hammamet to meet Shasha.

I first met George years ago when I was going to school in
Paris. At that time there was a group of artists drawing fashions
for *Vogue* whom I came to know well because my mother as
editor of the magazine was on amicable terms with nearly all the
contributors. There was Main Bocher who later made such a
name for himself in the French couture, and Douglas Pollard.
There was George Hoyningen Huene, the photographer, and
Porter Woodruff. Then there was George Sebastien. George did
not work for *Vogue* but he and Woodruff were devoted friends
and he was around.

I remembered George well. He was a Romanian, lean and
vulpine in appearance with dark hair growing in a deep V on
his forehead. He was married to an older and very rich American
woman named Flora.

In 1939 her car rolled over a cliff in Mexico while she was
in it. Her maid had got out to pick flowers and so had the
chauffeur forgetting to put on the brakes. The fall did not kill

Flora but it can't have done her any good for she developed pneumonia and, smoking up to sixty cigarettes a day, soon died.

I had not seen George in all the years that had intervened between Paris and this present visit to Tunis, yet when he stepped from the elevator despite his greatly changed appearance I was sure it was he. He had grown a bit portly, the saturnine features were now cast in pink cherubic mold and the strong dark hair had completely vanished leaving only a little white tonsure fringe.

He greeted us cordially and on the drive to Hammamet spoke with enthusiasm of his friends all of whom seemed to be well known figures in society and immensely rich. I think perhaps he was often lonely and had not a great deal of money himself and he found it comforting to talk about them.

During the time we were in Tunis whenever we saw him he spoke of money and of how expensive everything was, adding, "but then I never had any money." One day I said to him, "Oh come on, George, Flora was a very rich woman." Everyone had assumed he would inherit a packet.

He sighed. "That's just it," he said. "I've always been near money but I've never had any myself." Mrs. Sebastien had taken it with her.

To my surprise I learned he was seventy-four. "George! That can't be possible."

"Well, I'm seventy-three but I'll be seventy-four in September. I always add a year, then when my birthday comes, I am not surprised. The day I'm seventy-four I'll say I'm seventy-five." He was disarming.

In Hammamet we went to the Hotel Sinbad where Shasha was waiting for us warmly clad in a mustard yellow knit with a purple border, heavy brown leather boots and a leather coat. While she attended to a little business George took us around the hotel which he knew well. He knew all of Hammamet like his pocket, having lived there for many years.

The Sinbad is small and charming, every room having its own

patio, a sort of garden alcove opening on the beach. Full pension is $13 a day and Mr. Winkler, the manager, proved most pleasant.

Having organized her business affairs with typical dispatch Shasha presently returned. No languorous Oriental she. She devotes herself to her husband and four tall sons, runs several houses, works in ceramics and paints.

After luncheon we went to see the house the Guigas are building in Hammamet. It is set in an orange grove and will be a place of considerable charm with lovely carved stone lintels and door frames which they found lying neglected in ancient ruins.

Although it was not our business here once more a house was being built for a hot climate. For those months of the year when it rains and the dampness penetrates one's marrow it will be, I should think, cold and uncomfortable.

The guest cottage where they spend the night when they come out from Tunis to supervise progress was attractive and the abstract painting by Shasha that hung on the wall I thought colorful and good.

In the garden we saw a large handsome bird about the size of a crow. He was beige with white spots and a red head and he was in a tiny square cage madly beating his wings in his longing to escape. "Oh, Shasha," we said, "please let him out, *please* let him go."

"I don't know what to do," she said. "Originally I put him in there," and she pointed to one of the very large onion-domed cages like the ones we had seen in the souks, "but those two doves resented him and they kept pecking at his head. To save him I put him in this one," and she indicated the wretched little prison.

"But why cage him at all?" I asked. George was furious and started excoriating her. Two servants came out of the house to see what the hubbub was all about. Shasha looked vague, shrugged and went inside. "Go on," said George to the two men, "let him out and be quick about it." With obvious reluctance they released the prisoner who flew off into the orange trees. Once the bird was free George's good humor returned. He slapped one of the men on the back. "There goes your dinner. You would have eaten him tonight, I know you." The men laughed, there was no ill will.

We had come to Hammamet to see the community and to meet Shasha but also to see the house George had built in the thirties which had gained considerable fame because of its location and the beauty of its design.

It was set in a twenty acre garden he and Flora were able to create because of underground fresh water pools. The house of whitewashed plaster is large and open, more a beautiful rambling loggia than a conventional enclosed dwelling. There are not many rooms but all are spacious. The dining room is a terrace on the sea and the drawing room has an alcove furnished with a grand piano, I should imagine badly out of tune due to the climate. A long narrow swimming pool enclosed by arches lends a wonderfully Arabian Nights atmosphere.

George's room and a guest room are on the ground floor. Flora's room with its entrancing white-latticed terrace is on the other side of the pool up a steep little staircase.

When his lifelong friend, Porter Woodruff (Dick as he was always called) died of cancer, George got permission from the government to build a small mausoleum on the property. It is a typically Tunisian structure, cube and dome, shaded by eucalyptus trees.

Adjoining the land the municipality has recently erected a peculiarly ugly outdoor theatre in the style of the Greek amphitheatre. Unpainted cinder blocks are cemented together and bare scaffolding towers to hold the lights are silhouetted like gibbets against the sky. The only inoffensive part is the artist's quarters down the hill.

These are like underground bunkers but they are roomy and low windows open on the sea. The actors sleep two to a room. The idea of a theatre was a good one but why couldn't they have set it back in the orange groves, any place where it wouldn't defile the view?

George lived on in the house after Flora's death, but in 1943 he came to the United States and General Erwin Rommel installed himself in the romantic surroundings when he was in North Africa.

After the war George returned and although artists and writers began coming back again as they had in the old days, the days were not the same.

The government took over the property allowing him to keep only two or three acres. Eventually in what was perhaps a squeeze play or perhaps he could no longer afford it, he said he sold it to the government for $100,000 dollars. He has always been bitter about that, feeling he should have got much more and today it is undoubtedly worth twice the amount. If I understand correctly, the Rockefeller International Fund later repaid the $100,000 to the Tunisian government and the house is now used as an International Cultural Center where artists and writers may stay for limited sojourns. The prospect is tempting but not in early March.

George did not go to his house with us. Since Woodruff's death and the passing of the property to the government he has never seen it.

We rejoined him at the Sinbad and he took us to the Casbah. Having lived so long in Hammamet he has become a kind of unofficial official town planner and is now engaged in skillfully restoring the ancient fort. In its new incarnation the ancient stronghold will be a simple and picturesque seaside café.

From the Casbah we went on to Nabeul, a village famous for its pottery, where the indefatigable Shasha sometimes works. It was amusing to see hundreds of earthen pots and roosters and tiles and vases in various stages of creation. While I watched a child modeled for me a tiny pitcher which I still have.

The next day, our last in Tunis, we lunched at the Hilton. The food was not outstanding with the exception of some absolutely delicious prawns, the most flavorful and succulent I have ever tasted. They were big fellows with whiskers and hard little round eyes and we learned that the shrimps of Carthage were famous in Roman times too.

Since it was a beautiful day we decided to take advantage of so rare a treat, stopping off again at Carthage en route to the airport. In sunlight it was more appealing, also Dr. Brown did not get his fingers smashed and this time we saw an upper area we had missed before. At one time it had been a great square and a broken column and ancient statues still stand against the sky.

The air terminal when we reached it was an Arab madhouse with huddled heaps of exhausted dirty white-veiled Arab women crouched on the floor, their dejected postures the essence of misery. They were either going to or returning from the hadj—it was the height of the season for the annual pilgrimage to Mecca —but the poor souls seemed to be deriving small comfort from their religion.

The Tunis-Tripoli flight is one hour and Tripoli time is an hour later. Pan American's crack ground service was at our disposal and as we drew nearer to Saudi Arabia, although not very near, the long arm of Wanda Jablonski, our friend in oil, reached out to us.

The Esso Company had sent a car to meet us and we were handed a note from the Ken Millers. Mr. Miller, a friend and associate of Wanda's, represents *Petroleum Intelligence Weekly* in Libya and he and his charming wife have lived there for some time.

Thanks to them, we had a reservation at the Hotel Uaddan instead of the Libya Palace where we had been booked originally. With all that oil I am sure the Libyans will someday build a good hotel. Until they do, the Uaddan is the lesser of the two evils available to the traveler.

The note said that the Millers regretted their inability to meet the plane but that they would be at our hotel a 10 P.M. No one should go to the airport unless he has to because it is an eighteen-mile drive from town. They built it just before the war and, airports being popular targets, placed it where they did in order to save the city from destruction when the inevitable bombs would begin dropping. A new terminal building is in the works. They need it.

We had barely got to our room when the Millers arrived and a delightful couple they turned out to be—warm, helpful and knowledgeable. Ken is a dear, a notably able newspaperman and Leyna is a blond, blue-eyed Greek at home in seven languages.

It was getting late and we were hungry but the hotel dining room was a mistake: the food frightful and the blaring band an assault on the eardrums. We had literally to shout at one another.

Afterward Ken suggested a drive around the old city walls and we gazed with awe upon the four-sided staunch chunky arch of Marcus Aurelius which has been there since the second century A.D.

It just goes to show that when something is built to last it can render unexpected service to posterity. We were amused when Ken told us that in the early days of the flicks the arch was used as a movie house. The seating capacity must have been limited but the exclusive audience was able to see the silent silvery wonders of the cinema in all their glory.

Leaving the arch-cum-theatre we said to the Millers, "Isn't there some nice little café where we might have coffee?" Sadly they shook their heads. "Unfortunately not. Nothing of the kind exists." Oil is wonderful but you can't put it in a little cup and drink it. Libya understandably is still so excited about her new wealth, who wouldn't be—from zero to 3,000,000 barrels a day in ten years—that she hasn't had time to learn the lesson so cogently brought home to King Midas.

Back at the hotel we leaned from our windowsill overlooking the harbor. A battleship lay at anchor and, as Marrakech had been, the town was gaily decorated, this time for a Trade Fair that was opening the following day.

The Tripoli harbor is large and as old as the history of the

Mediterranean world. The town lies on the site of the emporium or market established by the Phoenicians about 1000 B.C. They called it Macar Uiat. Later, guess who came along, and it was named Oea and with Leptis Magna and Sabratha formed the land of the three cities—treis polis—or the Tripolitania of the Romans. Supposedly it was the land of the Lotus Eaters who caused Ulysses so much trouble although as a small guide book states with candor, "All that story is rather vague."

Thrusting its mammoth wedge deep into the Sahara between Egypt and Algeria, Libya is as large as France, Spain, Italy, and West Germany combined but before the discovery of oil, once the 1300 mile sea coast was left behind, sand was its principal product.

We had been invited to the opening of the Trade Fair—in which among other things the glorious new product was to be featured —and early the next morning we were picked up by Mr. Donald Snook, press representative extraordinary, of the Esso Company.

We had very good seats in the reviewing stand and while I have never thought of a reviewing stand as a homey place, this one was. It had great charm, the canopy and draperies being of the prettiest printed paisley cotton one could hope to see. Although King Idris at that time was still on the throne, he was not present but the Libyan Prime Minister, Mr. Wanis Geddafi, was, and he reviewed the troops who marched and presented arms to that old Muslim chant, "Daisy, Daisy, Give Me Your Answer True."

As the Prime Minister was speaking a helicopter passed overhead squirting out leaflets that fluttered down like glittering confetti, orange and green and white, the colors of the Libyan flag although there is black in that as well. It was a pretty sight but my sympathies went out to those who would later have to clean up the mess.

Flags of nations participating in the Fair whipped in the breeze from the top of the main gate but that of America was not among them as this year the Libyans had belatedly changed their minds deciding only at the last moment to make the fair international instead of national as originally planned.

Flags on poles are scarcely news but the Libyans did something else with them that we had never before seen and that created a gay and shimmering spectacle. Small flags of all nations were shot from cannons and attached to little silken parachutes frolicked down the sky chased by puffs of white smoke. It was a joyous sight and Mr. Snook told us the Libyans are past masters of fireworks. One never guesses a nation's hidden talents! He also told us that with the discovery of oil in less than ten years the average annual Arab income has risen from under $100 to $1000. They are very pleased.

Driving to the Fair we had been just behind the car of the American ambassador who, I understood, had been posted to Iran. Since Norton and I were going there I said, "Wouldn't it be nice if we could meet him. He might give us a few tips."

As we were visiting one of the exhibits sure enough there he was too and we were introduced to him. All smiles and dimples, relishing the delicious title I said, "I understand, Excellency, that you were in Iran."

He stared at me a moment. "Iraq," he said and with a brief bow turned on his heel and departed. So much for helpful hints from the top brass.

One feature of the Fair that was entertaining if unexpected was a band of Scottish pipers—trousers not kilts, too bad—who marched and countermarched through the grounds, the pipes skirling merrily.

Pavilions had been erected by many nations including Poland and the U.S.S.R. Russia had machinery but she also had Vodka, ranks and ranks of bottles of all sizes.

Thinking how educational it would be for Russians to sample American bourbon whiskey, the thought naturally followed—why should we not sample their contribution to human betterment? In this hands across the sea spirit—let the people speak and never mind the politicians—I tried to buy a bottle from a decorative young lady but she explained that nothing was for sale.

This seemed curious. Were the bottles mere decoys? Filled with water perhaps? For advertising purposes only? We never found out.

Since this was an industrial fair I cannot say I was entranced by the exhibits although the enormous Esso models of heat exchange systems for liquefying natural gas were quite handsome and because of their colors and forms looked remarkably like Léger paintings. I said as much to Mr. George Culp, director of the Esso Company in Libya. I said, "They look like Léger paintings don't they, Mr. Culp?" Mr. Culp said, "They made the models first and the blueprints afterward." Dr. Brown said, "I imagine that is a revolutionary procedure." Mr. Culp said, "It is." That was not my morning. Nor did noontime bring improvement. For luncheon Norton and I were on our own and we went to a restaurant that had been recommended to us, the Akropol, an unattractive spot where a modest but inedible meal for two came to $15.70. That was our initiation into the standard procedures in the city.

In the restaurants the food and service are deplorable and they rob you blind. I expect it's because of the oil. Everybody in the country knows it exists. They know that oil and money are synonymous and if they personally can't get their hands on the former, they'll settle for cash. I believe there are other explanations having to do with supply and demand and interest rates, with the difficulties of transportation, plain lack of sophistication in the culinary department and endless other fol de rols but for the hapless tourist, victim of poor food and high prices my theory will suffice.

In the afternoon our good spirits revived for Leyna picked us up and we went to the souks. They could not compare with those of Fes but it is only fair to say that many were closed because of the Fair. We stopped off at a rug souk where Leyna chatted along at a great rate in German with some German friends and dropped in on the proprietor of a tiny gold souk and listened, awed, while she and he conversed in spirited Italian. I know enough to know when these languages are well spoken and Mrs. Miller spoke with the tongue of a native, under the circumstances preferable to that of men and of angels. It was her Italian chum who was our undoing.

"He's a very honest dealer," she assured us, "and his things are good." This I could see with my own eyes. I could see especially a gold necklace and it was love at first sight. Strung on a gold chain was a flexible bib formed of fish, crescent moons and thin Turkish gold coins. I was seduced by the merry marriage of the Christian symbol of the fish, the moons of Islam and for good measure the tender of mammon, each piece stamped.

We priced the pretty bauble and gulped at the honest merchant's reply. Although I had had no success with it before I thought to try once again the system of Dr. Charles Poindexter. Haggle. I enlisted the aid of Leyna. Perhaps the beauty of his native tongue, fluted so dulcetly by a charming woman would move the man. He cocked an ear, he smiled, he spoke. The figure stood. I sighed and we went away. For two days I held out and finally it was the doctor who undermined me. "Dear, it isn't all that much and it's a very pretty thing. If you have your heart set on it let's get it." What kind of discipline is that? "Of course," he added knowingly, "we've got to bargain." "Of course." We corraled Leyna. We went back to the jeweler and began our overtures. He sighed. "You see," he said, "it costs more than I told you the other day. I've been weighing it." Indeed his scales were on the counter before him. "I made a mistake the first time, it's heavier than I thought." The price he quoted was seventeen dollars more than the original. We bought it. Moral: Strike while the iron is hot.

Seated in the shop we had noticed a young Arab woman, her toes and the tips of her fingers heavily hennaed and her veil undone exposing her face. She was, said Leyna, a prostitute and certainly the veiling of the virtuous was more complete in Libya than in any other Arab or Moslem country we visited. A Libyan woman on the street, wrapped in her barracan, looks like a tent on the move. Visible are two small padding feet, one eye, the right, and nothing more.

The Millers told us of an Arab friend of theirs, a woman of considerable education who spoke Italian and English, who would never come to their house to see them and who, when she wished to speak with Leyna, had one of her children call the number in case Ken might be home and answer the telephone. She would receive both male and female Miller in her house but when they went there to dine they parted at the door. Leyna went into the women's quarters and Ken spent the evening with the men. They met each other on the threshold when it was time to go home.

Yet curiously enough at a dinner party the Millers hospitably gave for Norton and me the woman's husband and one of her daughters, unveiled, were among the guests. His name was Fuab Kabazi and he was, Ken said, *the* intellectual of Tripoli. He wore a small pointed beard and had at one time held a post in the oil ministery. He was a witty man who wrote poetry and he had translated D'Annunzio into Arabic. To us it seemed strange that with such a temperament he should be married to a recluse. The old customs, of course, are slowly fading and I imagine that the children of the girl who accompanied her father to dinner will hear with amusement and incredulity the story of their veiled and cloistered grandmother.

There was another couple, the Sherkasis. Mr. Sherkasi, a Libyan, was grave—not a smile all evening. But his wife, Maria, was animated and extremely intelligent. She was small and dark with a sharp profile and had traveled extensively and with real knowledge throughout her native country, Italy.

Another dinner guest or more accurately host was Bongo, the beguiling Miller poodle. The party had gone with commendable smoothness but with disillusion I learned that the servant problem is not confined to the U.S.A. The Millers had one man, Mohammed. Leyna said he was very good but he refused to peel onions or potatoes or to appear on Fridays or Sundays.

We were also invited to dine with the George Culps who had a big house on the water. They lived in what was considered a swank residential area but the streets were unpaved. It was a buffet party, twenty or more people and dinner was served about ten o'clock. Norton and I were very hungry but it was good training for what was to come when we would be introduced into the frenetic social life of Jidda in Saudi Arabia.

The Culps had an organ which George played very well and after dinner we all gathered around and sang. It was a cheerful evening but we had a full day ahead so when an attractive southern woman offered to drive us home we gratefully accepted. In a moment a man came up and said politely, "We'll be glad to take you." Thinking he was her husband we followed him out to his car and were somewhat shaken when his wife, a totally different non-Southern belle got in beside us. The first one must have thought us singularly rude or perhaps touched in the head.

The project for which we had wanted to rest up was our day at Leptis Magna that glory of the Romans in Africa which ranks as one of the largest and most splendid ruins in the world.

On the way a short detour brings one to an area of considerable fascination. Altogether modern, this one was worth seeing in its own right. It is called the Sand Dune Stabilization Program and is in part the brain child of the Esso Company. The great problem of all arid lands is how to make the desert blossom like a rose and while roses still do not blow in the Sahara, the program the oil people are developing is transforming thousands of barren acres into fertile forests of eucalyptus and yellow flowering acacia trees which become commercially valuable in from ten to twenty-five years.

Growing rapidly these trees send down firm roots and establish their own windbreaks but when first planted the seedlings must be protected long enough to allow those roots to develop and get some kind of purchase in the ground.

The trouble has always been that the desert sand and the dunes are constantly shifting in the hot winds and the struggling infants would be buried or uprooted, left to wither and die in the baking sun. They used to try to protect them with windbreaks of dead grass but it was a laborious and not very satisfactory method.

One fine day in 1960 Mr. Tad Les, an Esso research man, presently the company's manager in Bengazi, got an inspiration after, one may assume, a good deal of thought, sweat and experimenting. Now, just prior to setting out the seedlings, and sometimes afterward, strange enormous vehicles move into the areas to be planted and spray them with a coating of special oil that not only stabilizes the sand but is so formulated that it allows rain to enter the ground and prevents evaporation. The blackened surface by absorbing more of the sun's rays than is normally the case increases the earth's temperature and hastens the development of the plants.

Frankly it looks perfectly awful but it does promote extraordinary growth and in time the black surface crumbles away, the trees and a carpet of grass remain.

Not far from this modern marvel we stopped to admire a small ancient one, a recently excavated villa at Tagiura. It is directly on the sea and has some enchanting mosaics. Ken Miller said that in the Roman days the whole coast line was undoubtedly heavily settled with the villas of the well-to-do. Like Santa Monica and Malibu except that the houses were done in exquisite taste and each was very self-contained even to the extent of having its own kilns for making pottery.

The guardian of this pretty treasure was much annoyed when he saw us taking pictures, because nothing from the digs had yet been published. Ken shrugged him off. "Pay no attention," he said. "We aren't going to beat the authorities into print. He has nothing to worry about."

The drive to Leptis Magna took about two hours. Arrived at the gate we stretched our legs, drank cold soda water and ate the best pistachio nuts I have ever tasted. Leyna had just received a package from Greece.

Like every city of the ancient world Leptis or Lepcis (one has to make up one's mind) Magna was built on the site of an older city dating back to the Phoenicians or the Egyptians or somesuch. This time it appears to have been the Phoenicians. They called it Lepqy and built it on a flat plain near the sea in 800–700 B.C.

The Romans landed in North Africa in 207 B.C. and on an April day in A.D. 146 Septimius Severus, who was to become emperor of Rome, was born in Leptis. Wishing to do something for his home town he drew up plans for enhancing the city which at its height was inhabited by some 80,000 people and greatly patronized as a winter resort.

Apart from starting this operation he cannot have devoted much time to it, for he was constantly fighting and governing and traveling around the then known world. He behaved in a fashion that was cool, cruel, and contemporary and died at York in Britain in the year 211, supposedly poisoned by his son, Caracalla.

The destruction of Leptis was caused by enemy raids, the encroachment of desert sand, the wadi Lebda in full spate, the erosion of the sea and more than one violent earthquake. Nature was doing an effective job but she was helped along by ever impatient man. Generations of barbarians plundered the city for building materials and the civilized weren't far behind them. Three hundred of the columns which enhance Versailles were sent to Paris by Louis the XIV's consul in Tripoli and in the nineteenth century one Mr. Smith of the British Navy transported several columns and marbles to Virginia Water near Windsor.

Today the awesome ruins rise from the desert sand but in Roman times Julius Caesar, because Leptis had sympathized with his enemy, Pompey, over whom he triumphed, imposed a tribute of 240,000 gallons of oil a year, testimony to the wealth of olive orchards that surrounded the city.

The first sight that meets the visitor's eye is the arch of the founder Septimius Severus but unfortunately when we were there the majestic impact was lessened by the elaborate scaffolding surrounding it. However since it was built for preservative and restorative purposes one should not complain. A wide paved road leads from that arch to another one, a fair distance off, which was dedicated to the Emperor Trajan. Trajan was arch prone, he also had one in Ancona and another in Benevento. Septimius Severus had one in Rome too.

To me the history of triumphs and triumphal arches is fascinating and I cannot do fairer than to recommend reading the account of them to be found in the Encyclopaedia Britannica, preferably the eleventh edition, the great vintage year 1910–11.

By way of baksheesh I will toss in the information that some generals, who not having served as dictator, consul or praetor and who therefore were not entitled to a triumph regardless of their achievement, might be honored by a minor celebration called an Ovation. I was surprised to learn this was minor having always considered an ovation quite grand and gratifying—the sort of reward a great actor receives for a great performance on opening night.

Although in the case of the Romans a sheep rather than a bull was sacrificed at an ovation, signifying a lesser honor, ovis which means sheep, is probably not the derivation of the term. It stems I believe from a Greek word meaning joyful shouting and makes more sense from an actor's or anybody else's point of view.

But to get back to Leptis Magna. That which impresses most is the scale and magnitude of the city. Magna is right! The thought of what such stateliness and craftsmanship must have cost is staggering.

The majestic Basilica that served both as law court and stock exchange with its exquisitely carved columns measures approximately 368 feet in length and 152 feet wide. It was roofed with timber and was about 60 feet high.

The Forum was paved with white marble, the columns and galleries faced with marble. The side porticoes were formed of 98 columns and between the arches great heads of Medusas and Gorgons gazed upon the passing scene. They were considered good luck omens by the Romans.

Hadrian's baths, started by him in A.D. 127 and considered the most palatial of the Roman provinces, are admirably conceived and executed and between the frigidarium and the tepidarium the citizens must have glowed with antiseptics.

As the names imply, the frigidarium was a cold bath, in effect a very large swimming pool paved with mosaics and the tepidarium a room for warm baths heated by circulating hot air. The laconica was for steam as in Turkish baths or saunas. There were dressing rooms, small rooms for massage and hair dressing rooms. Possibly even restaurants. Women and children, as well as men, had access to the baths, one paid a token fee to enter and they were open day and night. The latrines were sociable. In Corinth we had seen those in the market but they were small in scale, three- and four-holers. At Leptis they were of the same Magna proportions as the rest of the city: whole rows carved in marble-faced stone set over channels of running water.

I should say that the two other places of the great city that most spark the imagination are the theatre and the market place.

The latter is an enormous rectangular area and the ghosts of merchants and shoppers seem very near, evoked not so much by the arches and columns, as by the practical earthy properties of any market: counters among them, one with deep ridges formed by the ropes on which hung scales for weighing food and other merchandise.

Two charming circular kiosks in the center were surrounded by Ionic columns with counters where goods were displayed for sale.

In another spot are the hollowed out stones used as measures, small ones for oil and liquids, larger ones for grain. Nearby a marble slab is marked off with a comparative measure for Greco-Roman and Phoenician lengths for all the world like the yard goods counter in Bloomingdale's. Those togas! The fish section is especially fine; small individual counters or slabs flanked by handsome carved marble fish. It is easy to imagine the jostling crowds, to hear the strident bargaining, chaffing, and laughter all part of the routine as the prosperous beautiful city went about its daily business.

To get a view of the theatre before visiting it and also to see the port, we climbed steep and fairly difficult stairs to be rewarded at the top by a yahoo playing a horrible transistor radio. The rasping din was deafening, an insult to one's sensibilities and eardrums. Leyna and I turned on him and between us managed to quell him. She was gentle in her plea, honey as opposed to my vinegar. I suspect hers was the approach that brought peace but I feel an unbridled sense of outrage when the tranquillity of ancient or sylvan places is destroyed by hideous inescapable noise.

Considering the number of idiotic laws which prevail in every country we can only wonder when a sensible and universal one banning such mayhem will be passed.

The port of Leptis was at one time one of the busiest of the Mediterranean. The ships putting out to sea bore oil, grain, wild animals, and slaves to every part of the Empire. The destiny of the slaves was unenviable, that of the animals violent death. It is recorded that in the reign of Titus five thousand animals were massacred in a single day. Where blood was involved the Romans were insatiable.

Of course it doesn't do to point too indignant a finger at the ancients. Murder of animals is prevalent in the twentieth century too. In September of 1969, for instance, *Town and Country* published an article—both magazine and writer apparently condoning the event as nothing short of glamorous—about a distinguished member of the French aristocracy who with ten companions ranked as outstanding "guns" in a few hours slaughtered

1487 birds and small animals and considered it a perfectly splendid day. There was another chap who all by himself dispatched seven hundred birds in one day. The Romans surpassed them but one can't say our boys don't try.

But to return to Leptis. The port boasted big warehouses, a lighthouse and a temple dedicated to the god of sailors. A cistern from which the ships drew their fresh water still exists. However, a great deal of excavation remains to be done, so since the port was a relatively long way off we decided to be satisfied with the view through Norton's powerful binoculars rather than trek all the way there and back again. The theatre was something else. We scrambled down our precipitous staircase and walked over to what is actually more a stadium than a theatre in the sense that it is standing free rather than being built into a hillside as are so many Greek and Roman theatres.

It was not excavated until after the Second World War and is the only Roman theatre with a perfectly preserved auditorium up to the first gallery columns. It was built in A.D. 11–12 and was surmounted by a double colonnade interspersed with statues. Of the few that remain one is a large seated female figure with a child on its knee, presumably a member of the audience.

Actually it was a vaudeville house, the Palace of its time, as only variety shows were performed there, never dramas or comedies and as Mortimer Wheeler points out in the magnificent picture book, *Roman Africa in Color* (photos by Roger Wood, text by Wheeler himself) "The Imperial Theatre must have been a pretty low grade affair." With the exception of the younger Seneca in the time of Nero and Terence in the second century B.C. there were no Roman playwrights.

Today the view over the water is magnificent, the whole setting reminiscent of the Antico Theatre in Taormina. The view was a fringe benefit denied the Romans, the stage and its surroundings being then so built up as to shut out the sea.

From the theatre we returned to the car and drove toward the amphitheatre or arena. Ken the indefatigable was all for seeing everything at once but Leyna and Norton and I were of feebler fiber and plumped for eating our picnic lunch then and there. We installed ourselves on a windy bluff overlooking the harbor and dug into the sandwiches and tomatoes and eggs and good white wine of Cyrene that Leyna had thoughtfully provided.

Fortified we walked over to the edge of the amphitheatre and gazed down into the great stone strewn oval surrounded by crumbling tiers of seats. Sometimes it was flooded for water battles but more often it was used for the dreadful gladiatorial combats in which human beings were pitted against one another and against famished beasts who demolished them. Occasionally if a man was armed he might triumph. Usually he was doomed.

Doorways were set at intervals along corridors under the stands through which men and animals, prodded out of cages and as terrified as their victims, blinded by their sojourns in semi-darkness were thrust or hauled into the glare of the open arena and sacrificed before twenty or thirty thousand roaring bloodthirsty spectators.

It was Ken who told us of the ingenious system for quick scene changes perfected by the Romans. Sometimes the victims were tied to stakes and wheeled into the arena on small go carts on platforms. The lions and panthers were released and when the carnage was over and the agonized shrieks of the dying had ceased the platform was wheeled away and the new act was brought on. Interest never flagged. In the Castello Museum of Tripoli well-depicted scenes in mosaics preserve for the present some of the more grizzly exhibits of those happy bygone days.

I commented on how strange it was that the Romans with their genius for acquisition, law, and administration should at the same time have been capable of such barbaric cruelty. "Well you know," Ken said, "many people regard the United States as the Rome of the twentieth century." The point of view is understandable. We can boast unmatched achievements in science, medicine and industry. We can get to the moon and we can also get to Vietnam. Our wanton destruction of our natural resources and of wildlife must certainly be regarded as barbarism and the spectacle of a coterie of our higher intellects devoting themselves to the development of nerve gases and germ warfare is not an edifying one.

Subdued by man's inhumanity to man we felt the need of a change of scene and, leaving the amphitheatre, crossed over to a small complex of ruins, the Hunter's baths, their low domes and vaults emerging from a fold in the sand dunes. The work of preserving them has altered them in only the smallest degree from the original forms. Lead pipes through which water flowed into the tanks and pools are still in place and on the interior walls fragments of enchanting frescoes may still be seen. There are men battling leopards with long spears and in one sequence I was pleased to see the leopard besting the hunter.

On a wall above a large deep swimming tank two men are fishing from a boat wearing visored caps that might have been manufactured today. They were living, I am sure, in the charming country villa that rises on the bank behind them.

About seven o'clock we returned to our hotel and although exhausted my conscience began nagging me. Should we not dine out in order to have another restaurant to write about for any readers who might be going to Tripoli and who would appreciate a little guidance? Maybe we should have but the chances were strong that the food would be no good and we had had a long day. The doctor gave me a look half-pleading, half sour and poured a couple of drinks. "Couldn't we just eat here? Who are those tourist readers that they can't dig up their own restaurants?" I agreed although at that going out might have been the better choice.

Since we could not subject ourselves to the din of the hotel orchestra a second time we called for room service. Quite a while later a waiter arrived bearing a small tray on which were crowded two beat up covered metal serving dishes, a fish exposed on its platter, two glasses and that was it. No plates from which to eat, no knives and forks to eat with and no table on which to set anything down. It was so wildly inadequate we could only dissolve into helpless laughter. Bewildered and resentful the waiter finally did rustle up a small table and the necessary implements but one cannot say that elegance was the keynote.

The next morning was bright and sunny but a cold wind blew and we feared the dreaded ghibli. Generally speaking the ghibli is a hot wind, scorching and sand laden and highly destructive to crops but I believe it is capricious and can also blow cold and last for three days at a stretch or even longer. If in thrall to a goblin you may talk your way out but beware the clutches of the ghibli!

We were not sorry to find shelter in the Castello Museum originally a cross between fort and palace. It contains some fascinating mosaics, many from Leptis Magna, as well as an imposing relief-chariots, horses, togaed Romans—from the arch of Septimius Severus.

Our afternoon was devoted to Sabratha, Leptis on a smaller scale with a distinction all its own.

On the way we stopped for lunch at the Swan Restaurant in Giorgimpopoli. That is where the George Culps live and where we had dined but I believe the locality was so named before their arrival. As at the Akropolis the food was not very good and it was very expensive.

Sabratha lies about forty miles from Tripoli and although a settlement had existed there before, like Leptis it came to flower in the first and second centuries. It was thriving in the third century, had its ups and down—down via the Vandals in 455, up by the Byzantine emperor Justinian in 533, and down finally by the Arabs.

The winds blew, the sands covered it until 1923 when thanks to the start of prolonged excavations it began once more to bask in the sun. There is still some way to go but now on view are houses, streets and public squares. To date no houses have been uncovered at Leptis Magna although obviously they must have existed. At Sabratha from holes for floor joists and remains of staircases it is deduced that many of the houses were at least two storied and frescoes and mosaics were conventional decoration. The gem in Sabratha, however, is the theatre, partially and admirably restored by the Italians who, when they first unearthed it, found only the lowest parts in position. By careful study they were able accurately to replace most of the scattered remains. As in all Roman theatres the auditorium is semicircular, with benches rising in tiers. It faces a rectangular stage of equal height, the most compelling feature of the building. The front is decorated with panels of carved stone, alternating rectangular panels and curved bays. The subject matter is varied: masks, bulls, dancers, philosophers—whatever the imagination of the sculptor dictated. The back of the stage, the permanent set, is superb, a three storied free standing Corinthian colonnade with high and princely portals through which the lucky actors made what had to be marvelously impressive entrances.

The Sabratha museum while small contains a magnificent mosaic floor from the Basilica of Justinian, a lovely thing of branches and birds and flowers, a rectangular abstract panel set in the wall and the famous "Ocean" mosaic, a head of a water god with waving blue-green seaweed hair and beard set in a hexagonal frame.

Chapter 2 THE MIDDLE EAST

The following day we left the scenes of ancient glory—not that they were the last of the glories we would see—this particular trip *abounded* in ruins—and headed for Beirut.

Our departure was somewhat soured by an exorbitant charge for excess luggage and the information that we could not clear customs in Tripoli. This rite was performed in Bengazi, the eastern capital of Libya. Everybody and everybody's luggage deplaned, nothing was opened, white squiggles were sketched on every bag, every bag and everybody re-enplaned and we took off. The most inefficient and flagrant example of made work we were to encounter in all the miles that we and the crow would fly.

Having experienced the food at ground level we were dubious as to what Libyan air would offer but there we misjudged them. We had a very decent meal. Not Lucullan, not Epicurean not, thank God, poor weary overworked Gourmet but nice food nicely served and with alcoholic accompaniment.

A passenger with whom we fell into conversation spoke English with a pronounced accent.

Me: May I ask what nationality you are?

He: Swiss.

Me: We are Americans.

His laughter was explosive. Not rude exactly but a wholehearted guffaw. "That I could see," he said when he had gained enough control to speak. "You do not need passports." Our cameras? Our clothes? I looked at Norton carefully to make sure he had not sprouted a Made in U.S.A. sign on his back.

When the stewardness told us we were passing over Mykonos we were not surprised, since we didn't know the customary route. The Swiss, who did know it, *was* surprised. We were making the detour to avoid flying over Israel.

When traveling with Pan Am one certainly has the impression that His eye is on the sparrow for as in Tripoli so in Beirut. We were met by a helpful member of the staff, although there perhaps it was more to be expected, Beirut being a pivotal stop in the company's famous round the world flights Numbers One and Two.

We were also met by Emil Bishuty, the associate of Suliman Olayan who had given the Arabian flavored dinner party in New York. He drove us to the Phoenicia, a big fine commercial hotel. I like my hotels intimate and cozy or I like them big and grand and the Phoenicia is indubitably B and G. It also has on sale in its lobby a remarkably catholic selection of pornographic literature. The Swedes and Danes may match it but they surely can't outdo it. Book jackets writhe with naked bodies and sexual orgies and there are such titles as *Three in a Bed*. Great stuff.

The hotel, one of the Intercontinental chain is presided over by a Swiss manager Mr. Hans Sternik who for fifteen years has been married to an American wife from Scarsdale, New York. They have four children.

We became friendly with them and they told us they had been offered a hotel in Nairobi and being crazy about animals and the idea of Africa in general had been strongly tempted to accept. The children's education was the deciding factor against it.

Thanks to Mr. Sternik we were furnished with a copious bar and thanks to him and the Messrs. Olayan, Bishuty, and the extremely helpful and amiable Mr. Frank Guzzardo of Pan Am we tiptoed through the tulips and the daisies, the freesias and the snapdragons all the time we were in Beirut. Our suite was a garden.

On our first evening Mr. Bishuty and his wife had asked us to dine and at about half-past eight they came by to pick us up. They had said something about a nice nearby restaurant and being pretty tired we welcomed the idea; something near and cozy would be fine. What they had in mind, however, was not the corner bistro but a long drive into the mountains to a palatial affair called Al Bustan.

We drove around the crescent of the city got out of the car and dutifully viewed two large rocks in the harbor, Les Rochers des Pigeons. It used to be fashionable to jump off them and commit suicide for love or something but today's young generation has seen the light. They look at the rocks, they watch the pigeons and they let it go at that.

We reached the city limits and started winding 2500 feet up the mountains through fog and rain. When we arrived we found ourselves in a delightful place, a hotel as well as restaurant where the food and wine were first rate and our hosts proved such companionable people that all thought of fatigue was swept away.

Mrs. Bishuty, Nuha, was five months pregnant. It would be their second child, for they already had a little girl. They were hoping for a boy, especially Emil who had been married before and already had two daughters by his former wife.

Their little daughter May was two years old and like many children enjoyed beer. Nor was she above swiping the last drop of Arak from a glass, savoring it as it went down her gullet and murmuring appreciatively, "This is delicious." As matters turned out we received a pink and frilly announcement in New York a few months later. Another girl.

We were obliged to creep back down the mountain in teeming rain but we decided that even so the Lebanese had a good deal to be thankful for. In summer they spend their days on the beaches and drive forty-five minutes up the mountains in the evening to sleep in cool comfort.

The next day the handsome Chrysler Imperial of the invisible Mr. Olayan in which we had driven to dinner was at the door to take us to the airport for our flight to Amman in Jordan. Although he had been largely instrumental in forming our plans for the Middle East, Mr. Olayan, like a character in a fairy story or a strange tale of science fiction, remained a power felt but never seen. When we were in Beirut he was in Saudi Arabia. When we were in Saudi Arabia he was . . . no one seemed to know. He had vanished in a puff of smoke.

While waiting for our plane to be called we watched the female personnel at the airport. They wore pastel-colored fezzes on their heads with buttons on top instead of tassels. Sheer, bead edged veils were drawn over them, crossed under the chin and the ends tossed over the shoulders. They looked very pretty. "Look dear," I said to my husband, "aren't they pretty?" My husband looked. "Lousy legs" he said.

We also amused ourselves by reading the destinations of other departing flights. Rome, Khartoum, Nicosia, Istanbul, Freetown, Prague, Tehran. Those names stir the pulse, they pique the imagination as Chicago, Atlanta, Detroit, or Dallas do not. Although it will be a long time before the word Dallas ceases to evoke in those who see or hear it a sense of shock, a sudden tensing of the nerves. Some names stick in history's craw. I imagine people who travel to Ekaterinburg, recalling that the massacre of the Russian Imperial family took place there in 1918 feel the same way. And who sees Ford's Theatre in Washington without thinking of the assassination of Abraham Lincoln?

In the Beirut airport we were pinpointing the places we had been or would like to go to and Norton raised his cherished Minox to snap the board.

That tore it. Up came a cop, revolver on hip. The little chap from Amlevco, the American Express Associate in Lebanon who was there to see us off quaveringly explained as we coached him how dull the domestic flight signs were in the States, how rich and colorful and *appreciated* by Americans were those of Lebanon. The gendarme stared at us with eyes like icepicks. His English was limited but he knew enough for his purpose. "Come. See, Captain." We followed him, quaking only a trifle, up a flight of stairs away from the hustle, bustle and any possible allies in the crowded waiting area. The policeman pointed to a sort of conference room. "Wait." We entered and sat down. Wait. For how long? Long enough to miss our plane? I hoped there was no physical indication my heart was bumping its way down into my shoes. In short order a grubby little man, also armed, appeared from an adjoining office accompanied by a satellite. Armed. While the representative of Amlevco launched into an explanatory torrent of Arabic I muttered to Norton that we had better brace ourselves for confiscation of the film but maybe if we were lucky not the camera.

We were luckier than that. Once he understood what the tempest in the teapot was about the Authority shrugged and walked back into his office and the original arrester shook our hands and apologized. We apologized too but were uncertain for what until Amlevco explained that it was not the policeman's fault but his duty. Since the Israeli raid in which thirteen planes were destroyed no one was supposed to take pictures in the airport. They had a point. "Also," he continued, "that man he speaks not English much. He understand Dr. Brown to say he was stupid."

"No, no," I said, "what Dr. Brown said was 'This is a stupid mistake.'"

Maybe that's what he did say.

Our hotel in Amman was the Jordan Continental run by a pleasant efficient woman. Like many people in a similar situation living near one of the marvels of the world she had never traveled the 169 miles to visit the ancient city of Petra, the magnet that had drawn us to her country. She said she couldn't leave her children.

To consider Amman as an old country is fair enough given the statement of scientists who believe that that portion of the globe was inhabited about a million years ago. Zeroing in on what is, comparatively, the present we know that in 1200 B.C. Rabbath Ammon, as it was then called, was the capital of the Ammonites who did battle with the Biblical kings and they and their country are frequently mentioned in the Old Testament.

Things moseyed along—battles, victories, retreats, lootings, burnings, triumphs—until the arrival in the third century B.C. of Ptolemy II, Philadelphus of Egypt, who rebuilt Amman and named it Philadelphia a fact that many people in Philadelphia, Pennsylvania, may not know.

That particular Ptolemy is a fascinating and glittering figure and the splendor of Alexandria reached its apogee under his rule. He has been referred to as the Louis IV of antiquity and like his illustrious successor had many mistresses all of whom apparently were women of intellect and charm.

In true Egyptian fashion his second wife was his sister, Arsinoe II, to distinguish her from his first wife, a relative stranger, Arsinoe I. After the death of number two he had her declared Philadelphus which is a bit confusing since the word means brotherly love but perhaps he was using it in the broad sense of mankind.

Assorted people such as the Selecids intervened next and in 30 B.C. along came Herod the Great. Despite ten wives and battalions of children of his own he was the one who unleashed the slaughter of the babies of Bethlehem.

There is incidentally an anachronism in the date of Jesus' birth. Since it is known that Herod died in what is referred to as 4 B.C. Jesus had to have been born earlier than is traditionally supposed.

In any event somewhere along the line Rabbath Amman settled down to calling itself Amman, and Jordan of course was for a long time a part of Palestine. After World War I when the League of Nations gave Britain mandate over Palestine, the name

Transjordan came into use and in 1949 it boiled down to the present Jordan.

Today Jordan has a population of about 1,500,000 of which Amman, a white city of limestone buildings spreading over seven hills, claims 350,000.

One of its finest sights thirty miles to the north is Jerash, a Roman colony dating back 2000 years. Since too abrupt a change would have been bad for our nervous systems our usual pattern prevailed and we drove to Jerash in the pouring rain. We were feeling sorry for ourselves until we passed a camp of Arab refugees from Israel who have been there since 1967. It was a wretched place of tents and tin-can shacks and mud. No running water, scant electricity if any, no schools, no toys, no medical facilities, clothing of rags—the condition of everyone, especially the children, was sickening.

We were told the Jordanian government gives the refugees a small allowance. Whether it is capable of giving more or of sheltering more people I do not know. Cynics claim that on the whole the government probably doesn't find the squalid conditions too objectionable because while harsh for the individual Arab they are powerful propaganda for the Arab cause versus the Israeli.

Statistics on the Lebanese population itself vary according to the speaker. Some say that 52 percent is Christian, 48 percent Muslim. Others insist on 60 percent Muslim, 40 percent Christian. For political reasons, loans perhaps among others, the government declares the majority Christian and were they to take in thousands of Arab refigees that figure would be knocked into a cocked hat. Therefore, runs the assumption, they tolerate a few for propaganda purposes but want no great influx.

Whatever the statistical or political or economic reasons, humanely speaking the passer-by must be appalled by what he sees for regardless of which side is right results such as that are wrong.

When I said as much to our Arab driver, adding that if only

mankind would give up war and killing and get on with the business of living how marvelous that would be and also how possible, I was greeted by grim silence. Our impression was that passions are too hot in those lands for an objective view. At that time it was not peace nor co-existence that either side wanted but the extermination of the opposition.

When we reached Jerash we found it a small but extremely interesting ruin with the theatre which could seat 6000 spectators in a good state of preservation. On a smaller scale than Sabratha it too has noble portals and pillars. The nine Corinthian columns of the Temple of Artemis soar high overhead and there is an extraordinary circular colonnade surrounding a huge paved flat area. A wide avenue rutted by chariot wheels and lined on the west side by 136 columns leads away from it. The columns on the east side have toppled and it is thought the damage was caused by an earthquake which went so far and no further; similar to the local showers where it rains on one side of the street only.

The traveler who absorbs Jerash in the course of a morning or afternoon need not be accused of superficiality. While definitely worth seeing the area is not large and it is all there, on display. Our next junket was more prolonged and deservedly so.

Leaving most of our luggage at the hotel, taking only an overnight bag and wearing slacks and walking shoes we left at a quarter to eight the next morning on our way to Petra. The road leading south was excellent, virtually deserted, although from time to time we veered over to make way for big bus loads of pilgrims returning from Mecca.

The few private cars we passed made up in personality what they lacked in numbers. Fringe bobbed around the windshields and appliquéd plastic flowers bloomed in sprightly designs on the back windows. If you want to impede your rear view that's a good way to do it.

The countryside was bare and brown but there were occasional water holes beside the road and herds of camels clustered around them drinking. We saw an appealingly awkward frisky baby and somebody riding a palanquin which to our eyes appeared precariously perched on the back of a more mature member of the herd. The going was rough, pitching and tossing like a ship at sea. As we passed a group of nomads leading their flocks Norton observed that their one function in life was to stay alive, moving ever from place to place in search of water and grazing for their sheep, camels and goats. How the poor beasts survive I do not know. They nitpick their living from the pitiably sparse grass and low scrub which is desert verdure. What the humans eat is bare subsistence, little more.

In the course of our nearly four hour drive we traversed wild hilly country which though rocky was cultivated in small terraces, with green plants sprouting from every available crevice. Jordan is a traveler's goal for many historic reasons, Jerusalem and the unique monument of Petra among them, but why anyone would want to conquer and occupy that country is hard to imagine. It is an inhospitable land devoid of water, vegetation, or oil.

We finally arrived at Wadi Musa, an engaging little village of square mud huts and green terraces. It is also the site of a hotel where one may stay if, unlike us, he does not wish to spend the night in Petra. The hotel was quite new, partly man-made stucco, partly cut deep into indigenous rock. The dining room was a large picturesque cavern lighted by overhead lamps of pierced brass and vibrating with Jordanian musical discord.

A high steep staircase leads up to the small bedrooms which were clean and the beds looked relatively comfortable but our hearts were set on Nazzal's camp in the valley and preferably one of the cave rooms we had heard about. We would willingly have lunched at the hotel however, but when the management broke the news that there was nothing to eat it seemed wiser to push on at once, first taking the precaution of telephoning the camp so they could rustle up some food.

We knew that one went on horseback to reach Petra but not

having been on a horse in longer than I care to say I was secretly
relieved when what was led up for us to mount were not met-
tlesome Arabian stallions but three staid old nags with an Arab
at the end of each lead rein. Our luggage was strapped on the
back of a donkey. Norton and I mounted and set off with
Marwan our guide along the stony track which presently enters the Siq, the narrow tortuous defile winding for more than a
mile between towering cliffs, deep red and copper, ochre and
violet. Sometimes the walls are twenty feet apart, sometimes high
high overhead the rocks nearly join, a dramatic shaft of sunlight
knifing down between them to illuminate the trail.

An occasional fountain of green and golden vines or an oleander
bush spurts from a crevice in the rock face, a hidden deposit of
moisture giving it life. Other than the sound of the horses' hoofs
scattering the gravel there is no sound at all. The Nabataeans
themselves when they built the city in about 500 B.C. brought
water from Wadi Musa by way of a narrow groove carved along
the rock wall. Traces of it still remain today. Water was an ever-
present concern but they constructed cisterns to catch rain and
the few springs in the valley were carefully tended.

Emerging from the crepuscular twisting chasm the traveler is
confronted by a sudden burst of brilliance, the Kazneh or Treasury
with its double tier of pediments and Corinthian columns. Sheltered by overhanging rock it is the best preserved of all the
monuments of Petra, the tomb of a Nabataean king or possibly a
temple.

The columns and porticos, of the Treasury as they are in all
the tombs, are not built but carved into the rock face and the
proportions are elegant and graceful. When the sun strikes the
rose red sandstone it glows as though lighted from within. They
tell you that the bullet marks on the urn that tops the central
circular ornamentation of the upper pediment are the result of
assaults by those who hoped to shatter the building and release
the treasure that legend claims is buried there. Actually no treas-

ure has ever been found in the Nabataean tombs as it was in those of the Egyptians.

Although the peak of their prosperity and power was probably from the first century B.C. to the end of the first A.D. it is easy to understand how the Nabataean supremacy endured for several hundred years. In that narrow gorge, through which an enemy army was obliged to pass, a handful of men could stave off a battalion.

Petra, like Peter and Pierre the name means rock, grew rich from the tribute she exacted from caravans wending their way along the trade routes that passed through the valley leading to Gaza in the west, Bostra and Damascus in the north, to Elath on the Red Sea and across the desert to the Persian Gulf.

When Palmyra, northeast of Damascus, began attracting commerce and when the sea lanes became a swifter and more economical means of transportation the wealth of the Nabataeans faded.

Eventually they were engulfed by the tidal wave of the Roman army who in a last desperate effort to obtain the unobtainable swarmed over the undefended hills at the rear of the city and claimed it for themselves.

However, the story of Petra was not that of Carthage and although now a Roman province she again began to prosper and some of the finest monuments were built in that era.

From the clearing in which the Treasury stands the track narrows, lined on either side by tombs, opening out again when it reaches the theatre. The theatre was built by the Romans who after their arrival gave the tombs in their way short shrift. Probably their philosophy was: we're the living; they're the dead; let's get on with it.

One can picture them in all their efficiency, the commander, check list in hand, giving orders to his men. "O.K., fellows, here's where we'll lay out the road. Usual columns on either side, triumphal arch at the end. You, Leonides, get cracking.

Start now rehearsing the troops for the inaugural parade. We don't want any more historic snafus like the one in Volubilis.

"Over there we'll put the baths—damn dirty bunch these natives—and *there* by Jupiter is where we'll have the theatre. For once we get a break, good natural hillside. If there's anything I hate it's setting up the free standing stuff. We'll enlarge it of course but we don't have to start from scratch. Hop to it, men, start carving out the seats."

From the theatre onward the high rock walls diminish, the valley widens into an undulating plain a mile long, three quarters of a mile wide, ringed with low hills. Here and there rises an outcropping of higher rock formation. At the foot of one of these is Nazzal's camp, an unpretentious frame house without luxury but not uncomfortable. Happy to find ourselves in the ancient and fabled surroundings and fired by romance we asked to see the cave rooms.

Much depends on one's mood and point of view. When shown the small dark rooms of the Palais Jamai in Fes we considered ourselves insulted. How *dared* they offer us these black holes of Calcutta? The caves of Petra, true black holes, seemed merely picturesque. Not however picturesque enough to sleep in. They were real little caves hollowed from the rock. Each contained two cots with a small night table between them, one washbasin and a wooden door to insure privacy. The trouble was air. There was none. When the door was closed the only ventilation came from a small square hole cut out above it. We thanked the management and asked to see the rooms. The rooms were simple but they were adequate and we could breathe.

It was during luncheon, well seasoned canned food, that they divulged their big secret. No water. The system had broken down. They had a spring and a good pump but it had gone on the blink and it would be two days before parts could be brought in from Amman. One might think our strait was dire. On the contrary. We were reduced to elegance, drinking Vichy water and washing in Evian.

After lunch we went out to explore our valley. The conception of Petra was unusual and its execution extraordinary. For the most part the tombs are carved high up into the faces of the cliffs and it must have required not only imagination and skill but vacuum cupped feet to negotiate the perpendicular façades and achieve the sculptors design. Undoubtedly they used scaffoldings. Even so.

At times one thinks the cliffs must surely be of marble because of the markings; wavy streaks of blue and white and purple. In reality it is the natural coloring of much of the sandstone but the famous red predominates and when the afternoon sun bathes the great western façade it glows like a rose garden.

We entered two or three of the chambers, awe inspiring in size and in the precision with which they are cut. The cult of the dead which pervaded the lives of the Nabataeans as it did that of the Egyptians may strike us as curious but the tombs are an imposing expression of the creative urge and the building of them must have given artistic satisfaction to many.

Our valley guide, Marwan, who had come with us from Amman was a Palestinian Arab who before the week long war of 1967 usually referred to by Arabs as "the disaster" had worked continuously. He conducted mostly Germans since he had at one time lived in Vienna and spoke German, on three days' tours of Petra and the surrounding country. He told us he never had a day off and had made enough money to buy a little house in Jerusalem. Then came the fatal week and he and his wife were obliged to get out leaving everything behind.

Norton and I were in Petra in March and we were the second party he had had since the first of the year, most tourists considering conditions too unsettled to risk a visit. Marwan was not a young man to whom we warmed particularly. He herded us about in didactic fashion rather as though we were a large group of his accustomed Germans but just the same we sympathized with his plight. He had tried hard to get a Libyan visa feeling he could find work with the oil companies but the Libyans are chary in granting visas or work permits to foreigners. When we were there we had been told by some of our oil friends that labor was hard to come by. In a country of less than 2,000,000 when one subtracted the women and children the old and the unequipped there were few left to choose from.

People who have been to Israel say that what the Jews have done with the country since 1948 is an astounding feat of intelligent planning and dedicated effort. This is undeniable but when one sees suffering and dislocated lives and hardship no side can claim all the virtues.

The next morning, after a night of blazing stars attending a golden half moon across the sky, we set out to find the Lions tomb on the far side of Nazzal's camp. One climbs a long staircase part original part restoration to see a charming portal with a triangular pediment and two standing lions, one on either side. Their forms are blurred by time and eventually I suppose they will fade completely like the smile of the Cheshire cat. Indeed slow time is effacing everything for the sandstone is soft and in the end the carving will vanish and only the rocks remain until they too prove finite and crumble into nothingness.

We wandered away from the Lions tomb escorted by the crowing of a rooster pecking beneath an oleander bush and as we were clambering about the stony slopes enclosing the valley behind the camp we suddenly heard what the newspapers refer to as "sporadic gunfire." For a minute or two it ricocheted back and forth between the echoing rocks. Marwan's reflex was instantaneous. "Israeli," he said. I glanced at the sky. If there was to be any bombing those caves and tombs would make handy shelters. On the other hand why any air force in its right mind would waste fuel and ammunition on an ancient dreaming valley, inhabited that morning by a few cave dwelling Bedouins, their goats, the five or six men who composed the camp staff, Marwan and Doctor and Mrs. Brown, seemed mysterious. I looked again at the cerulean void which remained just that and as suddenly as it had started the firing ceased.

Marwan explained that we were not far from Aqaba which was in Arab hands nor Eliat which the Israelis occupied. "Every day they shoot a little," he said, adding bitterly, "just because the Jews are strong they think they own the Middle East."

Later when we were alone my husband said to me, "That was no more Israeli gunfire than it was Vietnamese. I heard shooting in the Pacific and no authoritative gun sounds like that. My bet is that it was one Arab poaching another Arab's black goat." He may have been right, he may not have. I preferred the Israeli theory, it was more dramatic.

As we walked about in the hot bright sunshine, so very welcome after North Africa, not to mention Jerash, we came upon a few Bedouin women who seemed to spring from the bushes. In their thin brown hands they held coins or bits of pottery wrapped in dirty cloth which they tried to persuade us were treasures from the diggings. These pathetic peddlers are to be found in all the ruin areas. They apparently do not realize that even the unsophisticated tourist is aware that all governments keep a sharp eye on authentic antiquities and are unlikely to permit their sale by individuals for a few dirhams or piasters or fillts or whatever the local currency is. Granted, here and there shards or old coins or a fragment of carving may be scuffed up by a random shoe or deliberate searching, but objects of real value are rare.

One woman had a small child by the hand and another unfortunately on the way. Norton said to Marwan, "Tell her I don't want to buy anything but if she'll let me take her picture I'll give her some money." Poor as she was she refused. Marwan's theory was that she did so because she feared we would print her picture in a magazine and everyone would say, "How poor and dirty the Arabs are."

Norton and I felt this was taking a longer view than was within her perspective. We doubted her acquaintance with *Look* or *Life* or *Paris-Match* and decided that like many of her countrymen, like many Africans too, she was superstitious about cameras.

Shortly before ten our Arabian steeds arrived to bear us back
to Wadi Musa where we would pick up our car for the drive
to Amman. As we ambled through the strange and haunting Siq
we heard a frightful racket. It was a small pickup truck grinding
and rattling its way toward us and we crowded close against the
walls to let it pass. Echoing between the rocks it sounded like the
earthquake of Marrakech and I was infinitely grateful that the
tragedy of a few years back had not befallen us and could never
be repeated.

At that time a flash flood poured through the narrow twisting
gorge trapping a party of travelers and drowning them all. Since
then the Jordanian government has built a dam and the danger
no longer exists but it was a terrible catastrophe and people
shudder today when they speak of it.

One may enter Petra by jeep instead of horseback but it seems
a pity to do so because the profound silence broken only by the
horses' hoofs and the creak of saddles is part of the magic.

When we dismounted and I remarked to Norton how lucky we
were not to be stiff, having not ridden for so many years, he
laughed. "Why on earth should we be? Those were rocking
horses." He was right and dear creatures they were too.

Returning to Amman we stopped for gas at a station surrounded by twenty-odd army trucks filled with Arabian soldiers
on their way south to Aqaba. The convoy was followed by
seven light tanks but it seemed to be routine procedure and
there was little excitement and we heard no mention of troop
movements.

I have never been at a war front and do not know what it is
like but I do know that what one reads in the papers while it may
not be fallacious often places emphasis on events and actions that
seem quite different to those on the spot.

I was interested in the soldiers but I was also interested in a
distinctly minor but curious art form indigenous apparently to
Jordan. They have a way of placing layers of different colored
sand in bottles so that it creates a decorative effect and the

mystery is that no matter how much one shakes the bottle the design does not disintegrate. Some were on sale in a little shop near the gas station and I bought a couple.

I made another purchase in a drug store adjoining our hotel. Like those in the United States it was stocked with items scarcely related to the drug trade, the most engaging of which were linen panels with appliquéd scenes of Egyptian life: pyramids, donkeys, camels, palm trees. I would not recommend blending them with Aubusson carpets or ormulu but in the right place they are colorful and fun. Inexpensive too.

Our ride to the airport next morning was swift. Our driver was so busy looking accusingly and for long periods at the driver of every other car—other cars on the road were demeaning to his dignity—that we nearly collided with oncoming vehicles. Once in the plane and taxiing along the runway we saw it was bordered with pits dug on either side furnished with antiaircraft guns, their crews beside them. The men laughed and waved as we rolled past them but they were there. Ready.

Before leaving for Petra we had been invited to lunch with a group of men from Tapline, the Trans Arabian Pipeline Company. The president, Mr. W. R. Chandler, was our host. There were ten or eleven men including the distinguished archaeologist, Professor Dimitri Baramki from the university. The American University of Beirut founded in 1866 by Dr. Daniel Bliss is considered one of the best in the Middle East.

Norton was impressed by the medical school which he said was a fine one although here and there a detail had to be ironed out. They had built a huge refrigerator but had no compressor and some of their butane gas appliances for chemistry students were faulty. However since they didn't plan to open until July there was time for rectification.

The Lucullus restaurant where the luncheon was held serves excellent food and Norton and I agreed that the fillet was the most delicious beef we had eaten since we first sampled the Kobe beef of Japan in 1959.

I was the only woman in the party and being surrounded by all those gentlemen was very pleasant but also they were good gentlemen: knowledgeable, able, humane.

The story of their pipeline is a challenging one, firing the imagination of even the non-oil conscious, a category of which I am a charter member. It is a story of imagination, courage and skill.

I owe my information to those we met at luncheon and to the *Aramco Handbook,* an account both historical and technical of oil in the Middle East.

The pipe through which the oil flows from eastern Arabia to the tankers docked at Sidon in Lebanon snakes its way across 1069 miles of land for the most part inimical to man. Temperatures range from a freezing 10° Fahrenheit to a baking 120°. In some areas whole years may pass without a drop of rain. The route crosses rolling sand dunes, rocky plains, an occasional dry water course in Saudi Arabia, dry lakes in Jordan, welcome agriculture in southeastern Syria and rears up the steep terraced slopes of the rugged Anti Lebanon and Lebanon Mountains terminating at last on a rocky hillside overlooking the Mediterranean.

The enterprise involved the movement of greater tonnages and more men—at the peak of construction 16,000—than had ever been undertaken in a single peacetime project.

Roads, camps, first-aid stations had to be constructed, wells dug, food imported. Some 350,000 tons of material were shipped halfway round the world and trucked enormous distances overland.

It will be surpassed by Taps the scheduled Trans Alaska Pipeline System—designed to bring oil from the Arctic north slope to southern Alaska, a lesser distance, 800 miles, but over terrain equally challenging in its own way and using 48-instead of 31-inch pipe.

Nearly half the Tapline pipe lies above ground, an ingenious innovation since the saving in cost compared to excavation amounted to many millions of dollars. Construction started in Abqaiq in Saudi Arabia in 1948 and at the other end in 1949. They came together in 1950. What a moment of exultation *that* must have been when the two ends actually connected! Was it a welcome surprise or was it an iron pipe cinch? A great sigh of relief must have mounted heavenward. Malt liquor must have foamed. Although probably it wasn't as chancy as tunnel building because working on the surface of the earth you could have a man in a helicopter waving to you, correcting your course. "No no, further over to the left. Hold it! That's too far. Back up a little." Then he could lean out grinning, thumb and forefinger joined. The On the Nose! symbol. It was nice they were so successful because they can now—how does one say it—Ship? Push? Flow? Anyway the capacity of the pipe is 480,000 barrels daily.

William Robinson, a lawyer for the company, told us a story unrelated to oil but it was a curious sidelight on everyday life. A redheaded American girl was coming out of a Beirut night club only a few steps ahead of her husband and friends when she was scooped into a passing car by two Arabs. She was young and strong and fought like a tiger pulling the driver back by his long hair so that he could not see where he was going. As the car slowed the husband and his friends rushed up and rescued her. There was a terrific fracas and one of the Americans was hurt. The Arabs' explanation for their action is hard to swallow but one must remember that Saudi Arabia and Jordan are violently anti-Communist and what they *said* was that to them a redhead meant an entertainer and entertainment meant night club singers and most of the night club singers were Russian. Perhaps they were planning to brainwash her into the ways of Capitalism.

We learned a little something of the background of our mysterious deus ex machina Suliman Olayan from two or three of the men at the lunch table. At one time he worked in a warehouse for American business interests. His job was humble and he spoke little English but the Americans offered work as contractors to those who seemed able. In ten years Olayan had mastered English and was the head of his own firm. Since his eyes were badly crossed he went to the United States for an operation, got on friendly terms with some of the biggest men in the contracting business as well as a few select bankers and is now one of the top international figures in his field and has amassed among other things the elegant Chrysler Imperial in which we were driving around.

Nuha Bishuty had generously offered to lend her services as guide, so after lunch while Norton went to see a colleague in the hospital she and I did a bit of shopping and sightseeing. The particular stores we went into I thought were something of a letdown. They were not picturesque like the souks nor did they have the merchandise and style of first-rate department stores. The more rewarding part of the afternoon came at teatime when we went back to the Bishuty apartment and I met the family. The Bishuty family was large and cohesive.

A maid brought tea, cup cakes, and a small delicious pastry, sesame seed fingers, a Syrian specialty fancied by Nuha and her sister who were Syrian themselves.

In that part of the world the countries are small and close together—Lebanon is 156 miles long and 31 miles wide—but even larger lands are close neighbors and it is hard for a Westerner to know whether he is consorting with Lebanese, Syrians, Jordanians, Iraqi, Turks, Egyptians, or Saudi Arabians. I was about to include Israelis but when we were there one could be pretty certain he was not exchanging a quip or raising a glass of tea with an Israeli. Nuha said, "It kills me to think of them in Jerusalem." Most of the people we met felt that way and without taking sides we ourselves were distressed to have been in Jordan and unable to go to the ancient city.

The next morning we drove to Baalbek. Leaving the city, from a bend in the climbing road one looks down on a grove of hundreds of umbrella pines. They grow to the same height and stop so that it is like looking down on a vast undulating green carpet. It was good to see the pines because the renowned cedars have all but disappeared. Today the Cedars of Lebanon is more likely to refer to a hospital in Los Angeles than to the superb forests that once covered the mountainsides. Here and there individual trees remain but there is only one place, the slopes of Mount Makhmal northeast of Beirut, where there is a stand of any importance and that contains less than four hundred trees, some of which are estimated to be 1500 years old, perhaps the next oldest in the world to the 3500- and 4000-year-old Sequoias of California.

Yet even this stark example has no message for the American Forest Service doing its busy best to destroy the magnificent giant redwoods, the oldest living organisms on the planet, to set up in their place "recreation areas" bristling with Laundromats, drive-in movies, and hamburg palaces.

As the road climbed higher we passed one tree looming through the fog like the solitary cedar on the Lebanese flag. It is a pretty flag with a red stripe at top and bottom and a white band in the middle on which the green tree is imprinted.

As the fog and mist shredded away we saw the summer houses we had heard about but they were disappointing. Some belong to individuals but there are many apartment buildings and many hotels with no grounds or gardens to speak of and virtually no privacy. Even villas, when they are five stories high, must inevitably look like apartment houses. They are built that way by rich Arabs who come to pass the summer in Lebanon bringing with them their four legal wives. Each wife has her own floor and the fifth is for the servants. The happy polygamists have a view and cool fresh air and that's it. Such blessings are not meager but countryside, gardens, charm, and privacy are also desirable.

The word Lebanon derives from the Semitic laban—white or whiteish—and probably referred to the white walls of chalk and limestone, characteristic of the central mountain masses, possibly including the snow on the summits.

At five thousand feet we crossed over the pass and into the

Bekaa, the high valley that was the granary of ancient Rome. We drove by the Ksara vineyards, their product is delectable but we were depressed by the relentlessly ugly buildings erected by the Jesuit fathers who grow the grapes. On a hilltop they have set up a truly odious concrete tower with a statue of the Virgin sticking up from the top like a sore thumb.

The ruins of Baalbek, however, more than compensate for these misfortunes. The name itself means City of the Lord. It was also called Heliopolis or Sun City by the Greeks but despite the magnificence of its temples little is known about its origin. What would appear certain is that it was always a sacred spot and as water flows there in abundance it must have been inhabited long before the Romans came.

Just when the building of the complex was begun is not known either but most archaeologists now agree that the Temple of Jupiter, of which only six gigantic columns topped by an entablature remain in place, was probably started in the first century A.D.

The dimensions of the columns are staggering. They stand 65 feet high from base to capital and measure 7 feet 6 inches in diameter. Much of the granite of which they are constructed was brought from Aswan in Egypt. It was floated down the Nile, across the Mediterranean, and hauled over the mountains to Baalbek. One can only say to oneself, what manner of men were these? Megalomaniacs yes, but in their way geniuses as well. The foundations on which the temples rest are remarkable. They are constructed of gigantic stones, three of them measuring approximately 62 by 14 by 11 feet each. In a nearby quarry lies the largest block of hewn stone in the world. That one is 69 by 26 by 14 feet and weighs about 1000 tons. It still lies there, and through the centuries there has been speculation as to what happened, why it was left where it was, never set in place beside the others? My own explanation is that one day, suddenly, the boys got sated. They had had enough of the Bigs. Foreseeing Gutzon Borglum, feeling something should be left for him, they

22. George Sebastien and Ilka in Hammamet

23. Swimming pool, Sebastien villa, Hammamet

24.   Tripoli Harbor from our window in Hotel Uaddan

25.   Leyna Miller, Ilka, Ken Miller in the Miller living room the night of the dinner party

26.   Haughty passengers met on the road to Lepcis Magna

27. One of the Gorgon heads of Lepcis Magna

28. Circular pavilion or kiosk in the market place of Lepcis Magna

29. Fish counter, market place, Lepcis Magna

30. Large lady, member of the
audience with her child. The
theatre. Lepcis Magna

31. Stage and permanent set of the theatre of Sabratha

32. *Left:* Burst of brilliance at the end of the Siq, Petra in Jordan. That exclamation point at the bottom of the picture is the rear view of Miss Chase and the rear end of her horse.

33. *Right:* The Treasury Building. Petra

34. The great western façade with tombs. Petra

35. The six towering columns
Baalbek

36. The Temple of Bacchus at Baalbek. Note the teetering stone
that never topples

37. Nawwaf Yassin's house in Jidda

38. Nawwaf with Nashwah

39. Left to right: our porters, our amiable wolf Mohamed Raschid, Norton

40. Ruined houses of Al Dir'iyah

41. Canal in the Hofuf Oasis

lay down their tools, went out for a beer and never came back. One must still gape in wonder at the skill that could detach in one unbroken piece so gargantuan a block.

Tumbled from the Temple of Jupiter a part of the entablature today rests on the ground. I copy the description in the guide book by Mr. G. Lankester Harding because the terms though learned give a feeling of the richness and intricacy of the detail.

"Above the columns was an entablature some sixteen feet high consisting of an architrave, a frieze of bulls and lions heads connected by garlands and a cornice of dentils, egg and dart pattern, medallions and rosettes, Greek key pattern and finally acanthus leaves and lions heads. These latter were the gargoyles discharging the rain water from the roof."

An architrave if you want to know is the lowest division of an entablature, that thing above the columns. It is the main beam and is also called the epistyle. Dentils, no relation to lentils, are small rectangular blocks resembling a row of teeth and medallions are brackets set in series. Got it?

The great "Bacchus" temple nearby in all likelihood began to take shape in the second century A.D. "Bacchus" is enclosed in quotes since the three gods worshipped in the sacred city were Jupiter, Venus and Mercury and it may have been dedicated to Venus but there are two representations of Bacchus in the interior, one seated on a panther, one with vine leaves on his head and since he was a popular member of the Olympic set well wishers wanted him to be enshrined too.

The "Bacchus" is of great beauty and in an admirable state of preservation. Broad shallow steps lead up to the central portal and the columns of the portico surrounding the cella or body of the temple are only a little smaller than those of Jupiter, 62 as opposed to 65 feet, most seemly and feminine, almost dainty in fact, if the building was indeed a shrine to Venus. Delicate stone work, carvings of flowers and vines frame the doors, in an enchanting marriage of grace and solidity. Inside high fluted Corinthian columns against the wall are separated by archways on the lower tier and triangular pediments on the upper. A huge stone appears to teeter at the very apex of the ruined outer pediment and looking up at it the visitor scuttles hastily out of harm's way. It is incredible that it does not topple.

At a little distance from the main complex another temple is in the process of being excavated and restored but this one is jealously guarded by the authorities until it shall be officially measured and annotated and photographed and the casual tourist cannot visit it without special permission.

We were casual and permissionless but from a little way down the road the slender white columns rising from flowering apricot trees foaming against the foundation stones and silhouetted against the dark tumbling clouds of a stormy sky were lovely to behold.

The history of Baalbek is the familiar chronicle of antiquity: war, destruction, fire, pillage, floods and earthquakes. Constantine came and Justinian and Islam came en masse, yet in changing guise and usage much of it survived. Today the ruined splendor is deeply impressive and it is a heady game, trying to imagine what it must have been at the height of its architectural glory when it rang to the music and chants of great and colorful processions and ceremonies.

Baalbek had proved a long and engrossing morning and returning to Beirut we stopped on the way to lunch at La Gondolle. They also have restaurants in town but the one on the roadside was particularly satisfying.

Preceded by a small glass of Arak, the potent local tipple, the enormous variety of mezzes tasted exceptionally good. Hors d'oeuvers in France, mezzes in Greece and the Middle East, these openers are a nourishing meal in themselves. We tasted a dish we had also eaten in Amman and that at first sight one might easily take to be mashed avocado but it is hommos, a purée of chick-peas with sesame oil. We found the recipe in a cookbook written in English on sale in the restaurant, *Lebanese Dishes Made Delicious*. I thought the title rather touching, as though the author were saying "Fundamentally they're not but with a few tricks, a little know how . . . you'd be surprised."

In the course of the Baalbek trip we had been chatting with our guide and had told him something of our plans when we left Lebanon. He had appeared puzzled by one or two of our projected destinations and driving back after lunch he said, "Why are you going to Saudi Arabia?" It was a question we had asked ourselves once or twice but I felt a truthful answer would only serve to confound confusion. I could hardly say to him, "Because our dogs met Wanda Jablonski's." Yet that was the root of the reason. Instead I said grandly, "We have friends there. We are going to see the King and the Hofuf Oasis."

"Insha' Allah," the doctor added piously. He was catching on. We were also rather glib with another phrase, "Ahlan Wa Sahlan," Welcome, in Arabic.

Our trip to Byblos, the other famed ruin near Beirut, took place on a bright and cloudy morning. It was Saturday and we were obliged to burrow our way through a great crush of people and along narrow streets choked with cars. One has to be brave to drive in Beirut for there are few traffic lights and who has the right of way depends on who is the most aggressive and who chickens out first.

The gold souk of the city is well known so we went to see it. It is a sparkling place, a short street crossed by two smaller and narrower ones, the shop windows crammed with gold necklaces and bracelets gold pins and earrings and rings by the thousands, glittering like sun-splashed water. It is a glorious spot if you are a connoisseur of gold for there are masses of everything to paw over and labor is extremely cheap. Since I could be sold a brass merry-go-round ring and be only mildly suspicious of my purchase I contented myself with my hallmarked loot from Tripoli. The labor part however is worth taking advantage of. The chain of my necklace was too long. In Beirut I had a piece cut off and the clasp resoldered. The charge was sixty-six cents. In New

York it would probably have been $20. If you have any gold you want remodeled take it to Beirut.

Extricating ourselves from the crush of traffic we headed for Byblos. Unlike Baalbek and Leptis and other ruins we had seen the appeal of the city lies in what it was rather than in what is there now.

Situated on a promontory jutting into the sea and today called Jbeil it is, according to legend and quite possibly in fact the oldest inhabited site in the world. People have lived there since the end of prehistoric times and the dawn of the Neolithic age about 5000 B.C.

Rather than being built up their shelters were pits cut into the earth like large graves with mats and hides stretched over them to form roofs. All that was wood is of course long gone but flint weapons and pottery survive.

By 3200 B.C. they were building above ground, crude pots and jars were replaced by ceramics shaped on the wheel and fired in kilns. They began utilizing their forests which unexploited until then were magnificent thick stands of giant trees but arid Egypt was hungry for cedar and juniper and pine. This promoted navigation, and was the basis of Phoenician trade and wealth.

The Greeks had a word for everything and Phoenician was their word for the people of that part of the world. As usual authorities are rarely in accord and the reason for the term Phoenician would seem to be largely a matter of personal preference. They invented the twenty-two letter all consonant alphabet, either as a complete innovation or an adaptation from the Egyptian. Phoenician might stem from phonetic: signs and characters and vocal sounds. Phoenix also means red. Phoenicia was the original land of Canaan and the dwelling place of the descendants of Ham son of Noah. Canaanite sailors were referred to as red men because of their sunburned skin. To further confuse the issue Phoenix may also mean date palm or a musical instrument shaped like a guitar. What is your pleasure?

Through the centuries Byblos expanded and diminished as

Egyptians and Greeks, Persians, Byzantines, Jews, and Romans ebbed and flowed over the citadel.

In 1098 the Crusaders arrived and built a great castle-fort and through the Frankish occupation, which lasted about two hundred years, things were pretty prosperous. Then along came the Mameluks in 1291 and what with continuous fighting and also the discovery of a way to the Indies around the Cape of Good Hope the caravans on which their prosperity had depended diminished and trade declined.

We then have the famed four hundred years of Ottoman occupation until 1918 when, whatever its horrors, World War I did succeed in forcing a withdrawal of the Turks into suitable territory; their own.

In a manner of speaking Byblos may be said to be the lazy man's ruin. This comment if superficial is not inaccurate. Because a part of the Crusaders fortress still stands it is not necessary to cover the entire area on foot in order to appreciate it. From the fortress tower one has a fine view of the ancient site bounded by the sea, the chief features of which are the remnants of walls that enclosed successive civilizations which down the centuries, with the vicissitudes of victory and defeat, through never ending warfare were built, destroyed, rebuilt and redestroyed. The trouble with antiquity is that it induces an immense lassitude. How long oh Lord how long will folly and fear, cruelty, ineptitude and sheer wantonness prevail? Apparently forever.

Scholars and the young ought to explore Byblos in detail. They will find it rewarding but I think the average traveler should behold it with awe, feel himself brushed by the wing of history, thank his gods that it is there and go on about his business. The most engaging detail is a bit of restoration. A few Roman columns have been replaced on top of a stone wall and silhouetted against feathery green trees and the blue waters of the harbor they are evocative and nostalgic. As funds become available further excavations will get under way.

Byblos is about 25 kilometers from Beirut and we returned

there to lunch with the Frank Guzzardos in their large comfortable apartment overlooking the bay. He is Pan Am's man in Beirut. While a little subdued at the time we were there, due to the political situation of the whole Middle East, Beirut is normally one of the great cross roads of the airlines routes, the gateway between Europe and Asia and not all that remote from Africa.

Our luncheon was delicious and dessert was the best Brown Betty I have ever eaten.

The Guzzardos are a relatively large family with three young sons at home, a nineteen-year-old daughter at the University of Kansas, and a poodle, Valentino, born in Rome on St. Valentine's Day. Her mother was afraid the girl might feel herself to be incommunicado because "Frank and I collect pictures as you see but at the University of Kansas . . . if our daughter were to say, 'My parents have eighty-five pictures hanging on the walls' nobody would understand." I felt that perhaps her fears were groundless. There is after all a good deal of money in Kansas and much of it finds its way around the world and I imagine some of the students have, willingly or not, been exposed to museums and galleries and surely *some* of their parents must have succumbed to a dealer's wiles.

As we were leaving the Guzzardos we were cheered by Frank's offer to have a bag we wanted to send back home placed in the custody of a Statesbound Pan American employee. On a lengthy trip it is an enormous help to be able to shed luggage one no longer needs but beware of dispatching it without a guardian. The rate of theft at our big airports is scandalous.

At eight o'clock that evening Nuha and Emil Bishuty arrived to drive us to the plane for our flight to Jidda in Saudi Arabia. In case you are thinking of going there prepare for a blow. The entry tax into the country is $15 per person. Only that day I had been saying to Norton, "If we *do* have an audience with the King what shall we ask him?" At the airport, anteing up the

$30 penalty my spouse said bitterly, "*I* know what to ask him. 'Why the hell do you impose that God-awful tax?'"

Our plane was a big one with few passengers but we did meet a vigorous young American, Mr. R. D. Samuels a field engineer for a Saudi project of the Raytheon Service Company. He liked the Arabs he worked with and said they were eager to learn. "Don't let anyone sell them short," he said. There were other Americans we met who felt that labor as such was not the Arabs' forte.

He told us that every two months he got ten days off to go to Europe. "It's vital because, after working hours, there is literally nothing, but nothing whatever to do." When I said it sounded like an admirable opportunity to take up guitar playing or a short story course by mail he smiled, "The hitch is the mails are few and far between."

In the plane Norton and I discussed what we would do in the event we were not met at the airport. Emil had assured us we would be but we were going into a strange strange world where we knew no human soul nor did we have an inkling as to hotels or anything else for that matter. Arabia! What were we doing there?

We landed after a flight of two hours and twenty-five minutes. The plane rolled to a halt, the door was opened and we looked down on three white robed figures, their heads covered with the Kofieh or native headdress bowing at the foot of the steps. Our very own Arabs!

As we reached the ground they bowed lower. "Dr. and Mrs. Brown?" "Yes." "Good evening." "Good evening." We are handed into a waiting car and driven across the apron. We get out and are handed into another with our two or three small bags. "May we have your luggage checks please for the large piece?" We hand them over. "They will follow." One of the trio disappears, presumably to look after them. The other two get into the car with us. As we pull away from the airport we see hundreds of Arabs sleeping on the ground. "They are waiting for planes to return them to their homelands from the hadj," one of our companions says. "They are told within about six hours what time their plane will leave but nothing more precise. They come here to sleep so as to be ready when it is called." The night was warm so the hardship was not too acute and certainly preferable to missing the plane. Nor can one blame the authorities for their vagueness. With thousands of pilgrims to cope with and limited capacity their job is a gruelling one.

We drove through the night for quite a while assuming of course we would be deposited at a hotel but we did not seem to be going into a city and finally we turned off the paving and bumped along a dirt road for a few minutes pulling up in front of a wall with an iron gate. The chauffeur tooted the horn, the gate was raised and we drove into the courtyard of what appeared to be and indeed was a private house. Headlines quavered across my consciousness—*AMERICAN COUPLE DISAPPEARS IN DESERT NIGHT . . . ARABIAN SEAPORT SWALLOWS DOCTOR AND WRITER WIFE.*

We were ushered into a foyer which gave into a large double drawing room. The place was very clean but had a curiously bare look as though it were not really lived in. A good many pictures were on the floor stacked against the wall and I was trying to account for their somewhat unorthodox placement when a tall good-looking young man also in Arab dress came in and greeted us. "Please," he pointed to a large foam-rubber sofa. We sat down. The young man sat down as did our two friends from the airport. The place was glacial and the air conditioner roaring full blast. The noise was so great we could not hear ourselves speak and the cold such that I feared pneumonia. At times air conditioners are indispensable but I am not an addict and resort to them only in a heat and humidity crisis. The night did not seem to me all that hot. "I wonder," I said, "would it be possible to turn that thing off?" This was done. We then sat in silence, the three Arab gentlemen and ourselves, Norton and I without any idea at all of where we were or who our companions were.

We glanced at each other, two minds with but a single thought: If this isn't the ideal time for a bit of schnapps to get the ball rolling there never was one! However we were in Saudi Arabia and Saudi Arabia is a Muslim country and drink is against the Muslim religion. I asked for a glass of water. It was brought by the young man. We sat on. How long would it take to get our luggage? How long were the three men going to stay? Who *were* they? Where *were* we? If and when they went what would we do? Something had to give. Strained and total silence is not my forte so I said briskly, "And Mr. Adham whom we met in New York and who is so charming . . . we hope very much we will be seeing him."

"Tomorrow morning at ten o'clock."

"That will be nice." Silence. I embark on a sprightly little monologue about the earthquake in Marrakech and the various ruins we have seen.

"They must be very interesting" say the Arabs courteously.

"Yes indeed. You can't imagine . . ." The momentum is running down again when Norton hits on Beirut. "Have any of you been there?" They have all been. We all agree that Beirut is delightful. "The Paris of the East" say the Arabs in one voice. The Paris of the East we concluded sometime later if one must spend much time in Jidda. By comparison Beirut would be a seething caldron of activity.

As the night wore on and our luggage didn't arrive I suspected darkly that they were riffling it for liquor of which we had neither jot nor tittle.

We had been cautioned that under no circumstances should we try to smuggle any into the country, an admonition we scrupulously obeyed the more so because we were being sponsored by a member of the court, the brother-in-law of the King. At that particular moment however I thought enviously of an American couple we had heard about who bought a large bag of oranges in Beirut, filled a syringe with vodka and injected it into the fruit which they prudently carted to Saudi Arabia. It seemed an in-

spired idea although as we were to learn Saudi Arabia is about
as dry as the United States was during Prohibition.

People import liquor or they make it in their own stills. The
homemade variety is known as Brown and White. Brown is
whiskey white, gin or vodka. It is not very good but the alcohol is
pure and you won't die or go blind. The imported liquor is perfectly authentic and when ordering over the telephone one uses a
code with the bootlegger. Coca-Cola means whiskey, 7-Up is gin
or vodka. Vodka is a little more difficult but it can be had. Beer,
desirable in a hot country, is rare the reason being that boot-
leggers demand and get two hundred dollars a case for hard liquor
whereas a case of beer which is just as heavy and costs them just
as much effort to bring in is infinitely lower in price.

I had always assumed that Saudi Arabia was dry because it is
a Muslim country and that is one reason. We were told another
was because during the reign of the old King, Abd Ar Rahman,
one of his sons got drunk at a party in the British Embassy.
There was a fight over a woman and the Arab prince killed
an Englishman. It is said that according to custom the King went
to the widow and offered her his son's head in recompense. She
refused but it was then that the edict went out that alcohol should
not be obtainable in the country.

Our luggage came at last and as soon as it arrived the two airport Arabs departed. We then began to realize that the young man
was our host and the owner of the house we were in. He did
not know us, we did not know him but like an occupying army
we had been quartered upon him. Later we learned the why and
wherefore.

I felt extremely embarrassed because it occurred to me that my
request to have the air conditioner turned off had been rather
peremptory, perhaps more in the nature of a demand, but I was
completely baffled as to my whereabouts.

We learned that our host's name was Nawwaf Yassin. He
asked us if we would like some fruit juice but as it was now
2 A.M. we demurred and he showed us to our room. He also

showed us the room switch that turned the air conditioning off and on. We thanked him and as soon as we were alone turned it off and opened a window. The air was balmy and there was a slight breeze. The ways of Allah surpassed those of man.

About eight-thirty we woke to a clear and lovely morning. We dressed and went downstairs to find our host also up and moving gracefully about in his long white cotton robe but this time minus the headdress.

In the dining room—shuttered and air conditioned—breakfast was served by Bourrie a young Ethiopian maid in a swinging Ethiopian skirt. Bourrie is how it sounded and I *hope* that is how it is spelled.

Eggs were brought, I suspected out of deference to our quaint native folk ways although Nawwaf ate them too. There was butter and yogurt, cheese, olives, delicious jam and tea. Norton had to make do with powdered Sanka. I was later able to remedy this— I trust tactfully—but not that morning.

About ten as predicted Sheikh Kamal Adham arrived accompanied by Mr. Ramzi Wassif. Mr. Wassif had a keen intelligent face and was we inferred chief of the Travel Bureau. I did not know so many people traveled in Saudi Arabia but I was thinking in terms of tourists from the West. If one thinks in terms of pilgrims going to Mecca they number, of course, hundreds of thousands, over the years millions. We had a little shock of surprise in seeing Kamal Adham in Arabian dress because when we had dined together in New York he had been in a business suit. His native garb became him as it does most men.

We exchanged greetings and since the three men spoke excellent English Norton and I did not anticipate the prolonged silences of the previous evening. In this we were wrong. Once we had said how good it was to see them all and how eagerly we were looking forward to visiting as much as would be feasible of their fascinating country a pall of silence descended. I went into my act about the ruins. Nawwaf looked like a man who had heard it before. I was sorry about the repetition but it had a good effect for it at least galvanized them into a brisk three way conversation in Arabic.

In our minds a weaselly suspicion began to raise its little head. In effect might they not be saying "Now that we have them here what the hell are we going to do with them?" Yet they had invited us, surely they must have made *some* plans?

Kamal Adham finally volunteers the information that we have an appointment with his sister, the Queen, next Wednesday and he adds something about going to Riyadh on Friday. I burst out, "Friday!" This is only Sunday. "Oh we couldn't dream of it. We can't possibly impose on you to that extent. We don't want to be a burden, you know."

"There is no question of burden," he replies suavely. "We are doing nothing special for you. That is why we have put you here with Nawwaf instead of in a hotel. You will see the Arab way of life."

My house is yours. But we were rather sorry for our young host. He worked in the Foreign Ministry, Sheikh Adham was his boss and he had little choice but to bow to his requests, even bizarre ones like sheltering a couple of globe-trotting Americans.

We observe that we must leave Jidda before Friday because we have to go not only to Riyadh but also to Dhahran—we have been in touch with the oil people there and they are arranging a trip to the Hofuf Oasis.

Sheikh Adham observes that maybe we will have an appointment with a very high personage, it is not yet decided. We assume the King and he and Wassif leave. We have learned nothing.

For something to do Nawwaf drives us into town where there are still masses of pilgrims dawdling about all looking scruffy and weary. There is a good deal of building going on and the city is obviously expanding but unfortunately, as is so frequently the case, charming old buildings, some with lovely wooden balconies and grill work, are being torn down to make room for concrete hideosities.

Oddly enough one of the attractive features of the town is the trucks, their sides gaily painted with marinescapes, mountains and flowers and with super structures of iron grill work studded with medallions and metal flowers that do much to take the curse off industrialization.

The name Jedda or Jidda, the spelling is interchangeable, means grandmother and they will tell you that it is here that Eve is buried although I do not believe anyone claims to have seen her tomb.

Jidda today has a population of about 250,000 and while the shops are not good they do have merchandise from all over the world and Sony transistor radios from Japan which sell in New York for twenty-five or twenty-eight dollars may be purchased there for ten. If you are going on to Hong Kong save your money as there they cost eight.

Dr. Brown bought a couple of drip-dry shirts, cost unremembered and uninteresting, and since we had expressed ourselves forcefully about wanting to see the desert we set out along the road to Mecca. Our way wound through rocky dunes and drifting sand tinged faintly with green because of an unusual amount of rain fall but when we got within twenty-five kilometers of Mecca Nawwaf turned around and headed back toward Jidda. We were after all infidel dogs and must not approach too near the sacred city.

As we entered the house he whipped off his kofieh, tossed it on a pouf in the front hall and uttered unexpected sounds. "How about a drink?" he said. Well! Because we were foreigners and guests, principles, as far as we were concerned, had been courteously suspended. To my surprise Dr. Brown refused saying he wished to abide by local custom and experiment to find out what no liquor at all was like. I suspected correctly that the experiment would be short lived but I myself being more self-indulgent and appreciative of the generous gesture of our host agreed to a gin and tonic. We all three partook of the pistachio nuts he provided.

Actually much of the sophisticated element in the country drinks and smokes but because of the shrines of Mecca and Medina, the pilgrims and the orthodoxy of a large section of the working class they maintain a pretense of abstinence. Also of course labor is more efficient if it doesn't drink. The attitude is a bit reminiscent of the English duchess who observed of sex that it was too good for the working classes.

During our pre-luncheon chat we learned that Nawwaf was married to an Egyptian girl who was presently back in Cairo with her family. The Jidda house had been repainted and decorated just before our arrival and that was why the pictures were stacked on the floor awaiting the mistress to return and supervise their arrangement. Nawwaf had been expecting her for some time and hoped he said that she would be back that week. Later in the day she telephoned him from Cairo and when he rejoined us he was obviously crestfallen. She was staying on he said for another month. "It's for a physical check-up." Although it was none of our business feminine intuition led me to doubt the need of medical attention and to speculate on the chances of her return.

"Next month," he said, "we will have been married three years."

We learned that they left Jidda to travel at least twice a year but I imagined the bride was bored. From the little we had seen there was literally nothing to do in the city and as far as housework was concerned the Ethiopian and, when Madame was in residence another servant, could easily cope with the six or seven rooms.

From what we saw during our stay my impression was that the social consciousness threshold of Arab women of the upper class is high and there does not appear to be much indulgence in Good Works to occupy their time. If they have children they also have any number of servants looking after them. The city has few shops, no museums, picture galleries, library, or restaurants. A large professional dryer at the Yassins indicated that hair was done at home so that even the sociability of a beauty shop was lacking.

When I remarked to Nawwaf that I thought a good hairdressing establishment in the community would be bound to flourish he said that a cousin of his had thought so too and had tried to start one but the enterprise had languished. Whether it wasn't good enough or whether the women still clung to the veiled psychology and shunned men other than their husbands I do not know.

Whatever the reasons occupation in general seemed sparse and if a young couple has no children . . . it was small wonder that as we discovered the women slept most of the day and stayed up as late as possible at night.

Shortly after two o'clock of our first day, luncheon was announced. Having seen no preparations whatsoever I was surprised by its lavishness. Mezzes followed by shepherd's pie followed by a roast with beans, rice, and salad, and for dessert fresh fruit, all passed by a male servant we had not seen before whom we took to be Nawwaf's cook or butler. We felt that in assuming Bourrie to be maid of all work we had greatly underestimated the staff.

Later the mystery was explained. The skilled provider did not live in the house but every day he brought food from the Adham kitchen reheated it at Nawwaf's and served it to us at table.

When I observed that the procedure indicated great consideration on the part of the Adhams—it insured us good food and certainly simplified Nawwaf's duties as host—he explained that his patrons establishment was extensive. There were three houses on the property: one for Mr. and Mrs. Adham, one for the children, and one where the Sheikh entertained business associates and that on an average thirty people sat down to a meal. "When my wife is away and I am alone," he continued, "I always eat with them." We hoped our company did not seem too anticlimactic and concluded that in Saudi Arabia the business of government is a profitable enterprise.

Although we were not to meet her there were a good many photographs of Mrs. Yassin strewn around the house and she appeared to be a seductive young woman with what used to be called bedroom eyes. She was twenty-three and Nawwaf was thirty-two or -three. Interestingly enough her husband owed her to Kamal Adham, dispenser of all bounty. We learned that his marriage had been arranged by the omnipotent Sheikh.

Nawwaf had told him that he wished to be married but where to find a bride? Mr. Adham had one up his sleeve. The suitor was whisked to Cairo where he met and with a speed I should imagine unusual in Arab countries wooed and married the fair maid within a few weeks.

He confided that on his honeymoon they were not allowed to sleep together because of a heart condition from which he was supposedly suffering. Pretty fed up with such an arrangement, and one imagines spurred by a few comments from Mrs. Yassin, he went to another doctor who told him the first one was a quack, that he had a heart of oak and to go to it. The bride and groom must have been pretty bitter when they recalled all that wasted time. I thought it explained one of the photographs taken on the honeymoon in which Madame is looking at Monsieur with what may fairly be described as a quizzical expression.

On that first morning when we returned from our abortive drive to Mecca I had heard a few meek little barks. "You have a dog?" I asked delightedly. "Where is he?"

"He's upstairs on the roof," Nawwaf said. "It's a she."

"Couldn't we get her down?"

Obviously considering this a harebrained scheme he sent Bourrie to fetch her. She was a lively little poodle and as dirty and unkempt a one as I have ever seen. As her story was gradually unfolded it developed that Sheikh Kamal Adham had been obliged to reap what he had sowed. He had arranged the eventually successfully consummated marriage. The honeymoon had ended, the happy couple had then returned home. *Then* the bride began to languish. Candidly the bride was bored. It seems likely that one morning in the office of the Foreign Ministry the distraught groom confided in his patron. "My bride is bored. What am I to do?" What kind of a patron is it who has no solution to the problem of the young lieutenant he has recently inducted into matrimony? A dandelion-headed patron that's the kind and this our Sheikh was not. To the rescue! Differing from many of their countrymen who hold that dogs are unclean the Ahmeds warm to them and I believe have several who are admirably catered to by a special groom assigned to the duty.

From their kennels they picked a poodle, one young Nashwah and gave her to the bride on whose hands time hung heavy. The little animal would amuse her and fill her empty days.

According to our host Nashwah was mad for the mistress and the mistress in turn adored her pet. Not to the extent of taking it with her to Cairo.

The little creature was kept day and night on the roof. The roof was spacious enough and off this barren playground was a kind of storeroom where she could escape the glaring sun and where her water bowl, filled when Bourrie thought of it, was kept but there were no toys, no care, no companionship. From what I could see her food consisted of rice and pastry when Bourrie had them for one of her own meals. The house was set in a large paved patio enclosed by a high wall and Nawwaf was genuinely interested in his small vegetable garden and lawn, trees and flowers all of which he had planted himself. The enclosure would have been an ideal place for Nashwah to run but he had a theory that it was not good for her to be on the ground.

We tried embarking on a gentle course of education. After all it was ignorance rather than evil that dictated the treatment. Understandably Nawwaf felt a certain resentment of what he could with some reason consider meddling in his private affairs. "I am already doing all I can," he said shortly. "I was brought up to believe dogs are unclean. My mother wouldn't allow one in the house. When she came to visit me Nashwah had to stay on the roof the *entire time* and I had a servant who left me because of her."

"Now Nawwaf," I said, "listen a minute. Allah made dogs just

as much as he made you and me. You're going to tell me Allah
made a *dirty* thing! Of course he didn't."

Nawwaf had no comeback to that but his expression clearly indicated that the hand of the potter had slipped. Whether in forming
me or the dog was not clear.

What was clear was that Nashwah—the name means a happy
state, a sort of euphoria and was a misnomer—was badly in
need of clipping and a bath. I had no shears and could do nothing
about the former condition but rallying Bourrie who seemed in-
trigued by the novel idea I rounded up soap and a pitcher, tumbled the dog into the tub and gave her a good shampoo. Like
all poodles she submitted miserably to the bathing part and like
all poodles was ecstatic with joy once it was over and she felt
fresh and clean.

As evening closed in we did a little grooming of ourselves and
around half past nine departed for the party to which we had
been invited by the Adhams. Theirs is a large and airy house
unobtrusively air conditioned and I thought what marvelous op-
portunities there were for sophisticated interior decorators in Saudi
Arabia. The bag of guests was mixed, colorful and entertaining,
twenty-five to thirty people: Arabs, Lebanese, Syrians, Turks,
Yemenites and Egyptians. With the exception of a woman from
the British Embassy Norton and I were the only Westerners.
Mr. Wassif who had accompanied Kamal Adham in the morning
was present, this time clad in a Western suit although most of
the men were in native attire.

Many of the women wore long elaborate brocaded evening
dresses. Mindful of excess luggage charges and packing and un-
packing on a trip around the world I was ill equipped to compete
with them. I wore a short white piqué dress with inserts of cotton
lace which had caused my husband some concern. "We're in a
very conservative country," he said, "that dress is pretty trans-
parent." I had put on another slip but compared to the mini skirts
that barely sheltered the behinds of two or three ladies in revolt
against longitude I was in a nun's habit.

There was a young girl at the party whom Norton and I took to be about fifteen or sixteen. She was the Adham's daughter and she was eleven. I have never before seen anything that age so well developed. Her mother, who is Kamal Adham's second wife and many years his junior, told us that next year she was to go to school in Switzerland but the young lady was already pouting.

She far preferred the swinging social life of Jidda. Observing her I said, "I suppose at thirteen she will be married."

Her young mother in a characteristic gesture raised her hand, lifted the long brown hair that habitually curtains one of her own eyes and peered at her daughter. "What else can I do with her?" she asked. Given the life and customs of that part of the world and the maturity of the daughter I imagine marriage was the answer.

At another party I was amused to overhear a conversation concerning a mutual friend of several of the ladies present who had recently wed. "And she ought to be grateful let me tell you," said one of them. "You know how *old* she is don't you?" Imagining a nervous and perhaps despairing spinster nearing forty, I asked, "How old?" "My dear, she's twenty-four!"

That first evening refreshments were passed accompanied by caviar and at eleven o'clock dinner was announced. We served ourselves at a buffet and sat at tables on the terrace. One of my partners was an amusing Egyptian woman, Mrs. LeBlanc. I will say that her first name was Fatima which it is not. The reason being that I was told the use of their real names might be offensive to some of the more conservative element. By male Arab reasoning the women could be accused of having sought publicity for themselves.

I think Fatima LeBlanc, a free-swinging soul if ever I saw one, wouldn't at all mind having her real name mentioned especially as she is married to an American who works for TWA but I'll take no chances. Mr. LeBlanc was not at the party. Now that the season was over he was busy shepherding those who made the pilgrimage to Mecca out of the country.

Since they come in their thousands from all over the Muslim world one would think that the hadj would be very profitable for Saudi Arabia. It cannot help but bring money into the country although apparently not the sums one might assume. Many of the pilgrims are extremely poor or they are frugal. They do not patronize hotels but bring their own food and sleep on the ground—we saw them doing it. Indeed they not infrequently smuggle goods into the country, sell them and depart with a nice little profit neatly serving God and mammon at the same time.

After dinner the party really began to swing. There was no orchestra but we didn't need one. They had a tape recorder and a loud speaker and the decibel count soared. People got up and started to do native Arab dances. Men and women faced each other, their movements undulating but sedate, accompanied by rhythmic hand clapping. One guest, tightly moulded into her girdle, did a very funny belly dance and having recently seen the Moroccan version and considering ourselves somewhat sophisticated in these matters Norton and I greatly enjoyed it.

During the long afternoon in the period between washing Nashwah and leaving for the party Nawwaf had instructed us in the terminology of male Arab apparel. The headdress is usually called the kofieh although precisely speaking that is only the round skull cap on which the superstructure is built. The veil draped over it, white, black or in the country frequently red and white checks is the ghotra and the black cord that binds it is the ogal. The floor-length tunic or robe is the taub and the long over garment usually trimmed with gold braid is the abayah or bisht.

I jot this down so you may really be With It when I tell you that as the merriment mounted most of the men whipped off their ghotras and tied them around their waists to free themselves for the contest and an especially talented member of the court kicked off his shoes, hitched up his taub and gave all. It was an innocent and spirited evening.

About two-thirty Norton and I with our effete Western background began to feel sleepy and as the gaiety showed no sign of diminishing we asked Nawwaf if it would be possible to make an unobtrusive exit. He looked distressed but agreed to drive us home which he did at a lickety split pace dropping us off and returning at once to the party. Norton and I went to bed and to sleep but about an hour later I thought I heard the metal door of the garage slam down and the next morning he told us the party had broken up shortly after we left.

Thanks to the prolonged entertainment of the hospitable Adhams we slept until almost ten o'clock and were grateful that at least that much of the day has slipped past since after dressing and breakfasting there was nothing at all to do. A car had been sent for us but as the driver had no instructions about taking us anywhere Nawwaf sent him away. He himself drove us into town later to buy a paper and a few postcards at which point Jidda struck us as being not so much a place as a bad idea.

Having learned the name of the American ambassador, the Honorable Hermann Frederick Eilts, I wrote a little note and later on when we went for another outing delivered it at the Embassy and then drove about viewing the complete desolation that is the beach; flat, gray, muddy. In the middle of nowhere Nawwaf proudly pointed to two sand lots he owns, where he plans to build. He is very investment conscious and dreary though it appeared to us he has probably made a good choice for the American Embassy is not far away and on land adjoining his property the British are putting up a new building of their own. Also in the neighborhood was the one really distinguished house we had so far seen, that of the Arabian Foreign Minister.

The physical set-up of the government is rather curious. The diplomatic corps is established in Jidda and for that reason the King and court are often there but the administration proper and the government offices are in Riyadh, in the center of the peninsula and that is the capital of the country.

Jiddans are convinced that a great boom is on and with the oil wealth the city is inevitably growing. On the other hand Riyadhans tell you that the real seat of government is there and

that it is only a question of time before the embassies will be
obliged to move to Riyadh.

Nawwaf's own taste in residences was catholic. That afternoon
as we sat at tea in the courtyard he questioned us closely about
New York. How much were rents? What were the advantages of
maintenance? How much did one save by living in the suburbs?
His dreams was to accompany Mr. Adham to New York the
following autumn and he told us what monthly salary he would
be paid. We thought it generous for the kind of work he would
likely be doing.

His future, his life in general, greatly concerned him. Had
the beach property *really* been a wise investment? He needed
money, his wife was so extravagant and what could he do about
it? "Sometimes," he said, "even when she is here I sit and think.
I don't want to talk to her and she doesn't understand that I am
thinking, thinking all the time." Norton smiled at him. "Not
worrying, Nawwaf? I hope not."

He had told us a story and we felt sorry for him because it
was an example of the disadvantages that those from the still
undeveloped countries undergo when trying to cope with technol-
ogy abroad. He had spent four years in Germany struggling for a
degree in Industrial Management but returned home when he
realized he faced what were for him two insurmountable hur-
dles: the language barrier, he could not master German, and the
fact that his secondary Arab education was insufficient prepara-
tion for the job.

His wife's family we gathered had money. They had owned a
department store in Cairo which Nasser had confiscated. However, they still had an apartment building and from that they continued to draw an income. There were echoes of money all
through the house in Jidda: a large imposing chest of flat silver,
obviously a part of the bride's dowry, many delicate-stemmed
wineglasses, although wine was virtually nonexistent, and while
the big wardrobe in the room we occupied had been emptied
for our use Norton said that when he went into Nawwaf's room

one morning to give him a physical examination at his request he had seen dozens of pairs of women's shoes ranged in the closet.

There was something a little eerie about being in the young woman's house, observing these traces of her, hearing her spoken of, seeing her pictures yet never seeing her. It was curious that at all the parties we went to the people who were her friends never mentioned her. I began to think of Rebecca and Manderley.

Wanda's statement that Arabs were hypochondriacs was exemplified by our host who poured out his medical history to Norton on our first afternoon and the next morning handed him his entire medical record complete with X rays.

Humanly enough, having been saddled with us, he probably considered himself entitled to a little free medical advice. Norton considered this fair for we appreciated the trouble he was going to on our account. Despite that, however, we felt ourselves to be under a benign house arrest. We knew no one, we had no place to go and nothing to do. To Arabs time is not of the essence but to traveling Americans who want to see as much as they can within the time at their disposal, it means a great deal. Norton minded the enforced idleness less than I for he is of philosophic disposition and on occasion—like Nawwaf—likes to sit and think. I feel I can think on my feet while I am going places and seeing things and if I am going to do it sitting down I want paper and a typewriter before me.

Occasionally there might be a bit of activity after lunch but then what to do until nine or ten when the evening parties began?

We couldn't budge without our host as the house was too far away from any sort of center or activity for us to walk to it and from time to time he did have to put in an appearance at the Foreign Ministry and naturally used his car to get there.

God knows we couldn't cope with the Arabian telephone even had we had anyone with whom to communicate. Still, we didn't feel too stupid about that as the Arabs obviously couldn't cope with it either. The brain child of Mr. Alexander Graham Bell is not really firmly entrenched in the Arabian peninsula.

There was a phone on a low taboret in the front hall of
Nawwaf's house and he spent long periods crouched beside it
hoping it would respond to his pleas. He would take the receiver
off the hook, turn a crank, replace the receiver and wait. This
action supposedly summoned the operator but it was more theory
than performance. Once in a great while there *would* be a ring,
an answer to prayer, and he would dive for the phone tossing us
a triumphant glance. "You see! I have summoned the genie, he
has emerged from the bottle!"

It reminded me of Glendower's boast in *Henry IV*, "I can call
spirits from the vasty deep," and Hotspur's pertinent response,
"Why so can I or so can any man; but will they come when
you do call for them?" Once contact had been established with
the outside world Norton and I would be submerged in the
torrent of Arabic swirling around us.

As far as using the car was concerned I am sure Nawwaf would
have had no objection when he didn't need it but he was guardian
as well as host and, since he was responsible to Higher Ups for
our welfare, he was taking no chances.

On one occasion when we happened to be talking about cars
I learned that women are not permitted to drive in Saudi Arabia,
not even Westerners. "But why not?" I asked. Nawwaf explained
that in case of an accident and someone is killed a jail sentence
for the driver is mandatory. Furthermore he must stay in prison,
whether he was at fault or not, until the family of the victim is
satisfied. "You wouldn't put a woman in jail, would you?" he
asked. "The settlement, don't forget, may take several days." I
said that in the United States women had been known to go to
jail. "Not a Saudi Arabian jail," he said grimly. He may have
had a point.

The Arabs are much more practical about damages than we
are. There is none of this business of suits and how much can
you collect from the insurance company and how grave an injury
have you sustained and long drawn out court cases. Compensa-
tion is cut and dried and set ahead of time. If you kill a Muslim

male the top blood price is 16,000 riales about $3600. You can get yourself a Christian male for under a $1000. A Muslim female is progressively less and a Christian female . . . how insignificant can a human creature be after all? Mow 'em down, they're bargains. Should you deprive someone of an arm or leg the price varies accordingly. Selon grandeur as it says on French menus when a lobster or a steak is in question.

In Jidda we benefited from the first prolonged bout of hot sunshine we had experienced on the entire trip. In mid-March it was not unbearable and when Nawwaf went out Norton and I often turned off the air conditioning surreptitiously and opened the windows to enjoy the breeze, keeping a sharp lookout for our host's return in order to re-establish the status quo before his arrival.

Bourrie was amused by these shenanigans and sometimes through the long afternoons she would come and sit with me when I was writing or reading or doing needlepoint. She had a few words of English and a little French. She was curious about the countries we had passed through before coming to Jidda and she blossomed when I told her we had once been in Asmara the town that was her home in Ethiopia. We had only been at the airport during a stop on our way from Addis Ababa to Cairo but I didn't tell her that. The magic syllables were all she needed to make her happy. The child must have been lonely although she did have a friend, another Ethiopian girl who sometimes came to call, her white gauze skirt swinging, her baby in her arms.

In one of our talks with Nawwaf we had got on the subject of domestic help and the lack of same in the United States. Nawwaf assured us it was not much better in Jidda. He was not overly enthusiastic about the service rendered by Bourrie although acknowledging that she was an excellent laundress. "That's the first thing I ask when I interview them. I change all my linen at least twice a day. They must know how to wash and iron."

It was true that his white garments were spotless. He reminded me of the ads of my childhood that featured Phoebe Snow the damsel who owed her immaculate appearance to the fact that she rode the trains of the Lackawanna, the Road of Anthracite. Bourrie achieved for Nawwaf the same radiance and without benefit of washing or drying machines. Yet he found her wages irksome. "When you think she gets her room and board for nothing! The money they want."

It had a familiar ring but on the morning when I had first gone upstairs to release Nashwah from the glaring solitude of the roof I had seen Bourrie's room. It was the landing at the top of the stairs. There was a chest of drawers and a small mattress on the floor without sheets or a pillow.

The bath was a sink and the sanitary facilities eastern; a hole in the floor of the roof shed where Nashwah's water bowl and a few household tools were kept.

From an American point of view the arrangements were meager. Compared to what she may have been accustomed to in Ethiopia they might well have been an improvement and in a hot country bedding can be informal yet still adequate. Although Bourrie was clean, judging from her appearance her toilet night and morning could not have been time consuming. She wore a sleeveless blouse and skirt and like many eastern servants went barefoot.

About six o'clock one evening when the heat of the day began to abate Nawwaf and I drove into town to buy stamps. I also wanted to buy a toy for Nashwah. The idea of a dog having a ball or a chewy toy or any other means of amusement was totally unthought of and Nawwaf looked at me strangely when I suggested it. This lack of imagination annoyed me but the stamp selling restored my good humor. In Saudi Arabia you do not do anything so square as go into the post office to buy stamps. They are sold by a fellow sitting at a little table in front of the building. He keeps them in a drawer that sticks and he has to wrestle to open and close it. He also sells airmail stationery which is weighted down by stones. When he gives you your stamps he

puts them in the corner of a torn envelope and hands them to
you and you may then enter the post office to mail your letters.

This ceremony accomplished we went in search of a toy store.
Nawwaf was vague as to where one might be found and if Jidda
is an example Arab children fare poorly. We finally unearthed a
shabby little shop where they had a few plastic toys but no balls.
In the end I bought a bag of wretched plastic ninepins because
there was a small ball enclosed. I said I would take it before
asking the price. A mistake! It cost over $3. I was about to put it
back but I couldn't bear to think of the boredom of poor little
Nashwah and also I had made such a fuss about getting her
something and had expatiated in such superior fashion about
the happy lot of American dogs, I didn't have the nerve to return
to Nawwaf empty handed. He, by the way, had been circling
the block waiting for me, the parking problem in downtown
Jidda being not unlike that of New York.

Arabs would think us mad were they to see the dog shops of
America's large cities or were they to be presented with the gross
business figures for animal foods and accoutrements. I cannot
even imagine their reaction to something like New York's Animal
Medical Center.

Sometimes in the night in Jidda we would be awakened by
packs of half-starved dogs barking in the streets in wild cacophony. The bedlam would cease as abruptly as it began.

It is probably not fair to say that Arabs are cruel to animals,
although they are, but it is more out of indifference than intent
and because they are totally uneducated to their requirements.
For the animals the results are the same either way. I was told
the story of a woman in Jidda who had gone away for two
weeks inadvertently shutting her cat in her clothes closet. The
cat had given birth to a litter, eaten her kittens and torn the
woman's clothes to shreds. No female, Arab or otherwise, could
be expected to enthuse over that but I thought it curious that no
one commented on the agony of the cat.

The evening of the day I had bought the ninepins we were

invited to a party given by Sheikh Ahmed Abdull Wahab, the Minister of Protocol, and his wife. The minister we had met the night before at the Adhams'. He was a tall good-looking chap and had been one of the most convivial of the guests.

This time Nawwaf drove us but he did not come to the party. Norton and I entered the house by ourselves and I was directed to one drawing room, he to another. The rooms were large and they were adjoining but it was obvious that the party was segregated at least until dinner was served.

My salon was full of women in elaborate clothes. They were perhaps not altogether to the Western taste, but they were certainly dressed. I, as usual, looked plain Jane by comparison.

The ladies greeted me courteously, they all spoke good English, and relapsed at once into Arabic and the gossip my entrance had interrupted.

Pretty young Mrs. Adham was there holding up her curtain of hair, her black chiffon dress more flattering to her figure than the glittering brocade of the night before had been. She was making a noble effort to diet and in that small closed community every friend could and did comment on every gram lost or gained.

One of the women, a forthright type who was, I learned, half German, half Palestinian Arab, came and sat down beside me gallantly attempting a bit of hands across the sea rapport. She stuck it out for a few minutes then she too took the easier path relapsing into Arabic with her playmates. I couldn't blame her. Conversation with a stranger is not very entertaining. I sat there smiling and trying to look alert and intelligent and as if I understood all they were saying and dutifully sipped the tomato juice that was passed. I glanced through the open double doors into the next room to see what the chaps were having and wondering if Norton might be able to slip me a little serum. The chaps were having tomato juice. I knew Dr. Brown must be charmed.

I thought to myself, if this is going to be like last night, no food till eleven, the going will be rough but to my relief dinner was announced at ten-thirty. Like the previous evening it was a buffet served under blazing chandeliers and it was abundant. Among other dishes were half lambs served on beds of delicious Iranian rice. The butler, or steward perhaps, he was not the classic English butler type, began carving the roast in the usual way but as he got near the bone it became more difficult. He struggled for a bit then coping with the crisis in pragmatic fashion he dropped the utensils and started tearing the meat from the carcass with his bare hands. The high ranking court official onto whose plate he tossed a couple of slabs accepted them with nonchalant good grace scooping them into his mouth with his fingers.

There was a Damascus specialty, meat balls in cream sauce, salad and tiny tiny little roasted birds, so pathetic I couldn't eat them.

The desserts were for my taste excessively sweet made more so by the demon steward who before I could stop him poured a sort of Karo over whatever it was on my plate. I set it down as unobtrusively as possible but unfortunately my hostess saw me. Her pretty enameled face puckered into a distressed frown. "You do not like it?"

"It is delicious," I said, "but I have eaten too much of this wonderful dinner." We smiled at each other. Our little social gambit was well played. As we returned to the drawing room the indefatigable servant rushed after me with a plate of fresh fruit which showed I thought quick thoughtfulness on the part of my hostess and if I could have had a small cup of black sugarless coffee I should have been very content. What was served was sweet sweet tea.

During dinner and afterward the sexes had mingled to some extent and I met two elderly men to whom I warmed at once. They looked and were distinguished members of the community. One who was small and frail with a white goatee had studied medicine in his youth but he preferred politics and had been for a long time an adviser to King Faisal. The other was the King's friend of thirty-five years standing, an historian and archaeologist.

They wore Arab dress and there is no question that those robes
are becoming to the male sex. They are simple, imposing, and
right for their climate and life. Next to them the women tend to
seem garish.

We had hoped very much that Fatima LeBlanc would be at
the party, for the night before she had been busily making plans
to take us on a picnic the following day to a pretty creek we had
been told about where we could swim. Mrs. Craig from the
British Embassy had joined in saying she would come by in her
boat and pick us up. It sounded pleasant but the junket was to be
the next morning and having heard nothing all day we assumed,
correctly, that the deal was off.

In the afternoon Ambassador Eilts' secretary had phoned to say
the Ambassador could receive us at ten o'clock Wednesday
morning. In the meantime we had learned that I would be taken
to a reception given by the Queen on Wednesday and from Mr.
Adham we also gathered—one has to gather and surmise since
they don't come right out with it—that an audience had been
arranged with His Majesty. That would be on Wednesday too.
But when? It would be ironic if with all that time on our hands we
were suddenly to have a conflict of engagements.

Apparently nothing would interfere with the embassy appointment since the Queen's party was a tea and the audience, if it did
come through and it was not yet certain, would be sometime in
the evening. That may not sound overly definite but Norton and
I felt a certain satisfaction. We had at least extracted a smidgen
of information, a commodity that Arabs do not freely toss around.

We awoke the next day to a morning that would have been
ideal for the swimming party so cordially offered by Fatima Le-
Blanc but it was a figment. We had asked several times if we
might drive or be driven to the creek but it never materialized.
We were always put off with some vague excuse. I suppose the
simple truth was it was a nuisance for them to take us but Norton
and I began to entertain dark suspicions. Was it a secret missile
site? Was it in reality a dreary little place they were ashamed of?

I doubt it but we had nothing to do but give our imaginations free rein.

It did occur to us to put in a call to Dhahran to Mr. Robert Brougham, the president of Aramco, to whom Wanda had written a lengthy letter about our arrival in Saudi Arabia. Actually we had hoped we might hear from him and a telephone conversation seemed as good a plan as any. I approached Nawwaf.

"Nawwaf, will you be a dear and put in a call to Dhahran for us? We'd like to speak to Mr. Robert Brougham." Nawwaf agreed to try but said with a shrug, "Getting Dhahran on the phone you understand, that's not easy." However, he made the effort. After a really heroic attempt lasting a couple of hours it became clear that we had reached an impasse.

I then had a bright idea. "I tell you what, we'll send a telegram. How shall we tell him to address his answer? To your office in the Ministry?" Nawwaf smiled at my naïveté. "But he will only get it tomorrow. Then he will reply the next day and maybe we will have the answer the day after but that will be Thursday or Friday and you will be gone."

"Oh. Here telegrams don't go and come right away?"

"Here nothing is right away."

Americans used rightfully to be proud of the native telephone and telegraph service. It is still superior to that of Jidda—as of this writing—but if the present trend continues I would just as soon not hear Nawwaf's crowing laughter if he does come to the United States and has to deal with it.

Still he was game. He telephoned to Mr. Wassif. Apparently Ramzi Wassif had more pull with the telegraph company than he had. To someone in the office he read out Mr. Brougham's name and address in Able Baker Charlie fashion. B for Beirut R for Roger. When we got to M he hesitated a moment. "Mary," I suggested but he was on his own. "Mother," he said firmly. Nothing came of our mutual effort.

Norton had expressed interest in the new desalinization plant he had heard was being constructed and that visit they were helpful in arranging. Later in the afternoon we set out to call on Prince Mohamed, one of King Faisal's sons who headed the project.

The Prince and his family live on the shore of the Red Sea in a big air conditioned house set in a large garden or what will be a garden when it is completed. When we were there it looked like a gray sand desert but they were busily setting out trees and bushes hoping I imagine that the desalinization work would advance quickly so they could syphon off some of the greatly needed water. It might be the abode of a Prince but on a second-floor balcony laundry fluttered from a line giving the place a homey lived in touch.

We were shown into the drawing room where we were recieved by Her Highness, a slim dark young woman who was, we learned later, an Egyptian. With my husband's conservatism in mind I hoped my dress would be acceptable and was relieved to see that Her Highness was not so conservative that she couldn't wear pajamas in her own home.

In a few minutes His Royal Highness came in. Prince Mohamed is a delight; a big man, handsome, humorous, simple, and straightforward. Besides the Prince and Princess, Nawwaf and ourselves, there was an Arab whose card read *Adnan T. Samman, Office Manager for H.R.H. Prince Mohamed al Faisal,* and a tall lean American named Ted Modine. He was a good American. Later we spent a little time with him and his wife and found him to be able, intelligent, efficient and kind. He was the resident manager and boss of the saline water conversion plant, the man who was doing the job.

The Prince and Princess proved both democratic and entertaining and had the gift of making one feel at home at once. They have an apartment in New York's famous old building in the West 70s, the Dakota. They had met each other, we understood, in the United States and their three children were born there, the most recent, a baby girl, only two months old.

The older daughter, a child of seven or eight, came in carrying a bag of schoolbooks and wearing blue jeans. She gave a polite little bob when introduced to us but her real concern was the jeans. "These pants keep falling down the whole *time*," she said. I didn't wonder. There was very little to hold them up. I asked her mother if she had come from school but she said no, the children were tutored at home. The Jidda school system, especially for girls, is sketchy in the extreme although, thanks to the Queen, it is improving.

The Princess was fully aware of today's cogent problem for any housewife and hostess; the lack of servants. "That apartment," she said laughing, referring to the Dakota, "it's so *long*. If I'm dusting in the living room and the back doorbell rings I have to sprint to get there and the delivery men never wait."

They both like it though and the Prince accepts the neighborhood with commendable open-mindedness. "When the Israel Arab war was on," he told us, "I came out of the apartment one day and a young Jewish boy passing out handbills tossed me one. 'Give a buck to kill an Arab,' he said. He was full of enthusiasm."

We were served tea or more precisely sweet lemonade and afterward set out with Mr. Modine to see the desalinization project. He told us it would be operational in October or November and capable of converting fifty to sixty million gallons of salt water into about five million gallons of potable water a day. Eventually they hope to get twenty million a day. I respected Mr. Modine but couldn't help wondering if these mighty engineers ever consider what will happen to the planet when the seas are dry and the forests decimated.

I am told it would take such an infinity of time to drain the seas that nobody worries, but I do. So does Senator Claiborne Pell, at this writing chairman of the Foreign Relations Committee's Subcommittee on Ocean Space, although he worries more about the underwater activities of the nations of the world. We both assume they will be nefarious and should be watched with a sharp eye and stringently policed.

Ted Modine told us that the year before the United States Congress in one of its sporadic, if ill directed, frenzies had decided that the U.S. taxpayer was being mulched of funds to pay for the Arabian project. It must have been around election time for as we all know for long periods that august body never troubles its curly collective head over what is happening to the American taxpayer. The furor was a tempest in a teapot, the desalinization being one project for which Saudi Arabia itself is footing the bill. What they want from Americans is expertise.

After walking around the huge plant directed by Mr. Modine we returned to Nawwaf's. In the walled patio the afternoon light was lovely and the air soft. We discovered he owned a pretty little cat who led an independent cat life but who occasionally deigned to come and sit in his lap. He had become reconciled, at least during our stay, to allowing Nashwah to come down from the roof so she could have some affection and companionship and exercise. In the morning when I would go upstairs to fetch her the poor little dog would whimper with happiness at having some attention paid to her.

That evening as far as we knew no party had been planned so Norton and I asked Nawwaf if for a change we couldn't take *him* to dinner at a restaurant or hotel in town. He said no, there was no place, literally no place to go. This information depressed me since having raided the icebox earlier in the afternoon hoping to find something to eat with a cup of tea, I was aware that we were kin to old mother Hubbard. If there were no public eating places prospects for dinner were dim. But how foolish I was! How could I have forgotten the Adhams, dispensers of manna?

Nawwaf, apparently not having given a thought to qualms which he would have known to be unjustified, suddenly volunteered the information that Fatima Adham and Fatima LeBlanc were coming over later in the evening and bringing dinner with them. That sounded cozy, a small quiet fivesome and early bed. That's how it sounded but we had forgotten where we were.

Dinner was for sixteen, guests did not start arriving until after ten, two tables of bridge were set up and we dined at twelve-fifteen. After dinner the tape recorder and dancing.

We had been under the impression we would be leaving Jidda on Thursday—two days later—but Mr. Wassif came hurrying in to say they had been able to get hold of an army air force plane to fly us to Mada'in Salih on that day and therefore we could not leave until Friday, just as Kamal Adham had said at our first morning meeting. The flight was an honor and could not have been easy to arrange but ungratefully perhaps we wished the honor had befallen us sooner during one of the empty days. It seemed strange that the possibility of such a fascinating trip had not been mentioned but in all probability they had not wanted to say anything until they could make sure of the plane. Arabs feeling as they do about time what was a day more or less anyway?

Mada'in Salih was a place we were eager to see. It is a desert valley north of Medina and has the same kind of cliff tombs as Petra but is wilder and more desolate. Norton and I began to perk up, things were moving. Two or three engagements for the morrow, the ancient valley the next day and the day after a new Arabian city, Riyadh.

The next morning we drove to the American embassy for a pleasant and informative half hour with Ambassador Eilts. At that time he had held the Arabian post for four years but was an experienced hand in the Middle and Far East. Although the day was hot he wore a dark pin-striped business suit and looked fittingly ambassadorial. We liked him at once. He was a tall man with dark hair, totally lacking in any affectation and while most amiable we got the impression that he puts up with no nonsense.

His liking and respect for King Faisal seemed genuine although he felt His Majesty took too many details on himself and would delegate no authority. "He's at his desk eighteen hours a day. Once I went in to say goodbye to him when I was off on a holiday, his face lighted up and he said, 'I used to be able to take Fridays off but not any more.' He imprisons himself in unnecessary detail."

Considering him in most respects a moderate man our impression was that the ambassador thought the King tended to emotionalism on the subject of Jerusalem. "You must realize that to him it is the Arab homeland. Americans don't understand this."

The majority does not. When I was a child—I blush for the misconception now but in childhood I entertained it—I thought the name was Jewrusalem. Why wouldn't it be, it was where the Jews lived. Even today many adult Americans forget that Arabs dwelt there thousands of years before modern Israel came into being.

Irked and dismayed by the behavior of the Saudi Arabian delegation to the United Nations, Ambassador Eilts had candidly informed King Faisal that his fiery deputy was the enemy's best ally. "He has only to open his mouth and sympathy *flows* to Israel." Others too feel that the Saudi Arabian government's instructions to its overseas representatives are not sufficiently specific.

On leaving the embassy we drove to the offices of Aramco. It should have taken us possibly seven minutes. Due to the disorientation of our Jiddian chauffeur the journey consumed one hour.

We had learned that Aramco had a local office the day before through Mr. Modine, although why we had not thought of it ourselves was an imbecility worthy of the chauffeur.

Staffing the office were Mr. Max Carter and his wife. "There you are!" they cried when they saw us. "Where on earth have you been?" It seemed that having received a letter from Wanda Jablonski about our arrival Mr. Robert Brougham in Dhahran had signaled Mr. Carter in Jidda. "Find out where those Browns are." Max had tried. First the hotels, such as they are. No Browns. Knowing that the life of the city flowed through channels directed in large part by Sheikh Kamal Adham he had got in touch with his office asking that we get in touch with him. This message we had not received.

"Do you suppose," we asked, "is there *any* way we can put a call through to Dhahran?" Mr. Carter looked at us as though we were crazy. "Why not?" He pressed a button. The Dhahran office of Aramco was on the wire and I was on the phone with Mr. Brougham.

There had been some discussion that in order to see more of the country we might drive to Riyadh. "I wouldn't," said Mr. Brougham, "unless you're nuts for sand. But in any event when do you plan to arrive in Riyadh?"

"Insha Allah we'll be flying in Friday morning."

"Good. Our man Mike Ameen will meet you and we'll send a company plane in the evening to fly you here. You'll make it in forty minutes. It will be good to see you."

I nearly fell on his neck over the telephone. Never in my life have I been so grateful for American know-how.

It is true that while we were in Jidda King Huessin of Jordan was visiting King Faisal seeking his country's support against the Israelis. Sometime later we read in the paper that Saudi Arabia had given him ten million dollars so the visit may be said to have been successful. Because of this meeting ministers of the Court had been very busy and it is hardly surprising that their undivided attention was not devoted to Dr. and Mrs. Brown, but it was interesting to contrast the Eastern and Western modes of life.

Had the circumstances been reversed, had an Eastern couple been invited by a ranking government figure to come to the United States and the host found himself tied up on business a capable wife would have taken over. I think that kind of marital cooperation does not exist in the Arab world although no one could have been more gracious and indeed efficient than Mrs. Adham when she took me to be received by her sister-in-law the Queen.

She arrived at Nawwaf's house about five-thirty in the afternoon clad in a long dress and with a sheer black veil over her head. Any time we passed another car or a pedestrian, as we were driving to the palace, she drew it across her face. What with lifting her long chestnut hair from over one eye in order to see me and covering and uncovering her face with the veil she was occupied and conversation was sporadic. I was interested in the little ceremony because this was a lady who had an apartment in Rome and a flat in London and who must go about those streets in European fashion. At home she conforms to the customs of her country. Old habit dies hard. It was like Boul de Breteuil, on other occasions not notably religious, crossing herself in Marrakech the night of the earthquake.

As we arrived at the palace, really an immensely large town house and were mounting the few broad steps into the lobby King Faisal passed us coming down. Mrs. Adham presented me, we shook hands and he went on out. I thought he looked grave and tired and as if he should be taking those Fridays off.

We were shown into a very long narrow drawing room with gold framed overstuffed chairs and sofas lining the walls. Fatima led me to a chair at right angles to a sofa at the far end of the room. "You sit here," she whispered, "Her Majesty will be here," and she indicated the sofa. It was thoughtful of her to place me so strategically.

There were two or three other women in the room and presently the Queen came in. She looked young to be the mother of nine grown children, five sons and four daughters. Her soft brown hair was drawn back into a knot and she wore a long black dress. She and Fatima Adham greeted one another with an affectionate kiss. I was introduced to her and to a lady-in-waiting who accompanied her and who acted as interpreter, although the Queen herself speaks more than acceptable English. Like her mistress the lady-in-waiting was Turkish with a rather prim little mouth, brightly hennaed hair and a great deal of eye make-up. She sat beside me in a chair placed in the angle formed by my overstuffed chair and the sofa.

The Queen was simple and cordial in manner and as we sat down more guests started drifting in until there were I should say twenty or twenty-four women in all. They were mostly, Fatima had told me, the wives of ambassadors: Spanish, Turkish, Italian, Pakistani, the last a fragile-looking elegant woman in an exquisite cocoa brown and gold sari who sat on the sofa on the other side of the Queen. Of the Europeans I thought the wife of the Turkish ambassador the best dressed in her simple little eight-hundred-dollar Yves Saint Laurent natural silk suit with a print lining.

Those of us who were near Her Majesty found the party interesting but the women at the far end of the room must have had a thin time for the Queen did not move about and they could only talk to their neighbors on either side.

As conversation became general I said to the Queen that we had had the pleasure of meeting her son Prince Mohamed the day before and I added, "What a beautiful man he is."

"Not beautiful," said his mother, "big."

She has a good many grandchildren and I observed—somewhat fatuously I fear—that she must be devoted to all of them.

"Not at all," she said briskly, "I don't know them all. How can I like the ones I don't know? They're born all over the world": and turning to the lady-in-waiting, "How many is it now?"

"Nine," said the lady-in-waiting.

"There you are," said the Queen, "and it's difficult to remember who belongs to whom."

Learning that Her Majesty travels a good deal I asked if she enjoys shopping. "Only for certain things. Shoes and lingerie, that's what I buy." She is wise. I doubt that anyone would be enthusiastic about the shoes and lingerie of Saudi Arabia. I suppose she must also pick up an occasional jewel as she was discreetly ablaze with emeralds of startling size and purity. Earrings, pendent, rings. She confided that she also likes pearls and turquoise but is cool to rubies.

I was wearing my own modest pride, the gold bib necklace we had bought in Tripoli and the Queen assessed it with a practiced eye. "What you're wearing is very pretty," she said.

"Thank you, ma'am but your jewels . . . superb!" It was true, why not say it? Besides, maybe she'd suggest a swap. People had said to us, "Be careful what you admire in Saudi Arabia. Their hospitality is such they're likely to turn around and give it to you. You don't want to hurt their feelings by refusing and it can be embarrassing."

At the risk of a fleeting moment of personal embarrassment I would have accepted the Queen's emeralds but they were not forthcoming. Her Majesty is Turkish after all. Possibly she had not heard of the old tradition.

When months later I related the incident to Wanda and Ken Miller who was home on a brief visit they cried as one, "But you made a fatal mistake! You should have offered *your* necklace to the Queen. She'd have been on a spot and maybe she'd have made the switch." I doubted it. Her Majesty looked to me a shrewd woman. I couldn't quite picture her reaching for the short end of the stick.

The conversation drifted to houses. The royal family had them sprinkled around Europe and five or six in Saudi Arabia alone and apparently they have the same trouble that Americans with a house in the country and an apartment in town experience in microcosm: What you want is always in the other place.

The Queen seemed regretful that we were in her country at that particular time. Because of the hadj and the throngs of pilgrims who were obviously unsheltered and with few resources she may have felt we would get an impression of inefficiency and poverty. But inefficiency and poverty exist all over the world including the glorious U.S.A. Pilgrimages to Mecca have been going on even before Mohammed growing in popularity with the rise of the Moslem era in A.D. 622. I see no reason to apologize for them.

As the party progressed two maids came in bearing tiny cups into which they poured bitter cardamom-flavored Arabian coffee from the long spouted brass pots used by Arabs of all classes no matter where they may be, in cities or in the desert. These were followed by glasses of the, for me, overly sweet hot tea and then in a few minutes more coffee. It made a little liquid sandwich. A large box of tinsel wrapped candy was passed and as I took one the lady-in-waiting said, "It's dates." I like dates so I unwrapped the gold foil greedily. Milk chocolate. Oh well, I like milk chocolate too.

About seven o'clock the reception broke up. As we were driving back to Nawwaf's house Fatima told me that the Queen takes a great interest in education for girls. She started the first girls' school in Saudi Arabia and had an uphill fight with tradition. At first the conservative lower classes were dead set against it. They considered the removal of daughters from their homes outrageous and also having them set to learning Allah knew what and subjected to strange and unaccustomed influences. Within three years they were bitter if there were no girls' schools in their neighborhood.

On arriving at Nawwaf's, Norton told me we had an audience with the King at nine o'clock that night. Nawwaf explained it would not be in the palace from which I had just come but in His Majesty's office, a building we had passed several times in driving around the city.

Shortly before nine he drove us over and after a short wait during which we chatted with the Minister of Protocol Sheikh Wahab, at whose house we had dined a couple of nights before, we were shown into the Presence. The room was large, not uncomfortable but lacking in any taste or personality. King Faisal himself is an imposing figure. He is not very tall but he has great dignity and his white Arabian headdress with it's heavy ogal or black silk cord forming a square with knots at the corners becomes his somewhat saturnine features. Neither his expression nor his eyes are humorous and he did not smile throughout the interview. Perhaps, his mood lightens when he is with people he knows.

The only people in the room were the King, the interpreter, Norton and I and a somewhat mysterious character draped at the far end of the long-cushioned banquette on which we sat. Possibly he was the hatchet man with a snickersnee concealed under his robe in case we developed regicidal tendencies but his manner was mild and he took part in the proceedings only once or twice when the interpreter turned to him for confirmation of a translated remark.

His Majesty has spent considerable time in the United States. He was his country's representative at the formation of the United Nations in San Francisco in 1945; he has been operated on in an American hospital and he visited Lyndon Johnson at the White House in 1966. His English is good and he certainly understands everything that is said but for reasons of protocol or perhaps to give himself time to consider his statements he prefers to communicate through an interpreter. At least he did when we were there. The interpreter that night appeared rather tense and repeated our remarks to the King with a disapproving air. We learned later that he was a replacement for the usual one so perhaps it was opening-night nerves.

The going at the beginning was a bit sticky. Hoping to get the ball rolling I said I had had the honor of being received by the Queen that afternoon and had been so interested to learn how much she concerned herself with the education of Arabian girls. This passed through the interpreter who then broke the news that His Majesty had said that it was the duty and privilege of the Queen to interest herself in the betterment of her people.

"Yes, indeed," I said, "but she seems genuinely to care." Silence. I glanced at my husband. I love that man but it cannot be said that he is tempermentally a chatterbox. He looked relaxed and obviously had no intention of sparking any light social intercourse. I bethought me of the desalinzation project. "Your Majesty's son, His Royal Highness Prince Mohamed, we had the great pleasure of meeting him and his wife yesterday afternoon . . . all he's doing to make fresh water available in this part of the country, what a splendid job he's undertaken."

"It is," replied His Majesty, "the duty and privilege of every member of the royal family to place himself at the service of his people." Silence.

A servant came in with the tiny cups of bitter coffee followed presently by a chap with the sweet tea followed in turn by the coffee bearer. The little procession kept up throughout the audience. Good Dr. Brown strolled to the rescue by remarking that it was unfortunate that Congress was or had been under the impression that the United States was pouring money into Saudi Arabia when really all the country was asking for was guidance in developing her oil resources. His Majesty said sharply, "The United States gets $500,000,000 worth of oil a year out of us." This I understand is true but since it is in Arabian territory the Arabs do much better than that so the arrangement would seem equitable and each year they receive more and we less. A stop clause doubtless exists in the contract but even if the American share diminishes to only a small percentage such is the supply it still means enormous wealth. Having polished off the oil industry our little party again relapsed into silence.

I was beginning to think to myself, this is going to be a stimulating interlude, when suddenly His Majesty swung. From the floor. He launched into the Israeli problem. We had, of course, been warned, "Don't bring up Israel," but I have found more than once in my life that the forbidden topic cannot be ignored and that it is brought into play very often by the very person who was not to be reminded of it.

Were the matter to be touched on at all Norton and I had anticipated bitterness, that was no more than human. We were unprepared for the almost fanatical attacks on world Jewry. Jews and Communism. In King Faisal's opinion they are inextricably intertwined. Jews, he said, started Communism in ancient days. "Read the Talmud. They were Communists in their small rural communities." We had not read the Talmud but Communism seemed far fetched. "Surely," we said, "that was not political. Was it not more a cooperative way of life? By pooling their resources of agriculture, herds and so on, were they not able to live better?"

"So they said," retorted the King, "but it was a ruse and from there they penetrated industry. And it is not true that Russians are ani-Semitic. That is a hoax to blind the world to the fact that they actually work closely together. There are many Jews in the high Soviet Council. And in America. They penetrate American life. The Rotary Clubs, the Lions, the Elks." I thought to myself, Knights of Columbus too, no doubt.

"Your Majesty," Norton said, "that is simply not a fact."

The King backtracked a little. "They may not have succeeded but they tried. When they failed to dominate those organizations they turned to other aspects of American life. They are all powerful in your government. Men like Henry Kissinger, so close to the President, so influential. And all your communications. Dominated by Jews! The press, television, radio."

We said it was true there were some Jews, remarkably able men in high positions in those fields, and there were hundreds who were not Jewish.

Back again to the Communists: "Engels, Marx, Lenin, Trotsky . . . all Jews!" In this his majesty was in error. Engels was not Jewish, Marx had one Christian parent.

King Faisal continued, "And why will America not accept the facts? Israel is attacking us, the Arabs, and did in the war of 1967. It was not Egypt who attacked Israel. Why not *see* that?"

"Well, Your Majesty, some of those statements of Mr. Nasser's were pretty bellicose. All that about pushing Israel into the sea . . ."

The subject switched. The Saudi position vis-à-vis Egypt is that of a precariously balanced tightrope walker. Egypt is an Arab nation, yet, on the other hand, Mr. Nasser's flirtation with Russia, his acceptance of arms and money do not sit well with the profoundly anti-Communist sovereign of Saudi Arabia who relented to the extent of saying that all Jews were not objectionable perhaps but that Zionists were. In more moderate fashion he observed he had nothing against the Semitic race. "We ourselves are Semites. It is the Israeli grab for territory—the tragedy of the refugees, the people forced from their homes—you have not seen them." Thinking of Lebanon we assured him we had.

He then returned to the United States asking in tones at once angry and pleading, "Why is everybody in your country pro-Israel? Why does nobody understand the Arab side?"

The Arabs do have a side. Having been in what is now part of Israel for a few thousand years they naturally think of it as their native land. But as far as the American attitude is concerned I think what we said is true. "Your Majesty must understand that in America very few people know any Arabs whereas all Americans know Jews. Our Jews *are* Americans. They're home folks." We do not know how home folks came through in Arabic, in-digenes perhaps but we hope he got the idea. Whether he did or not he spoke with renewed heat, "The Rosenbergs, Ethel and Julius Rosenberg, Jews!"

"Some people are still not convinced they were guilty—that sentiment actually is on the increase—but their action was de-plored by thousands of Jews as well as Christians and they were sent to their deaths by a Jewish judge." On and on and on.

The audience lasted for an hour at the end of which time Norton and I were spent. The King finally rose, we rose, thanked him, returned home to pick up Nawwaf and went on to the night's scheduled party, a barbecue at the LeBlancs and the biggest crowd yet. We gratefully gulped down the refreshment that was immediately handed to us.

We hadn't been there five minutes when who should come charging in but the interpreter. He was a changed man from the tight and prissy one of the audience, hearty, outgoing, relieved that the strain was over. Whether or not he availed himself of the hospitality offered to American guests I do not know. If he did Allah surely winked.

The barbecue party was a swinger, a jiving Texas cookout but instead of the suburban host in a chef's hat and white apron printed with I GOT MY JOB THROUGH THE NEW YORK TIMES we were ministered to, I was pleased to note, by professionals.

The merry-eyed Minister of Protocol whom we had seen briefly in the King's office was there as were the Adhams, Fatima in a long pink dress sparkling with passementerie and Kamal in an elegant black taub with a little standing collar looking like a gray-haired blue-eyed Chinese mandarin. The black taub was his own idea, a fashion he was initiating for evening wear. "It is our answer to your dinner jacket," he said. He looked very handsome and I thought quite grand for a barbecue but the grandeur was counterbalanced by several nearly invisible mini skirts.

I forget at what time dinner was served but I remember it took the prize for being the latest yet. It must have been around midnight or after and we fell upon it ravenously, especially the chicken unusually succulent and flavorful for having been cooked on an outdoor grill.

It is funny how the hour one dines seems a barometer of sophistication. In the United States seven-thirty to eight-thirty seems reasonably sophisticated. Asia, Africa, and Europe clock in anywhere from nine to eleven but in Jidda . . . ah, Jidda, even Spain must bow, it's from eleven on. More sophisticated than that I do not care to get.

As at the other parties, after dinner there were at the Le-Blancs' tape recordings, loudspeakers, and dancing. Norton and I as usual left the festivities at what they must have considered the weakling's hour and it wasn't until we were dressing early the next morning that I was smitten belatedly, in true classic fashion, with an attack of staircase wit: that scintillating bit of repartee that occurs to one long after the opportunity has passed by. "God what a fool!" I cried. "Why didn't I say it?"

"Say what?" My husband who was shaving at the moment suspended operations and looked at me in the mirror.

"Well what else? When the King said that about Julius and Ethel Rosenberg being Jews why didn't I say, yes and how about Bobby Kennedy? Sirhan Sirhan was an Arab." I must have looked pretty pleased with myself because Norton grinned but after a moment he said, "I wouldn't regret it too much, it may be just as well you didn't. There were only two of us remember and he had a palace full of guards."

Our flight to Mada'in Salih had been scheduled for early morning to give us time for several hours of sightseeing. Glancing out the window my heart sank. The empty days had all been warm, bright, and sunny. Now for the first time ominous thunder heads were building up in a dusty sky.

Nawwaf drove us to the airport where after some difficulty we spotted our plane fairly far removed from the terminal. Our pilot was a young Texan and there was another American about too, a sort of superintendent. On seeing how small the plane was, and a glance took in the lack of facilities, I said prudently I thought I should attend to a few needs before taking off. Mr. Shaw, the other American, said, "Hop in my jeep I'll drive you over." We headed toward the terminal building where a great crowd of Arabs were milling around still waiting for planes to take them home. As we veered away from the terminal I said, "It's all right, I'll go in there."

"Oh no you won't," said Mr. Shaw, "you have no conception of the filth around there."

He drove me to a nearby hotel positively sparkling with hygiene and aromatic with disinfectant sprayed by a gnome who plowed ahead like a small bulldozer, totally indifferent to sex and signs on toilet doors. Nawwaf had said there was no place to go for dinner but I wondered if the hotel restaurant might not have been worth a try.

On the way back Mr. Shaw said most of the horde had pretty well gone although there were still many hundreds sleeping on bits of carpet on the ground and getting their breakfasts from the food booths that had been set up in the streets radiating from the terminal.

We were joined by a young Arab who spoke excellent English. He was also eager to see Mada'in Salih. We took off at seven forty-five on what was to be a two-and-a-half to three-hour flight five hundred miles to the north. As we were flying through heavy clouds at high altitude the plane grew very cold and I began to hope the ancient landmark would be worth the discomfort. There was little to divert attention for even the desert below us was obscured by haze and overcast.

We struggled for about an hour and then the pilot announced it was no use. When it proved impossible to spot Medina, where we were scheduled to refuel, he headed back to the coast and following the shore line returned to Jidda and the joys of a long empty day.

I had, however, the satisfaction of knowing it would not be my death day. When we were children we used to say that the day you didn't learn something was the day you died. What I had learned was that the Prophet Mohammed fled to Medina, the flight became known as the hegira, to escape the wrath of the Meccan leaders. They cared nothing at all for the theory he constantly preached, that there was only one God and that the worship of idols was wrong.

On the way to Medina he and a faithful disciple Abu Bakr hid in a cave. Legend has it that Abu Bakr knowing they were being pursued trembled with fear saying, "We are but two." Mohammed comforted him. "No, we are three, for God is with us." Working in mysterious ways his wonders to perform God had a spider weave its web across the mouth of the cave. When the irate Meccans arrived they peered in but seeing the web and a pigeon quietly sitting on its nest concluded the cave had been unoccupied a long time and continued on their way.

Spiders have played quite a part in the history of the exalted. There was that spider who inspired Robert Bruce, remember? When the Scottish King was fleeing from the English he hid in a dilapidated hut and lying on a dilapidated cot watched a spider swinging on one frail thread trying to attach its web from one beam to another. Six times it tried and failed. Just like me, thought Robert who had fought six losing battles against the English. If that spider tries again and succeeds . . . well what he can do I can do. The spider tried once more and won. The King went forth and did the same.

We had been invited to tea at the Ted Modines should we get back from Mada'in Salih in time. Since we had ample time, all day in fact, we wanted to get them on the phone to say we could come.

Returning to the house from the airport we found Nawwaf had left for his office but our new-found Arab friend struggled with the phone. Having no better luck than the master he said, "Come along down the road, we'll try the Callahans."

Virtually our next door neighbors, we had not met Mr. and Mrs. Callahan. They were attached to the American Embassy, but the Arab knew them and although they were out he also knew their servant who had no objection to our using the phone. The lovely thing worked and it was arranged we would go the Modines in the afternoon.

We looked forward to it with special eagerness because no lunch had been ordered since we expected we would be in Mada'in Salih. The pickings were slim in the icebox. We speculated on what Bourrie ate much of the time since Nawwaf, fed by the Adhams, like Elijah by the ravens, rarely stocked up apparently. Happily at the Modines there were sandwiches and cakes and splendid things like that.

There was also a couple from the British embassy Mr. and Mrs. Monty Banks. He was the commercial attaché and a philosophical observer of the Arabian scene.

"These people may seem backward to you," he said, "but you must realize that in the last fifty years, actually less than that, say from the early thirties when the oil business really got under way, they have made greater advances than in the previous two thousand years."

But it takes time. Some of the oil people told us that when working around oil rigs, for their own safety, they tried to persuade the Arabs to exchange their taubs and kofiehs for pants and hard hats but were reviled as infidel dogs wishing to impose foreign ways on holy Islam. Patience, patience. And a few accidents.

We spoke of the prohibition of alcohol and of the theoretical asceticism of life in general. "Because of Mecca and Medina Saudi Arabia considers itself the holy place of all Islam," Mr. Banks said. "That's why Ramadan is strictly observed, why there are no cabarets, no theatres, no smoking. And," he added, "it's understandable. Rome itself may be a swinging or a go-go or whatever you like city but no one is surprised that there are no night clubs in the Vatican."

"Agreed," said Norton, "but the Vatican is a comparatively small area. Saudi Arabia is a country." Mr. Banks shrugged. "That's how it is."

On the way home Ted Modine stopped at the Arabian equivalent of a White Tower and insisted on buying us two shishkebab sandwiches on hero rolls. I took a bite of one and seared my gullet but they were to stay us, he said, in the event that the routine of lunch was repeated at dinnertime.

Nawwaf was upset to learn of our fast. "Why didn't you wake me up?" he said. "I would have phoned and had lunch sent over." We had not known it but he had come back from the office and was in his room asleep. We assured him it was unimportant and he assured us dinner was on the way.

We sat in the garden waiting for it. The air was balmy, the poodle and the cat played together, we discussed Nawwaf's health and his future . . . a cozy domestic scene.

I had tried introducing Nashwah to the joys of her three-dollar ball but the whole concept of toys and play was so foreign to her I was meeting with only modest success. She would chase it for a minute or two and then her attention span collapsed. I once owned a poodle who would retrieve a ball and expect it to be thrown again for twenty-four hours at a stretch if his partner had the stamina.

We had learned that the Arab word for friend is sadic. That evening, for the next morning we would be away very early, I bade farewell to Nashwah my little sadic and urged Nawwaf to make sure her water bowl was always filled. I can only hope, with no great conviction, that our proselytizing did some good. After we had left Saudi Arabia I wrote twice asking if he and his wife would consider selling us the dog and shipping her to the United States but never received an answer.

The next morning at the airport we met a group of visiting English journalists and introduced Nawwaf. "Mr. Yassin has been our host for five days," I said, "I'm afraid to him it must have seemed like five months." Our host did not gainsay me. Poor fellow, if he found us a burden it was not unnatural but for our part despite some fallow hours we were grateful to him and all the others for they had enabled us to participate in a way of life we could never have learned about on our own as casual tourists in a hotel.

We urged him to leave us and go on about his business. "Have fun at the party tonight Nawwaf, no matter where it is." We felt he would not be lonely for he had assured us a night in Jidda without a party was unthinkable.

We made our way through the jammed airport between crowds of the holy still waiting to return to their homes from the hadj. They were propped up against their bedding rolls, clutching plastic water bottles, their white robes crumpled and dirty. They looked exhausted and we hoped that spiritual satisfaction compensated for acute physical discomfort.

A Pakistani woman with a dark pock-marked face and prominent intelligent liquid eyes sat down on the bench beside me and said briskly, "Good morning, Madam. Are you enjoying yourself?" I say I am. "I think," she continued, "we are on the same plane." I think not as she is going to Karachi and we to Riyadh, nevertheless we engaged in conversation. She lives in Africa but enjoys seeing the world. She had just been to Mecca and is planning on Kashmir in the new future.

I was right about different planes and on ours we were served the by now familiar little cups of pungent coffee and almond stuffed dates. Very good. During the flight we discussed how to handle what might prove a ticklish problem of protocol.

During our sojourn in Jidda no mention had been made of any plans for our stopover in either Riyadh or Dhahran and having been entertained for five days we felt our Arab hosts had amply discharged any duty they might have contracted toward us. However, as we were taking leave of Nawwaf he mentioned that the Minister of Petroleum was meeting us in Riyadh. Knowing from the phone conversation with Mr. Brougham that Mike Ameen the Aramco representative in the capital was meeting us I was rather shaken by Nawwaf's information. "It probably isn't the Minister himself," I said hopefully, "maybe just a minion."

The plane landed, taxied to a stop, the door opened and we emerged to see at the bottom of the steps a crescent of bowing Arabs, dramatic and handsome in their long cloaks and head-dresses. We also saw an unmistakable American whom we took to be Mr. Ameen. "Uh oh," I muttered to Norton under my breath, "here's a pretty kettle of fish."

As we set foot on the runway Mike Ameen whisked us aside. "You are in *my* care," he said firmly.

"But what about them?"

"Don't worry, I'll fix it."

It was a relief to find that the entire welcoming committee was not for us. Fortunately our wish had been granted for the Minister of Petroleum was not present, and although some of the Arabs were there to meet us others were greeting the British journalists.

The whole party moved into the terminal which was very pleasant, infinitely superior to the shambles in Jidda. When we observed how nice it was, they said proudly that an even better one was about to be built.

Our group of Arabs had been instructed by Jidda that we were their booty but any small social crisis was tactfully dissolved by Mike Ameen. Like Solomon's babe we would be equally divided, spending the morning with the Ameens, the afternoon with the Arabs and, the topper, we would all lunch and dine together.

We drove en masse to an attractive cottage that had been reserved for us in the grounds of the Hotel Sahari where we dropped our bags and after coffee and a small breather went on to the Ameens' house. They had a lovely garden fragrant with frangipani and shaded by tall trees that they themselves had planted. They also had two enormous cages, the homes of ringed green parrots. The birds are not very large but their coloring is brilliant. In the winter they migrate from Karachi to southern Arabia and the Ameens had trapped them when they settled for food and rest. Despite the spacious cages and the fact that they were obviously well cared for it was sad to see such strong fliers penned.

Mrs. Ameen is a slender redhead and her husband is proud of the impressive bargains she has picked up in the souks of Arabia. "See that," he said, pointing to a large mirror on the dining-room wall, "best Venetian glass money can buy. Hand-carved Italian frame all gilded. She got it for twenty dollars." It was a lot for the money. My own favorite piece was a handsome nail-studded brass-locked cedar chest. They are not rare in Saudi Arabia but this one was outstanding.

The Ameens introduced a friend of theirs, Ralph Sherman, and the five of us went off to see the souks of Riyadh. In one shadowy little hole a blind woman kept her wares in a small chest and fished about and hauled them out knowing every bracelet and ring and trinket by touch. In another I bought a long spouted brass coffee pot for which by this time we had developed quite an affection. Pat Ameen here demonstrated her bargaining abilities. We had already paid thirteen riyals, a little over $3.25 for a small one when a few yards down the street she picked up a large one for us for only ten. My husband tossed me a husbandly glance. "Why can't you be like that?"

However, Mrs. Ameen herself acknowledged she had small influence in the spice souks. "The powdered cardamom seed they

mix with the coffee is terribly expensive. Seven-fifty a pound."
We weren't all that keen on it.

As it was Friday the souks closed early so we strolled about
absorbing local color and admiring the local vehicles, one especially, a cream-colored Ford truck with a light iron grill work
superstructure also painted cream and bedecked with brass medallions. I imagine that when it is very hot an awning must be
stretched across it creating a festive and amusing means of transportation.

Unhappily the local color included many dogs running unfed
and unwanted through the streets and Mike Ameen told us of a
child who had been bitten by one. In a city of 200,000 there
was not a drop of anti-rabies vaccine. "It cost my department
about six hundred dollars to fly some in," he said. "There was a
good deal of beefing about it but what was I supposed to do? Let
the kid die?"

We passed a mosque with hundreds of cars parked outside and
an overflow crowd listening to a sermon over a loudspeaker.
"Very popular preacher," said Mike. The other side of the coin
was the not infrequent beheading of criminals in the public square
and I wondered if one was taking place when we were there
whether I would have stopped to watch it or fled. I was glad I
did not have to make the decision.

Two of our Arab friends from the airport joined us at luncheon
in the Sahari Hotel and said they were sorry we had not arrived
from Jidda a day or so sooner. They had been making plans to
have us spend a night in the desert. Our regret at missing the
experience was greater than theirs.

The hotel luncheon was very good especially the mezzes. As
they were being removed the waiter said, "We have steak then
turkey and rice." Assuming he meant steak or turkey and rice I
said I would have turkey. Steak arrived anyway and then turkey
and rice. In Riyadh they say what they mean and they mean a
lot of food.

In the afternoon we took a siesta in our cottage and at half-past four a distinguished wolf, Mohamed Raschid, with dazzling white teeth and sparkling intelligent dark eyes, positively brimming with vitality, came to fetch us and drive us to Al Dir'iyah, an oasis in Wadi Hanifah about eleven kilometers northwest of Riyadh. A wadi is a valley or river bed and sometimes water roars or trickles through it but most of the time it is dry.

The ruins of the city lie on an elevation above a deep green palm oasis. The buildings are of clay but the crumbling walls have lightness and elegance thanks to rows of triangular holes cut into them to admit light and air that form an open pattern not unlike hemstitching. Al Dir'iyah was founded in about 1446 and after the customary vicissitudes destroyed for the last time in 1818.

Today it is deserted but the walls bathed in the light of the late afternoon sun were powdery gold against a clear blue sky and we wandered for some time through the empty silent streets and the open roofless houses.

Our wolf—I call him that because his sharp white teeth flashed in the fashion of those friendly animals every time he spoke—stood at the edge of the cliff a dramatic figure in his long robes and mused on a vanished world. "Do you not wonder . . . I wonder, I imagine how they slept and what they dreamed about and how life was for them." I imagine and wonder too.

We were accompanied on our journey through time by two small boys who acted as porters for Norton's camera cases and my handbag. He gave them each a riyal and an American dime as a souvenir. He tried to explain to them what they were, even mentioning President Roosevelt, and the kids doubtless thought him an old American nut but they looked pleased with their mysterious wealth.

We returned to the Ameens' for dinner and at eight o'clock we were at the airport to board the Aramco Saberjet, promised over the phone by Mr. Brougham, for the thirty-five minute flight to Dhahran. Although I have flown on countless planes any small boy can tell you more about them than I can but I can tell you that the eight-seated Saberjet is a love and were I rich that is the one I would like to own.

During the flight I said to Norton, "This time I don't imagine there'll be any Arabs to meet us. This bit is the American segment."

What we failed to appreciate was that as long as we were in their country the Arabs considered us their guests. It was perhaps remiss on our part not to realize this but in our defense it must be said that we considered they had done enough for us in Jidda and also no one ever breathed a word to us as to what plans if any had been made.

When we stepped from the plane there was an American to meet us, Mr. Schneider from the College of Petroleum and Minerals, but there was also an Arab with an authoritative Arab name, Mr. Nasser. Apparently both Jidda and Riyadh had been on the hot line.

They drove us to the college where accommodations had been prepared for us but at this point Dr. Brown took over. "Just a minute," he said as they were about to take our luggage from the car, "Mr. Brougham is expecting us and we have to get in touch with him."

Mr. Nasser was put out. His boss, the Minister of Petroleum, had told him to take care of us and he felt he had better do it or else. We told him politely and I hope comfortingly that we were ignorant of any arrangements and explained that at this point we were the guests of Mr. Brougham. To be considered such desirable plums by one and all sounds flattering but it is distinctly uncomfortable for the plums.

Mr. Nasser gave ground to the extent of telephoning to Mr. Brougham. "Where on earth are you?" he demanded. "We've just been to the airport to meet you but you were whisked away." Within minutes he and his wife Hazel were at the college, gracefully explained the situation to the Messrs. Schneider and Nasser, and took us off to Hamilton House, a large attractive guest cottage owned by the company where we had tea and cookies and discussed the next day's plans which included a trip to the greatly anticipated Hofuf Oasis.

The morning plane, a De Havilland Beaver, was even grander than the Saberjet, but for me it did not have the sex appeal of its predecessor.

We were accompanied by an attractive man from Aramco, one Mr. Stormy Weather. Those poor Weather and Roads people, Stormy and Dusty from birth till death. Our day was sunny but we flew over desert dunes and drifts and a bay of the Persian Gulf veiled by haze.

At Hofuf we are met by a couple of young Arabs involved in agricultural projects and by his Honor the Mayor. The small airport building was a pretty pillared pavilion but with hunks and bits of concrete and rubble littering the ground. It looked rather the way places do that have been submitted to machine-gun fire. "Heavens," I said, "what's happened here?" Stormy sighed. "Nothing. Not a thing. They just let it decay." Quite often one sees these examples of instant deterioration.

Our first goal was the souks which were colorful and fun and having seen so many in use my loved one had been inoculated with a passion for worry beads and bought several strings. Slipped through the fingers like a rosary they are as efficacious as prayer. At home I have never seen them used but they are better than smoking and many people must find solace in the habit for it prevails in Greece and North Africa and all through Asia.

One of the entertaining features of Hofuf is the donkeys; cream-colored donkeys with their heads and forequarters dyed a rich shade of henna. I thought perhaps it had something to do with filtering the burning rays of the sun but as any child can tell you it wards off the evil eye. I should think the women would prefer to settle for something of the kind rather than the black veils in which they are completely swathed and which must be suffocatingly hot.

Starting our tour we discovered that the oasis is enormous, really several continuous ones embracing some fifty-eight villages. When we were there they were digging a long water course for an irrigation project which will be completed in 1970. I expect they will replant and the palms will grow again, but at that time the working areas along the canal were so wide that it was nothing at all like my preconceived idea of an oasis and I was sadly let down. Norton guessed as much. "It's not what you were expecting, is it?"

"No. I thought there would be thick palms and here and there a well or a pool and little white sugar loaf houses and camel caravans." Instead the concrete walled canal and the big dusty town.

The Arabs however were optimistic and full of enthusiasm. Chinese were arriving to show them how to plant rice paddies under the palms and Germans were constructing the irrigation system. We were shown an experimental farm which seemed bleak compared to the lush farms of home, the soil gray and greasy and the plants spindly but they were getting water, life itself, and eventually their onions and okra, sunflowers and lettuce will be sturdy and prolific.

They showed us through a date processing plant, not of riveting interest as it was closed down but there were a few small orphaned packages of dates lying around and I asked if I might take one. My taste seemed to surprise them but they affably handed them over.

The town boasted a sulphur bath and several old men were immersed in the salubrious waters which I hoped did them a world of good because it was not one of the more compelling scenic attractions of the neighborhood.

For luncheon we were taken to the large house of an Arab construction man whom Aramco had helped establish in business. The owner was not in residence but he lent the establishment for occasions such as this. There was a huge indoor swimming pool and a series of salons opening one into the other, with high hung pictures, bright red rugs, plastic venetian blinds, and chairs and sofas upholstered in plush and foam rubber ranged along the walls. In all the Arab houses we saw the arrangement of furniture was that of a dancing school.

While waiting for luncheon Pepsi-Cola was passed. I tasted it for the first time in my life and couldn't believe my palate. Stormy Weather said, "It's not usually like that. They make it extra sweet for this part of the world to cater to the Arab taste."

When we went into the dining room, it was big, all the rooms were very large and I noticed several boxes of open Kleenex on the table and sideboard. I wondered about them but shortly understood the reason. There were great hunks of roast lamb on beds of rice and side dishes of peas, carrots and lettuce. Mayor Mohamed skillfully rolled everything into balls and stuffed the food into his mouth with his fingers so the Kleenex came in handy.

When we returned to Dhahran in the afternoon we were met by Jim Knight, Aramco's press representative who took us to the company theatre and ran the *Empty Quarter,* the Wilfred Thesiger picture which I had seen in New York but Norton had not. Its spell had not lessened nor had the dignity and simplicity of the Arab who, when Thesiger asked how he had survived traveling for weeks across the boundless sands with only his camel and no companions, replied, "God was my companion."

We also saw a film of Mada'in Salih and regretted again we had been unable to complete the trip from Jidda. To give an idea of what it is like I take the liberty of quoting a description by Mr. Parker T. Hart formerly the United States Ambassador to Saudi Arabia. Seeing it from the air in, I think, about 1963 he observed that "For forty miles the valley stretched north-south like a sea of yellow sand from which rose innumerable great islands of tawny pink sandstone, often sheer walled and several hundred feet in height, sculptured by wind and sand into columns, pinnacles, spires, saw teeth, natural bridges, profiles and every oddment of erosion conceivable to man's imagination. At the base of many the tomb entrances were clearly visible. The width of the great valley varies from perhaps ten to twenty-five miles, larger than the Grand Canyon and far more impressive than Bryce Canyon or Cedar Breaks." That is not a spectacle one is happy to have missed. Charles Doughty in his classic *Travels in Arabia Desert* also writes of Mada'in Salih.

That evening we dined with the Broughams, some of their family and friends. Their house was spacious with a delightful upstairs terrace overlooking the big garden. A new wall finished that day was deservedly the center of attraction. It was of white perforated tile in a graceful design insuring at once light, air, and privacy and it occurred to me that it would work equally well in a "development" permitting the all too near neighbors to withdraw into small worlds of their own.

We also met the Broughams' white poodle, a magnificent chap Monsieur Charlie de Gaulle with one of the most elegant topiary jobs I have ever seen. This triumph was a cooperative effort on the part of Bob, Hazel, and their cook. I thought sorrowfully of shaggy dirty little Nashwah.

The Broughams were enjoying their life in Dhahran and Hazel said the beaches of the Persian Gulf are superb and are likely to remain so because unless Islam changes its ways and sanctions liquor no one will venture to develop them as resorts. For those able to obtain a little private sauce the arrangement would seem ideal.

The Aramco compound itself is a meticulously maintained oasis of green lawns, trees and small neat houses. They have now had several years to settle in but in 1939 when they were comparatively new in those parts the King, Abd al-'Azia ibn 'abd ar-Rahman Al Faisal Al Saud, fortunately shortened to Ibn Saud, came to visit them.

He came accompanied by relatives, friends, and functionaries two thousand strong. The party was escorted by four hundred soldiers and traveled in four hundred cars some from as far away as Jidda and Mecca. Three hundred and fifty tents were pitched to accommodate the guests and the festivities lasted several days.

Since the inauguration things have come along nicely. In 1967 King Faisal the son of Abd al-'Aziz received over $909,000,000 in oil royalties to spend on his four million subjects.

As their annual income per capita is a little over $280, one hopes the government is doing something terribly intelligent with the difference. Maybe building nuclear weapons and developing germ warfare just like us.*

True to their promise to show us that part of the country Jim Knight and the others had arranged a flight to Rub-Al-Kahli, the Empty Quarter. That was one trip Norton didn't go on as he wanted to visit the company hospital with Dr. William Taylor. We were seven or eight in the group and we gathered at the airport early in the morning.

The terminal building of Dhahran is quite possibly the most beautiful in the world. Compared to the leviathans of capital cities it is small but it is exquisite. Designed by the renowned Japanese architect Mr. Minoru Yamasaki and built by the Ralph Parsons Company of Los Angeles, its lofty arches and disciplined open space not only delight the eye but efficiently serve the travelers needs. In 1963 it received the American Institute of Architects First Honor Award.

The reasons for building it are complicated and too involved to go into here but having paid $5,000,000 for it the United States government presented the pretty jewel to Saudi Arabia. Showing us around, Stormy Weather said wistfully, "Wouldn't you think they'd at least put up a plaque saying so?"

Two plaques actually existed, one engraved in Arabic one is English and the understanding was they were to be installed on either side of the main doors but they got lost in the shuffle. Who likes constantly to be reminded of benefactions?

* Since the above was written the President has decreed that the United States shall never resort to germ warfare. This must certainly be regarded as a step toward sanity but scientists and chemists are dedicated men reluctant to desert their test tubes. Let us hope that no one is stashing a can of germs in his bottom drawer just in case.

We rose from the beautiful concoction into a hazy sky so that visibility was poor but we could see enough to realize we were flying over ranges of sand mountains, dunes that rise five hundred to eight hundred feet from the desert floor, huge static waves blown up by the wind. The Empty Quarter covers 250,000 square miles. It is nearly the size of Texas and the largest continuous body of sand in the world. The Sahara is of course far larger but not continuous sand in the sense of Rub-Al-Kahli.

After about an hour and a half we landed at a place called Ramlah. Trying to pinpoint a particular spot in that vast area is like trying to locate a certain wave in the Pacific Ocean but our lads did it and sure enough, there was something recognizable as a landing strip to the experienced.

We met a few of the drilling crew stationed there who had come out in three red trucks to pick up equipment brought by a plane that followed us in and I recognized the co-pilot, young Jack Gillian who had flown us to Hofuf the day before. He was new with the company and I hope grows old in their service for he is an excellent pilot and a cheery companion.

We got out of the plane but didn't wander far because the shade of its big wings was welcome in what I took to be easily 100° heat.

As far as the eye can see salt flats and rust-colored dunes stretch to the horizon. Usually the dunes have sloping sides but sometimes they cut sharply down and the steep surface is known as slipface. When dislodged by heavy trucks the noise of trillions of particles of slipping sand roars like thunder and is referred to by the poetic Mr. Wilfred Thesiger as the "singing sands." Basso profundo.

Between the dunes flat valleys shimmer under the pitiless sun like rivers and ponds and lakes, and indeed beneath them is a table of excessively salty water. No good comes of that but in the northern part of the area the water is potable enough for camels and the Bedouins converge there with their herds.

Despite the intense heat and unutterable aridity the oil men work in Rub-Al-Kahli for six weeks at a time and then get two weeks off. Aramco labor sleeps in air-conditioned trailers, contract labor in tents. You have to love oil.

Helicopters and sometimes planes are used to transport personnel and equipment but monthly truck convoys carry the bulk of the freight, on occasion supplemented by sand buggies with oversize low-pressure tires more than five and a half feet high that supply traction in sand.

We flew back to Dhahran through thick red haze, a sandstorm for fair, the dreaded ghibli. Norton and I had experienced a worse one in Alice Springs in Australia and I had no wish to repeat the onslaught of sand that invades teeth, eyes, nose, and hair. Fortunately Dhahran itself was relatively unscathed.

When we exchanged stories of our morning's adventures Norton was enthusiastic about the hospital Aramco had established and which is open to the public as well as company personnel. "It's first rate," he said, "and I saw some fascinating cases, stuff I never meet up with in New York." We all take our pleasures differently.

The afternoon's pleasure was a trip with Hazel Brougham to Al Kohbar five or six miles down the road from Dhahran. In the mid-'30s it was a tiny fishermen's village of palm frond huts but was selected as the port for unloading supplies necessary to the establishment of an oil camp and the maintenance of the crews. Every bolt and can of beans traveled 11,000 nautical miles from the United States to the little harbor on the Persian Gulf.

Today it is, in essence, still a wide place in the road, yet it has become a kind of minute Paris in eastern Arabia. That probably does not hold for the food, although pointing to a small shop on the corner Hazel said you could buy there virtually any delicacy you might name provided you didn't mind what you paid for it. The merchandise in general is of unusual quality. There is an excellent tailor and a pharmacy which according to Dr. Brown carried more exotic drugs obtainable without a prescription than does the pharmacy he deals with in New York.

A comparatively large store sold exotic and colorful ornaments, furniture, and jewelry imported from India, and Eve, a little gold souk run by Mr. Ali, won our hearts and several dollars.

The sidewalks are paved but not yet the roads. Why should they bother? They are making money hand over fist right there in mother earth.

Returning home we passed a golf course where the greens are of brown sand mixed with oil and the fairways are sand unmixed. Hazel told us that the scores are about what they are on conventional courses, many people playing in the seventies.

That night we dined with James and Ann Knight, enjoying good food and pleasant company. A couple from Dubrovnik seemed to us especially attractive, possibly because we had fallen in love with the tiny fairy tale city when we were there in 1965. There was also a Mr. Perrine from West Virginia married to a Korean woman from San Francisco. She was a delight; small, tough, cute, and very smart.

When we were there the big focus of interest in Dhahran was the College of Petroleum and Minerals then under construction and which we wanted very much to see.

The builders are Caudhill, Rowlett & Scott of Houston, Texas, a firm famed for its campuses and the contractors are Japanese. It is going to be a handsome structure of sand-blasted cement which forms a rough grayish white surface requiring no maintenance. It would probably be too rugged for domestic architecture but as any homeowner can attest "no maintenance" is a lovely phrase. For students cramming for exams there is an Olympic swimming pool surrounded by a baby oasis of palms where they can relax.

In dedicating the college in 1965 King Faisal observed that "this institute was a dream to us a few years ago for we used to look around and find ourselves frozen in our position and bewildered, neither able to emulate nor to compete with other nations in their progress and their movement forward. God Almighty, however, has eased the path and erased the obstacles which blocked our way."

God Almighty would, I imagine, be the first to acknowledge that he got a leg up from the Minister of Petroleum and Mineral Resources of the Kingdom of Saudi Arabia, the Dean Emeritus of the Graduate School of MIT, the director in charge of Foreign Relations of l'Institute Francaise du Petrole, and the president of the American University of Beirut. There is also a tough-minded American, Dr. Robert King Hall, who is now whispering sound advice in God Almighty's ear.

He whispers things like: "Let us accept no excuse for backwardness. Our students must be able to compete with Americans, Russians and Europeans. A limping man is a detriment to his country."

As Nawwaf had found in a different field the obstacles young Arabs face are not easily surmountable and it takes guts and concentration to make good. The secondary schools do not educate students up to the university level so they have now established a transition period of one year, a sort of interval of orientation. "Furthermore," one of the professors said, "you've got to realize these boys don't have what is considered a normal background and childhood for an American kid. They don't have Mechano sets, tricycles, bicycles, and cars. It's a totally different culture. They have to start from scratch."

The college had three hundred students when we were there and they were anticipating five hundred in the next couple of years.

Classes are in English, standards are high and they are justly proud of the fact that their course of studies and program of experiments have been evaluated by ninety-seven accredited American and Canadian schools of engineering, ninety-six of which have indicated that if they accept an individual Saudi Arabian student his credits will be transferred.

When we asked one of the professors how he enjoyed Dhahran he laughed. "They can't pay you to spend your life on a sand dune, there's not enough money. You have to have something of the missionary spirit."

Petroleum and Minerals are not my forte but one gets involved, there is a tug of curiosity. Effort, struggle, determination have a magnetism of their own and I should not be averse to going back in four or five years to see how they are getting on.

Poor Mr. Nasser who had been frustrated the night of our arrival when we were whisked off to Hamilton House was again distressed when we could not stay for lunch. We wanted to but we were leaving Dhahran and were pressed for time.

That afternoon while waiting in Mr. Yamasaki's beautiful airport for the plane which would take us to Shiraz in Iran, I noticed that in that most contemporary of buildings black-veiled Arab women preferred to sit on the floor rather than on the benches. Part of the fascination of Arabia is that in biblical robes she is still crossing the wide threshold between yesterday and today.

IRAN

The flight from Dhahran to Shiraz is short, thirty-five minutes, crossing the Persian Gulf and arid shores that soon mount into green mottled hills. Travelers entering the country usually arrive at Tehran but we went in through the back door. Tehran is the large main portal of an austere house. Shiraz is the flowery kitchen doorway where geraniums grow and fragrant herbs crowd the steps. Except that in Shiraz they are roses. We were there too early in the season for them to be in full bloom but for eleven kilometers the median of the road from the airport to the center of town is a long bed of rose bushes.

Mr. Mashallah Behbahani of Near East Tours met us at the airport and he was my idea of a true Persian. Rather portly, dark hair, very full red lower lip, aquiline nose, dark liquid eyes.

From him we learned that due to our change of plans—our Arabian sojourn had somewhat discombobulated the schedule— we could not get into the Hotel Park Saadi. We learned this was just as well and that we would go instead to the Shiraz Inn, a government housing project that had been turned into a motel.

Our room was small and clean with no closet, a lack revealed when we opened a door of what we assumed to be one only to discover that there was nothing behind it but the wall. The bathroom wasn't any too efficient either; no hooks, no shelves, no medicine chest. The government must have thought its tenants were spirits although it did provide soft hot water in abundance.

I believe the lacks are being remedied and they are adding a large new wing. They already have a big swimming pool and when the planting has had a chance to grow—trees and masses of rose bushes—the place should be attractive. Even now it has certain virtues, a couple of old-fashioned horse-drawn barouches which make the tour of the grounds, spilling over with children bubbling with delight at the unaccustomed means of transportation.

Our first afternoon we went to the Park Saadi for tea and hopefully mail. Ever since writing to the Gyalmo of Sikkim in Marrakech I had been keeping an eye out for a reply to one of the addresses I had given her. So far no success, but Norton said, "Don't be silly. She's probably written to Tehran or certainly New Delhi. That's the logical place."

At the Park Saadi the mail system is informal. Letters awaiting claimants are all together in a pile on the front desk and anyone may riffle through them. We riffled and took our meager haul into the big old-fashioned lounge where we ordered tea. The table was still soiled from the previous guests, a condition that troubled the waiter not at all. He was about to set down our order but when I suggested that a little cleaning up would be appreciated he cheerfully complied whisking the sugar and cake crumbs onto the floor.

Later we drove around the city and a charming spot it is, a fertile oasis ringed by bare hills glowing rose and lavender in the late afternoon sunlight. They had had no rain for six months but Shiraz is rich in springs and wells and the parks and gardens and the foliage of the trees were a deep luxuriant green. A broad strip of water with closely spaced illuminated fountains runs down the center of Avenue Allam, a decorative and inviting thoroughfare where in the early evening the homeward bound traffic is unregulated but the atmosphere lively and bracing.

Their device for cleaning the streets is ingenious if challenging. Water flows through open gutters bordering the sidewalks like little canals. They are about a foot deep and perhaps twelve to fourteen inches wide and the debris flows along until it disappears into subterranean sewers. They are a hazard for car wheels which can sink into them with the greatest of ease and stepping from curbstone to road is a perilous enterprise, lethal I should think for drunks, and one imagines the hospitals must be crowded with fracture cases.

Returning to our hotel we went into the bar for drinks. In Iran liquor is legal and the choice wide and after the product of the household stills of Saudi Arabia one appreciates the professional touch.

An unconscionable number of children swarmed through the public rooms because of a big religious celebration that brought families out en masse for the holiday. This time not the Feast of the Lamb but Now Ruz the Persian New Year which continues for two weeks and is a combination of New Year and Easter or the arrival of spring and is a felicitous combination. Why shouldn't spring herald the New Year? Unlike the New Year of the West theirs does not occur always on the stroke of midnight but changes within a five-hour span during the night.

Looking around the bar we decided that their handsome Shah is a good ad for the nation because I should not say that on the whole modern Persians are a distinguished-looking race. The men have the best of it but the children are too fat and were I a Persian male I should certainly wait until nightfall before availing myself of a woman.

The food of the Shiraz Inn is not among its virtues. Ignoble: salad dressing made with prefabricated lemon squash instead of vinegar but one must face the fact that people who drink Coca-Cola and Pepsi with their meals are not going to eat with any discrimination. Although the Saudi love it, Coca-Cola was banned in Saudi Arabia because the company has a bottling plant in Israel. To the disgust of most of the citizens Fords were prohibited for a like reason; there is an assembly plant in Israel. Iranians don't give a damn about the conflict. Like the Lebanese they want to trade and to prosper and they import both.

Watching our fellow guests dine it occurred to me that in some respects Easterners are in the nursery of life. Arabs eat with their fingers, Persians with spoons and knives. Maybe forks will come along in a few years. Obviously one cannot pretend that eating with forks is a criterion of civilization—Hitler probably used them, Stalin and Joseph McCarthy too—but it does seem a more tidy method.

The reason for going to Shiraz, other than a driving desire to see the whole of this world before going on to the dubious pleasures of the next, is Persepolis that unparalleled achievement of an ancient empire.

An hour's drive from Shiraz brings one to the grandiose platform rising from the plain of Marvdasht northeast of the city.

Probably conceived by Cyrus the Great, who died in 529 B.C., the actual building was begun in the reign of Darius, 518–512 B.C.

Darius was a nice man. Although belonging to a younger branch of the Achaemenian dynasty he was, like his predecessor, a great statesman and organizer as well as a humane one who declared, "I am one who loves righteousness and hates iniquity . . . It is not my will that the strong should oppress the weak

. . . God's plan for the earth is not turmoil but peace, prosperity, and good government."

Darius also assumed that God would recognize beauty and splendor and harmony when He saw them and he set about organizing the magnificent monument. He was the instigator of Persepolis but two other Dariuses and Xerxes and Artaxerxes also contributed to it. The over-all time of its building was about one hundred eight years.

The first Darius' words are inscribed on the face of the platform ". . . I built it secure and beautiful and adequate, precisely as I ordered." It is all of that.

An interesting note on how the wherewithal for such magnificence was obtained we owe to an informative guide book called Persepolis written by Ali Sami and translated by The Reverend R. Sharp, M. A. Cantab.

Mr. Ali Sami may fairly be said to be prejudiced in regard to his ancestory and native land but he knows a very great deal about Persepolis. He was I understand involved in some of the excavating and if here and there one applies a small grain of salt the over-all picture is credible. He says for example:

"Since the Persian race is noted for agreeable conduct and kindly disposition, the Achaemenians, and especially Cyrus the Great, Darius and Xerxes being outstanding examples of these fine qualities, it is therefore entirely out of the question that the construction of the palaces at Persepolis should have been effected by forced labor . . . [or] were put up under duress by prisoners as the pyramids of Egypt and the Great Wall of China were."

In passing one may say that there is considerable evidence that the pyramids were not constructed by slave labor or certainly not for the most part but in all likelihood by farmers and fellahs who had little to occupy them during the annual three-months' flooding of the Nile and so turned a hand to the tombs.

Be that as it may, Mr. Ali Sami has irrefutable evidence to back up his own contention because tablets have been found in the treasury testifying to the fact that the Achaemenian Kings paid daily wages in silver to the workers; women and children, and boys as well as men. Even so the probability is that in both Egypt and Persia it would have been unhealthy to have refused to lend a hand.

Despite the ambition, the ideals, the labor and the material that went into Persepolis its glory was short lived for it was destroyed by Alexander in 331 B.C. when the Greeks overwhelmed the Persian Empire, and ostensibly in revenge for the burning of Greek temples by Xerxes.

Scorched and burned fragments of wood and fabric that have been recovered indicate that the superb complex was set ablaze.

Of the great stone columns, carvings, and bas reliefs that survived many were subsequently vandalized in the Arab invasion of 641, the Moslem religion forbidding the depiction of human beings but fortunately the demolition was not thorough and countless figures still remain. Curiously there are no temples dedicated to the deity, Ahuramazda, but that is because worship was in the open air.

Persepolis was thought at first to have been the capital of Iran, an idea now generally discredited for none of the thousands of clay tablets that have been excavated refer in any way to economic, military or political matters, all national concerns. Furthermore it was inconveniently placed for the purpose and Susa, Babylon, and Ekbatana were the seats of government.

Persepolis in any event was never designed as a permanent habitation. No homely signs such as worn thresholds or window ledges or hollowed steps attest to daily living. It was a ceremonial center where in the early months of spring the court kept the festival of the vernal equinox. Of course when they were there the royal family were not exactly squatters. They did live in the palaces on the platform and when people thronged to the area for religious ceremonies they lived in tents on the surrounding plain, tents of crimson and purple glittering with gold and ornamentation and at night their campfires dimmed the stars.

The rest of the year the center would appear to have been inhabited by artisans and their families who worked over several generations carving the incomparable bas reliefs and erecting the towering columns. They lived in tents, humble ones theirs, or in baked-brick huts long since disintegrated into dust.

A broad flight of stairs leads up to the platform and although statistics are tedious it may help to visualize the scale by saying that the platform itself upon which were superimposed the high-roofed halls and great palaces rises in places to a height of fifty-eight feet from the ground and is more than a quarter of a mile long.

Among the admirably preserved wonders that remain are two capitals of incredible size and weight resting in pits in the ground which apparently never were put into place atop the columns. One presents the heads of two lions, the other two eagles. Both beasts are highly stylized and are carved at either end of a heavy block of limestone.

The heads stare in opposite directions and despite their dignity and grandeur they evoke irreverent memories of Doctor Dolittle's Push-me, Pull-you.

Credulity boggles a bit when one is asked to accept that such enormous weight was raised to the top of the towering columns sixty-two feet in height and that the columns supported it but it was and they did and the flat space between the arching animal heads was a saddle on which were laid the beams of the wooden ceiling.

One of the most dramatic of the bas relief carvings and one frequently repeated is a lion, his claws digging into the hind quarters of a bull, his teeth sunk into its flesh.

Another superb sculpture shows the King fighting a chimera, a creature whose physique is to say the least unmonotonous for it has the head of a lion, a short unicorn horn which the King firmly grasps in his right hand, his left plunges a knife into the stomach, and below the mane, tight curled as the snails on Buddha's head, feathered wings cover the shoulders. He has a

42. The air terminal of Dhahran designed by Minoru Yamasaki
(photo courtesy of Ralph Parsons Company)

43. The Aramco plane and two trucks in the desolation that is
Rub Al Kahli

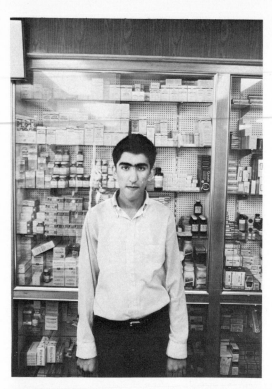

44. The sophisticated chemist of
al-Khobar

45. One of the imposing Push-Me Pull-Yous of Persepolis. These
capitals topped the great columns and the ceiling beams
rested in the saddle

46. Lion and bull relief, Persepolis

47. The chimera and the King. Persepolis

48. Double staircase of the Apanada. Persepolis

49. A buxom queen on the right and kings in ruffled britches

50. The Shahs palace in the Aram Gardens, Shiraz, Iran

51. Garden courtyard of the Hotel Shah Abbas, Isfahan, Iran

52. South gateway of the Masjid Jomeh or Friday Mosque, Isfahan

53. The delicate lace like stucco
of the prayer niche of the
Friday Mosque

54. The Lake Palace Hotel in Lake Pichola, Udaipur, India

55. Lake Palace courtyard, the setting where the Indian dancing took place

56. The island palace of Jag Mandir where the parakeets came to nest at night

57. The City Palace of Udaipur. There's no place like home

58. The Lofty Gate of Fathepur Sikri. The side facing the vast courtyard

59. Gateway to the gardens of the Taj Mahal seen from the garden side

60. Voila! The Taj Mahal. Agra, India

61. Back side, so to speak, of the Taj Mahal

scorpion's tail and clawed feet, one digging into the King's shin. He is a love. There is another enchanting carving of a warrior with a small antlered stag in his arms.

Farther off on a flat free-standing column Darius is walking tall as befits a king sheltered by a parasol borne by two human-sized attendants following behind.

Xerxes' famed Hall of One Hundred Columns 230 feet long by 230 feet wide is now a great space open to the sky and the encircling hills. Nearly all the low pedestals remain in place but the fluted columns themselves have toppled and disappeared as have the portals and the roof of cedar.

The greatest triumph of Persepolis, at least the greatest that remains today, is undeniably the eastern staircase of the Apadana. It is a double staircase, the steps purposely broad and shallow so horses could negotiate them during ceremonial processions, mount from either side forty feet up to the floor level and the façade is a miracle of precise delicate disciplined bas reliefs carved in stone. At the top is a crenelation of square stylized mountains with openings cut into them symbolizing God's entrance into the world. Below the mountains, and in descending scale, a border of twelve petaled rosettes, rows of cypress trees, the tree of life, then slim and stately palms of which they had an abundance. The true marvels, however, are the friezes, endless processions of the peoples who composed the vast Persian Empire.

According to the dedicated and patriotic Mr. Ali Sami [they] "are eloquent of history and indicate beyond all doubt the power and orderliness of this great empire.

"Feelings of devotion and loyalty are clearly shown in the features of those bringing their offerings."

This may be poetic interpretation it may be literal truth, what is undebatable is their numbers: Assyrians, Arabs, Ethiopians, Elamites, Parthians, Persians themselves bushy hair escaping from beneath their crowns, Medes in brimless derbies, Scythians with the stocking caps that children wear sledding.

On and on they come bringing gifts to the great kings, the produce of the known world.

Jars and vessels of every kind, double-humped camels, chariots, rams and oxen, horses, gold bracelets, rolls of cloth. There is no end to the offerings nor to the skill and beauty with which they are presented.

Curiously enough among the thousands of figures there is only one of a woman who would seem to be a servant of the Queen for she bears a jar of oil and a towel hangs over her arm.

We spent a long time at Persepolis, something that is very easy to do, and I should recommend to camera toters seeing it in the morning when the light is best for photography.

Returning to our driver we discovered he had become a hero. Strolling around waiting for us he had happened to glance into a car where he saw a struggling baby about to suffocate, its idiot parents having closed the windows tight and gone off to view the ruins. The doors were securely locked but he had the wit to break the window and saved the baby's life.

After congratulating him we drove to the necropolis, Naqsh-i-Rustam, a little over a mile from Persepolis. Two of the last of the Achaemenian kings lie on the slope of Mount Rahmat just to the east of the platform but Darius the Great, Xerxes, Artaxerxes the First and Darius the Second are buried at Naqsh-i-Rustam. Like the Nabataeans the Persians buried their kings in the faces of sheer cliffs. There are carvings here too of less precision and beauty than those in the city but the stone appears softer, perhaps sandstone instead of the gray limestone of Persepolis. One of the carvings depicts a buxom Queen and Kings in curiously ruffled trousers.

It was a radiant day and around the Hotel Apadana where we lunched pansies and petunias, nasturtiums and sweet william blazed in earthen pots. For roses I believe the ideal time in Iran is early April until perhaps the end of May. In late March we were rushing the season.

Back in Shiraz in the afternoon we went to stroll through

the Eram Gardens. Eram means paradise and the name is apposite. The grass is brilliant green velvet with nary a blade of crab nor a brown spot, the flower beds are illumined by millions of pansies. The planting is charming. Round beds are built up to a height of seven or eight inches and encircled by woven rushes so that they look like enormous flat baskets one could move about at will. The paths are bordered with cypress and pine and orange trees. Their 250-year-old star, naz, the Cypress of Grace and Femininity, towers 117 feet.

The Eram is a public park but also the setting for an exquisite pavilion and when the Shah and his family are in the city they live there, overlooking a broad shallow basin of water and a long avenue of trees with a canal running down the center.

The pavilion is three stories high and the façade of fairy tale coloring—lilac, plum and soft flushed beige—is in five sections divided by slender columns, banks of arched small-paned windows, grill work and deep balconies with slim balustrades. The roof is formed by five arches faced with flowered tiles. It is an altogether delicious affair and one envies the Iranian royal family their architectural luck.

A broad avenue sweeps around the garden and is the scene of the late-afternoon passeo, the promenade of the townspeople typical of the Eastern and Mediterranean worlds. In Iran some women walk veiled, draped in the long lightweight chador which while it covers their heads and bodies is not the eclipsing garment of the Arabian female.

Inspired by the beauty of Eram, Mr. Behbahani offered to show us his own garden and the house he was renting to an American. This sounded tempting so we drove out a short distance from town to his property which was walled and to which we could only gain entrance after much ringing and pounding at the big gate. We learned later that there are still antipathetic tribes in the hills who occasionally swoop down on raiding missions on relatively isolated houses.

The garden was large and ramshackle, the house small and

ramshackle but they both had charm and one's instinct was to
get out the pruning shears and paint brush and heave to. The
tenant was Mr. Odonel an American from Oregon who taught
English at the Shiraz university. He came out to meet us and
hospitably showed us around and in the course of the little tour
the horrid truth emerged. The garden was neglected because Mr.
Behbahani was about to cut it up and commit development.

When we went into the house the small open fire was very
welcome and another American, a tall bearded chap and friend
of Mr. Odonel, helped offer refreshments—beer, coffee, cookies,
and oranges. Portly Mr. Behbahani took cookies and oranges.
He will get portlier.

The two men questioned Norton at length, they were both
interested in catching up on recent medical developments, and
we learned that our host was shortly leaving for Pakistan to write
a book on an obscure religious sect and eventually planned to
return to Oregon. He had not been home in fifteen years.

Since we were so depressed by the wretched food and atmosphere of the coffee shop, the only dining room of the motel, on
the way back to town we asked Mr. Behbahani if he couldn't
direct us to a decent restaurant where we might dine later.
Our first stop was the Casbah, a real mess. They were just beginning to clear up last night's debris but then it was only seven
o'clock and they didn't open until nine.

The next one looked a little more promising. It was called
the Golden Bowl and a pretty garden stretched in front of it.
The tables were large and we gathered that many people sat
down together, a prospect of which Norton and I both took a
dim view, but Mr. Behbahani said he would be able to arrange
one for two and we urged that it be as far from the orchestra as
possible. He also obligingly ordered dinner in advance for us,
our Persian not being equal to it.

When we returned later the floor show was just getting under
way. A demoiselle in slinky silver brocade did a belly dance not
only not comparable to the virtuosi of Tangier but not even

up to the blithe corset bound amateur of the first night's party in Jidda. However she at least was understandable. It was the act following her that was the stumper: a pudgy girl in a mini skirt, middy blouse and derby hat who shuffled around the room vaguely in time to the music. Drawing even with the exit on her third or fourth revolution she shuffled off. To Buffalo we hoped and for good. Her black-clad singing successor was lighted by a perforated brass lamp set with pieces of colored glass swinging from the ceiling and interrupted by a small child who kept running back and forth from her parents' table. Dr. Brown remarked sourly that the conception of the baby sitter had obviously not reached Iran.

The following day we met a scholar. I assume my husband knows a few, dedicated scientists and philosophers being more in his line than mine but they are not a breed I often encounter. Intelligent people, able people, funny and kind and generous people, sometimes horrible people, yes. Scholarly folk, no.

Professor Arthur Upham Pope was all that a scholar should be. Old, eighty-eight, learned, immensely wise, objective, and an outstanding, probably *the* outstanding authority on Iran.

Jim Knight had spoken of him when we were in Dhahran and Norton had the feeling then that he might have known Dr. Allen Whipple who had been my husband's professor at Columbia and who was a devotee of Iranian culture.

Trying to get to Professor Pope had been a somewhat unnerving experience due chiefly to the complexities of Eastern courtesy and a communication gap between two languages. The first day we arrived as we were driving around Shiraz, Mr. Behbahani asked out of the blue if we would like to call on a distinguished American, one Professor Pope. We said yes, very much. We continue driving and Behbahani speaks.

Behbahani: There is his house. Shall we go in?

We: Perhaps not today. We are tired and besides we don't know him.

Behbahani: Tomorrow we will go.

We: If it can be arranged that will be very pleasant.

The next day our escort appears.

We: Ah, Mr. Behbahani, how nice to see you. Will we be able to call on Professor Pope do you think?

Behbahani: As you like.

We: No, not as *we* like. Do you know him? May we call on him?

Behbahani: Anything. As you like.

We: Yes but . . . never mind. It just seems odd to ring the bell of a total stranger.

Behbahani: I will call him if you want I should.

We: That would be nice. We want.

He places the call. I am slightly dazed but Norton takes over, mentions Jim Knight and I gather an appointment is being made.

When a day or two later we kept the engagement we found Professor Pope sitting behind his desk wearing a warm sweater under his jacket with a woolen lap robe over his knees and a gas heater nearby. He was spooning gruel from a cup. He had recently broken a rib and seemed very frail but although he yawned occasionally his manner was alert and he was courteous and interested in our travels. When we said we had been to Persepolis he spoke of it with the knowledge and intimacy of one who had not only helped plan the place but had been present at, indeed had been the instigator, of the magnificent annual ceremonies. His description of them was thrilling.

The splendor of the King, the crowds, the beauty of the tents and costumes, the music, the endless processions of the 10,000 royal guards, the animals; horses, camels, bulls, lions, the thronging multitudes from the farthest flung provinces of the empire . . . for him and for us his listeners they sprang to vivid life through 2500 years of history, the way a dark stage lights up behind a scrim and what has been a black void and silence is suddenly shocked into color and activity and sound.

Not only Persepolis but the mosques of Isfahan, our next

Iranian city, evoked from him descriptions of those who had built them and those who worshipped there. He spoke with special love of the purity and simplicity of a dome of the Friday mosque. "Be sure you see it, be sure you see it, it is unique." Love of the beauties of Iran glowed like fire through the fragile structure of his body. An intense caring seemed the very essence of his nature. When Norton asked him if he had known Dr. Allen Whipple his face lighted up. "I adored that man, my greatest friend. You are to be congratulated, sir, on having known him. Because of him your patients are in good hands."

During our visit two of his colleagues, a man and a Chinese woman came in and after speaking with the professor they telephoned and made arrangements for us to see Naranjestan a small palace built about one hundred years ago that was currently closed to the public because of the process of restoration that was being paid for out of Professor Pope's own pocket. Not wishing to overtax his strength we thanked him and took our leave.

A few months later in New York, the day after I had written the above paragraph, we read in the paper that he had died in Shiraz and would be buried in his beloved Isfahan.

Once at Naranjestan we had a little wait until the old guardian could be rustled up to admit us. We entered from the street through heavy wooden double doors and passed through a vestibule into a large rectangular garden festive with pansies and a shining narrow sheet of water down the middle.

From a pillared porch with richly carved plaster flowers in the ceiling one looks across the garden to the palace at the far end, its three arched façade covered with flowery tiles like those in the pavilion in the Eram Gardens.

Another American, a colleague of Professor Pope who was overseeing the work of restoration told us it had been built by Governor Gahvam of Shiraz who shortly thereafter was shot to death in his pretty garden by a political rival. When we commiserated with such a cavalier finish our American shrugged "It was better

than what happened to his grandfather. *He* was boiled in oil."
Politics in Iran is a chancy profession.

One may say that before misfortune befell him Governor
Gahvam's taste was joyous and ebullient. There are two mirrored
rooms in the palace which on first impact cause one to catch
one's breath and then to explode with delighted laughter. They
are so naïve and entertaining, so rich and grand. The walls
and ceilings are completely mirrored. There are narrow mirrored
pilasters flanking small mirrored slabs, there are faceted mirror
borders and chunky mirrored mouldings. When they flick a
switch and the rooms light up one is in the center of a million
glittering reflections, it is like being inside a brilliant flashing
diamond. The smaller of the two rooms, a real little jewel box,
is called Shah Neshin or Where the King Sits and it was here
the Governor used to receive his guests. Naranjestan is a looney
and lovely spot.

The idea of mirrors was not unique to Gahvam they were
used in other palaces in Asia and in Shiraz the shrine of Shah
Cheragh, into which we could peek but not enter, also sparkled
with them but the effect was nothing like as wholehearted and
gay as the entrancing toy of the Governor.

Since it was getting on toward noon we left Naranjestan for the
museum, a charming small octagonal building, it too decorated
with flowery tiles, its exterior more appealing than its contents
although it does house some notable bowls dating from 4000
B.C. and in the garden are a few fragments of sculpture from
Persepolis.

At our next stop, a mosque, a contretemps developed. I could
not go in because I lacked a chador, the all-enveloping veil of
the Iranian women. As the mosque adjoins a bazaar we went
there hoping to find one. Incidentally the souks of North Africa
and the Middle East become the bazaars of Iran and India.
This particular one was an enormous labyrinthine complex of
covered alleys like the great bazaar in Istanbul but although
we scurried after Faham, our guide, that morning very spruce in

a brown zoot suit with a vent in the back cut to the waist, feeling like the Alice in Wonderland rabbit scurrying to his rendezvous, nary a chador could we raise. I was not too saddened by this as the exterior of the mosque which I could gaze upon unveiled was a feast for the eye; a garden of tiles, all roses and iris and nightingales and our next stop was a special treat. It was the tomb of Hafiz, the great lyric poet, who lived in the fourteenth century. It is an enchanting affair set in a big garden abloom with flowers and shimmering with pools.

On blue rectangles inserted in the upper part of an open gallery that encloses the sarcophagus lines from his poems are engraved in white Persian script. To reach the sarcophagus itself we mounted a broad flight of steps banked with petunias and walked along the gallery on which were grouped hundreds of pots of geraniums and fragrant white stock. The white marble tomb is set under a high honeycomb dome upheld by slender fluted pillars, a kind of Temple d'Armour. It is said that if one strokes it light an inspiration will enter the soul. I stroked.

Iranians sometimes refer to Hafiz's collected poems, the Divan, as the troubled devout use the Bible, opening it at random and finding guidance in whatever verse their eye falls upon.

The garden was crowded with visitors and as at Persepolis we saw agile couples photographing themselves. One of them, usually the girl would stand in front of the famous monument, the fellow having adjusted his camera on its tripod would set the timing mechanism rush over to join her and click! They would be immortalized.

The Persians revered their poets and another beautiful tomb commemorates another one, Saadi, although he also wrote prose, who lived to be one hundred and seven years old bridging the thirteenth and fourteenth centuries. His tomb is a high elegant structure with a blue dome upheld by square columns and a long arcade stretches to the left.

We went to Saadi's tomb after lunch and in the interim our driver had thoughtfully procured a chador for me. It was his wife's and amid much laughter and advice from Iranian women crowding around us he draped it over me and I was able to go with Norton into the mosque forbidden to me when I was chadorless.

It is built around an immense courtyard paved with large flat stones and with a long pool in the center and faucets set at intervals where the faithful may wash their noses, ears, eyes, hands, and feet before entering to prostrate themselves facing toward Mecca.

The interior is spacious with a staircase carved from a solid block of alabaster for the Mola, the minister or priest to mount to his pulpit. We walked around watching them lay down rugs for Moharam the first month of a sixty-day period of mourning. The second month is called Safar and the mourning is for the prophet Emam Hosein who was killed near Baghdad in the eighth century. The mourning period changes with the calendar and may fall in spring, summer, autumn, or winter. When we were there it coincided with Now Ruz, the new year, although the word ruz literally means day. An unfortunate coincidence it was, causing a wild melee of traffic, tourists, and hotel accommodations.

That Iran is a mountainous country we learned on the flight to Isfahan and that every Iranian in the land was gathered in Isfahan we learned on our arrival at the Hotel Shah Abbas.

When we had mentioned that we had reservations there friends who knew it had said, "Oh you'll love the Shah Abbas, it's a dear place." From the affectionate manner in which they spoke we had somehow gathered the impression it was small. One of those dear *small* hotels like the parador San Francisco in Grenada or Bourdzi in Naphlion in Greece or the adorable Seteais of Pena in Portugal. Perhaps even like the Connaught in London which is not all that small but smallish just the same and lovable. Well, as they say, we live and learn. The Shah

Abbas is vast and was to be the first of the gigantic caravansaries we would be stopping at in Asia.

We entered the huge lobby, "the great and gorgeous entrance hall" as it is described in a brochure printed by the management, to find it seething with humanity. One would not automatically have assumed that the end of March would be the height of the tourist season but that is because one would not have known about the double jeopardy; Now Ruz plus Moharam cum Safar, the mourning period, propelling all Iran and all the children of all Iran out of their homes onto the roads and into the hotels.

Mr. A. Moshgforoush the assistant manager was a nice chap obviously distressed by our mutual plight, an unhonored reservation, and we did not have to make a tour of the hotel to realize that his rooms as well as his hands were full. He urged us to be seated while he did his best. Waiting we had ample time to drink in the glories described so glowingly in the brochure. "Colored convex mirror work in the ceiling, paintings on the wooden panels in front of the reception desk, plaster work, gilt and painting around the central hall, delicate carvings around the mirrors and pierced bronze shades on the floor lamps, large honeycomb pendentives from the ceiling . . ." We had got about so far glutted with splendor and there were pages more to go, when glancing once more toward the desk in the hope of catching the manager's eye whom did we spot but that urbane New Yorker, famed playwright, author, and man about the world, Mr. Marc Connelly. We leaped with shrill cries to his welcoming arms. Mr. Connelly had already been a guest in the hotel for a night or two and he had the coveted treasure, the Golden Fleece, the Holy Grail, he had a *room*. He had also read the Bible and taken to heart the bit about greater love hath no man. He was willing to lay down, not his life which while it would have grieved us would have done us scant good but, much more to the point, his precious room.

"I," he said, "have a double which I don't need. I'm off

tomorrow. If the manager can find me a corner for tonight, it's yours." The manager found, the move was effected and thanks to our generous friend we spent a couple of very comfortable nights.

The manager subsequently discovered that there *was* a room awaiting us but it had been booked under the name of Dr. Norton instead of Dr. Brown. This is the kind of thing about which the experienced traveler will develop a sixth sense but I do not think in fairness he can be expected to be born with it.

The Shah Abbas without false modesty proclaims itself the most beautiful hotel in the world. Obviously we have not seen them all but, particularly if one speaks only of the big ones, I'm not sure the claim isn't justified.

While the décor is rich rather than discriminating the enormous garden courtyard around which the hotel is constructed is lovely. There are lawns and walks, a small bridge crosses a canal and there are tall trees, I think of the poplar family, with slender trunks of palest blue. It was probably a trick of light but they were like trees in a fairy tale. The site was originally that of a caravanserai in the seventeenth century and was built by the mother of Shah Soltan Hosein and was known appropriately enough as the Queen Mother's Caravanserai. The lady must have subsidized it generously because the revenues derived from travelers went to support theological students in the nearby Chahar Bagh school.

Chahar Bagh means Four Gardens and streets and parks and assorted municipal features are so named. Although no one said so I should imagine the name derives from the classic design of the gardens of Iran and also many of India, that of the Taj Mahal among them. They are laid out in the shape of a cross dividing the area into four parts. The lines of demarcation may be canals or tree lined avenues or paths but they are set at right angles and the squares thus formed are usually of equal size.

The Hotel Shah Abbas' north wing is largely composed of the

original buildings but since the walls and roof were of unbaked brick they have been reinforced and plastered over.

The façades overlooking the courtyard are two-storied with the traditional Arch and Eye or double-arch vaulted roofs. Every room has a deep balcony, walls washed with softest blue perhaps to match the fairy trees and faced with flowered tiles.

It was pleasant to be ensconced in such luxurious surroundings because the sparkle of Shiraz was missing in Isfahan.

I do not refer to the architecture, the mosques of Isfahan are its glory but we went about our sightseeing under a cloudy sky. The royal square, Maidan-E-Shah built by Shah Abbas at the start of the seventeenth century is, next to the Red Square of Moscow, the largest in the world and the Ala Qapi, the magnificent palace gate and high pillared gallery from which the Shahs and their guests used to watch polo games still stands.

In 640 the Arabs invaded Iran. Isfahan was a rich and prosperous town, the climate was considered good and they made it the capital of the country.

Early in the tenth century a festival of such brilliance was held there that Iranians still talk about it. The Chevalier Mardavij on his way to the wars in Baghdad decided to give a great fete, to repeat a spectacle promulgated by his ancestors some three hundred years previously. "With this in view," so goes the story, "he ordered the people to spend some days in collecting brushwood and fuel from the desert and pile it upon the banks of the river. He brought oil in goat skins over great distances and engaged the men known as 'oil throwers' who used to dip the wood in oil and after lighting it throw it most skillfully over great distances. He prepared great candles, each as tall as a man, then treated them with camphor and placed them in position.

"On Garmkuh nearest the city and all the other hills he heaped up great piles of wood. He brought great trunks of trees and logs from outside the city, bound them together with iron bands in the forms of palaces and pulpits and placed them outside the city boundaries filled with shavings and brushwood. In addition hunters collected more than a thousand ravens and kites and bound oily walnut bark, wood and shavings to their beaks and legs.

"Then Mardavij gave orders that every hill and valley should be lighted simultaneously at the beginning of the festival and that the whole vast district should sparkle and flame as far as the eye could see. That same evening he spread such a board as the world had never seen; such lavishness, such generosity and such splendor."

Nor had it rarely seen such gratuitous cruelty as the flaming birds tossed into the sky to be roasted alive. It is fruitless, yet not unpleasant, to speculate on a suitable fate for the Chevalier Mardavij. Slow boiling in oil perhaps, or cancer of the prostate and in his day no morphine . . . that's a *good* one. The unjust truth is probably that the arson bug went to bed one night feeling tip top and died tranquilly in his sleep.

Although I myself prefer the Blue Mosque of Sultan Ahmed I in Istanbul, the Blue Mosque of Isfahan, built on the square by Shah Abbas, has its own magnificence. There is an enormous central courtyard surrounded by a great complex of chambers and the tile work and calligraphy are exquisite.

A more modest establishment is the Ladies Mosque. This one has no courtyard but a narrow curving corridor opening into a central apartment with a high-domed ceiling and cordlike ornamentation of turquoise enamel. There is a grill in the floor and below it a vault from which used to issue the voice of the mola as he conducted services so that he and the worshipping ladies should not look upon one another. Could he have caught a glimpse of a slim ankle, who knows, he might have developed a foot fetish.

The third renowned mosque of Isfahan, the Masjid-i-Jum'a or Friday Mosque, is some distance from the square and is a curious structure, a collection of architectural styles of every period of Iranian history in the Islamic era. There are twenty-eight component parts and it has been in the building from A.D. 1000 until the last century. One of its glories is a carved stucco prayer niche erected in 1310 with an intricate exquisite design of flowers and foliage.

The mosque, called by the Iranians Masjid Jomeh, covers several acres and while the part opening onto the central courtyard is tiled in blue the rest is of narrow fired clay bricks very similar to those used by the Romans. It is mostly earth-colored with the exception of a portion that breaks abruptly, into white-washed arches with no apparent rhyme or reason. There are hundreds of them outlined in bright blue paint, diminishing in long crisscrossing perspectives. There is also a small high-domed chamber with lofty columns constructed entirely of the narrow bricks where color does not count but the proportion and purity of line are memorable.

Returning to the square we went snooping through the large bazaar where one may pick up all kinds of souvenirs but those that caught my eye were sold more cheaply in small independent shops. They were the fat blue beads worn by donkeys to ward off the evil eye. Apparently the donkeys of Hofuf had not been in touch with their Iranian relatives to tell them about using henna on head and forelegs. The color of the beads is sharp and bright and they are fun to wear with summer dresses. Their only drawback if traveling is their weight. I accumulated quite a collection to give to friends and not wishing to pay excess luggage charges I would board planes with so many strings around my neck that my head was bent forward at the same angle from my body as the original wearers.

Mementos of more worth are Persian miniatures. Our guide Jaffrey had studied with one of the outstanding miniaturists of Isfahan and led us to the studio shop of his master Mr. Ali Sajjadi in street Chaharbagh ⚭100. Not surprisingly Sajjadi's own work was the best but many of the small ivories done by his students were fresh and delicate and not expensive.

Maidan-E-Shah, the Kings' Square, is a favorite subject but

there are also scenes with rich blue-domed mosques and cream puff cloudlike mountains and turbaned figures and fragile limbed horses and dogs. We bought four of them and as they are art they may enter the United States duty free. They were mailed to us and we received them in New York about two months later in excellent condition.

We visited the rug factory which because of the day of mourning was not functioning but the rugs were on the looms and out of curiosity we asked the price of a particularly beautiful one: about $66.66 a square yard.

Around one o'clock returning to the hotel we joined our benefactor Marc Connelly for lunch. Mr. Connelly in the old great days of the Algonquin Round Table was one of its bright stars and the years have not appreciably dimmed his luster. Referring to an acquaintance who had married an extremely rich man whom Mr. Connelly considered to be less than Lord Chesterfield he remarked that the lady was "living high under the hog." He has a warm spot in his heart for the Irish and had been tickled when a woman friend in Ireland to whom he was relating an account of the agreeable but notably uneventful day he had passed remarked, "You must have been emotionally drained."

That night we dined in the hotel and in the spirit of "What the hell, you only live once," ordered Iranian caviar. It is not cheap in Iran nor did we think it very good. Furthermore the doctor was under the weather suffering from a cold or some sort of allergy picked up in a dusty bazaar.

"What's the matter?" I said. "You sound testy." Brief interlude of muttering and wheezing then, surprising I thought as a seminal source of discomfort, "I haven't seen a decent pair of gams since I left home." He notices female feet and legs before faces and one must say in truth that the southern extremities of Iranian femininity, of most of the Middle East for that matter, leave much to be desired.

The Iranian women whom the legs support, however, are a good deal more emancipated than their Arabian sisters. They drive cars, the sophisticated element does not wear veils excepting perhaps the chador in mosques, and many of them sport pants in public. In so doing they err but for what it is worth they are With It.

I would say do not miss Isfahan but unless one were going to make an in depth study, a day spent there would be enough. Ideally one should arrive in the late afternoon of the day before, explore and enjoy the Shah Abbas Hotel, have a decent enough dinner and a good night's sleep in comfortable beds.

The next morning without any wild rush it is possible to see the three mosques—certainly two of them—then lunch, visit the third if it has been neglected, visit by all means the tombs of the two poets, go to the shop and enjoy the miniatures of Mr. Ali Sajadi, ramble through the bazaar and do not ignore the wonderful Allahvardikhan or Char Bagh Bridge. This beautiful and monumental structure with its double tier of thirty-three arches spanning the Zayandehrud River was built in 1602 on the order of Shah Abbas. Where would we be without him?

Having seen the bridge, one could then return to the hotel for a second night or leave for the airport and the next destination. This obviously is a superficial recommendation made by a transient and leaves out great chunks of history and architecture and many people will not wish to abide by it. But for the average traveler on a limited schedule, and a usually limited budget, who enjoys sampling and savoring the more renowned examples of an exotic way of life and exploring unique and beautiful buildings it can be reasonably satisfactory.

The next morning as we were driving to the airport we passed a funeral procession. The mourners draped in black were on foot, the pallbearers carried on their shoulders an open coffin with the corpse swathed in a chador that served as shroud. It was a fitting introduction to Tehran.

The capital is less than an hour's flight from Isfahan and arriving shortly before lunch on a gray and gloomy morning we were driven, by what perversion of fate I do not know, to the Hotel Sina where we had been booked by malign spirits from a baleful agency. Our room was large but there was only one window tucked into the corner where the building formed an L and we looked out on a dirty sky and a gray morose city. Furthermore it was Friday, the Moslem Sunday and because of the mourning period everything was even more shuttered than would normally have been the case.

Fortunately we found quite a stack of mail or I think we would have cut our throats. No letter however from the Gyalmo and Norton again repeated his sage advice to wait until New Delhi, now beginning to take shape on the horizon.

We were supposed to stay in Tehran until Sunday night but our mood was such that I started at once trying to get hold of every known airline to see if we couldn't leave sooner. My luck was nil. Did I not understand that it was Friday and a day of mourning? I explained that if I didn't understand it nobody did. Ah, yes, well . . . the airline offices would be open after 8 P.M. Since it was lunchtime we went to the hotel dining room. In the basement. No windows, no air, inexpressibly dreary and the food ignominious.

However even in the darkest hour sometimes, if one has lived right, if one has at least *tried,* a tiny ray of sunshine breaks through. In our mail had been a letter from our friend Gilbert Smith in New York. Dear and gifted Mr. Smith, by one of those providential twists of fate, knew the German ambassador to Iran. He had, he wrote us, sent him a letter giving him our arrival date in Tehran and the courtly friend of our friend sent a note to the hotel asking us to call him on our arrival.

This I did and he asked if we were free for dinner. Free! He little knew! Free for dinner, afternoon tea, the night, next morning's breakfast . . . we were it may be said uncommitted. "Would seven-thirty be too early?" "Not at all, Mr. Ambassador. Your convenience is ours." I refrained from adding, "We can come right now."

Somehow the lethal afternoon dragged to its close. We had engaged a car and chauffeur and shortly after seven set out on a long rainy drive to the residency, a large rambling one-story house of very modern architecture.

The household consisted of the ambassador, a German countess who I think was a relation and who acted as housekeeper, four of the ambassador's five children and a guest, an old friend, the Princess of Bavaria and her daughter. Ambassador Lilienfeld was a handsome man in, I imagine, his late fifties with simple delightful manners. Mrs. Lilienfeld and their oldest son were still in Washington, where they had previously been posted.

It is curious about Germans. When one meets people who were young or maturing adults in the years between 1933 and 1945 one cannot help wondering. . . . And what were you up to my fine and finney friend during that fateful span? Having been sprung from our gruesome hotel, sitting before a bright fire with this charming man and his friends I preferred not to peer into any pits and to assume him to have been of that rare species, an anti-Nazi German.

The Princess was a handsome woman who told us that she adored shooting. Flowers and bird shooting, she really couldn't decide *which* she preferred. I wondered why she didn't combine her hobbies and shoot the petals off flowers.

As we sat sipping our cocktails the countess observed glumly that she hoped we liked fish. We said we doted on it which is true. "The children," she said, "don't like it."

"Usually it is a cultivated taste."

"Yes." She looked depressed.

The non-fish enthusiasts came in and proved to be attractive youngsters with very good manners who spoke perfect English as did the adults.

Dinner as the ambassador had explained over the phone was extremely informal and we thought it more than courteous of him to have taken pity on two total strangers. We did feel that possibly that particular cook was not the one to persuade the children to the joys of seafood.

On our way back to the Sina we stopped off at the Tehran Hilton to reserve a room for the next morning. If we couldn't get on a plane we could at least improve our situation to that extent.

In fairness to the Sina one must say it is conveniently in the heart of town whereas the Hilton is a drive of about twenty-five minutes and as in Rabat and Tunis has been built with an eye to an expanding city and increasing tourist trade.

On our way out there the following day we stopped off for a brief chat with Mr. Ditto, the man in charge of Pan Am activities in Iran. He told us about Eisenhower. The general had fought the battle that we all must lose and had died the night before. Mr. Ditto also warned us to stay off the streets during the day and not by any means to go near crowds or large groups of people. "This is Ashura, their most holy day, and they work themselves up to a considerable emotional pitch and have small use for infidels. You never know what may cause trouble." We promised to be prudent and took ourselves off having gained the impression that Mr. Ditto had plans for an American holiday on an Iranian holy day.

Our room on the fourteenth floor of the Hilton was a poem in custard yellow and orchid, normally not my preferred color scheme but after the Sina, lyrical. We had a balcony and unimpeded view of the barren snow-capped mountains. All this bounty for $21 a day as opposed to the Sina's $16. The food at the Hilton is good. There is a very adequate hairdressing salon where one can get a manicure, a rare treat in both Asia and Africa, and all in all I should say the hotel has many features to recommend it.

Service is not among them. We found it negligent in the extreme and the attitude of the staff ranged from indifference to insolence. That may not be everyone's experience but it was ours.

When he had heard we were going to Tehran, Arnold Weissberger, the theatrical lawyer, had said, "But you must look up Ruth Matteson! She and her husband Curt Peterson are living there you know."

I had not known but it was a real pleasure to find them. Ruth and I had enjoyed a long-time friendship, one of those theatrical friendships that last through the years and in which the two parties rarely see each other.

We once appeared on Broadway together in a play I had written and when I joined the cast of *Barefoot in the Park* Ruth had been the standby for the part I played for many months. Even then we didn't meet much for the obvious reason that if one of us was in the theatre the other was not. We had to travel all the way to Tehran to get together but it was an enjoyable reunion.

Her husband Curt Peterson is an attractive man and his job in a very high sounding organization, International Executives Service Corporation, is an interesting one. He is the catalyst who brings together retired business, commercial or industrial executives from firms in the United States and people in Iran who have money to finance new businesses but need American know-how. The bag is varied. Supermarkets, filling stations, caterers, whatever the project may be Mr. Peterson matches up clients and advisers. The advisers as I understand it are paid only a per-diem wage, being for the most part men who have made enough to live on in any event, but they want to work or they may simply be altruists willing to give the other fellow a boost.

Ruth and Curt took us to the French Club to lunch where we again saw our Bavarian princess looming tall. They told us they had been living at the Hilton ever since their arrival two months previous and Ruth was elated because they were about to move into a comfortable house with a lovely garden. They liked Iran and were pleased to be settling in.

We had planned on sightseeing after luncheon but as our religious holiday was still with us it was a frustrating experience.

We drove to the bazaar which we understood was a good one. Bazaar closed. We drove to Golestan Palace. Palace closed and with any number of people clamoring to get in: a French group, a German family, two or three small buses loaded with tourists, ourselves . . . in vain. It is too bad that religion is so often inhibiting to culture but fortunately it had not spread to the archaeological museum.

Many of the exhibits were unique and of great beauty. They have a superb rectangular turquoise tile of an Assyrian warrior, another of two chimera, one of flowers, three small bronze lions forming a triangle. There is a lovely and intricate carved-wood staircase and gate from a mosque, rugs, samples of curling elegant calligraphy and a fine column from Persepolis. It has been cut down to fit under the museum ceiling and Norton said, and I thought it a good idea, that they should set it in a special alcove with a domed roof high enough to accommodate it and circled by a balcony so that people could study the great capital at eye level.

The Iranian government would doubtless consider it none of my business but from the traveler's point of view, and it is important if only because of the numbers of travelers who bring money into the country, their whole system of presentation should be reorganized. To begin with the signs telling you what you are looking at are written in Persian only. There are no catalogues, no postcards, no reproductions, no guides speaking foreign languages . . .

If Curt Peterson wants to bring together clients and an expert who could do them a world of good he should get Mr. Thomas Hoving from New York's Metropolitan Museum of Art to Tehran and plump his down across the table from the board of directors of the Archaeological Museum. The gentlemen would get an earful and let us hope act upon the advice.

We learned with pleasure that despite the holiday the bank vault where the crown jewels were on display was open to visitors so we went there from the museum.

I think anybody who writes, when confronted with a striking spectacle, a fresh experience, an unanticipated event, immediately starts writing in his head. How to describe it vividly and accurately? How to convince or move or involve the reader? When it is a question of beauty or splendor your writer reaches for the lofty adjective, the lyrical phrase, the winged word. I looked upon the crown jewels of Iran and my reaction was pure comic strip. Zowie! Wham! Pow! Speech, such as it was, emerged from my mouth in balloons and hung above my head.

There is something vulgar in such plethora, one's sensibilities are bludgeoned by the impact. Dazed one tends to mutter, "God is. The crown jewels are."

Not that it will dilute the opulence or magnitude nor matter really one way or the other to the viewer but the fact is that most of the treasure in Tehran was filched, commandeered, looted and just plain stolen, largely from India, during the perpetual wars and brigand campaigns waged between the countries of Asia.

As a guide book frankly states "We have tried to trace the histories of some of the more important pieces . . . but generally we have to admit that the origin of the greater part of this incredible collection is lost in the mists of history . . . weave around [a gem] whatever romantic history your imagination likes to fabricate. You will not be far wrong."

It seems reasonably sure however that the so-called Peacock Throne, although no peacock is to be seen, was in all probability constructed in Persia during the reign of the Persian Fath-Ali Shah early in the nineteenth century. The Shah was a lad who loved luxury and also loved to distraction a favorite, Tavous Khanoun, or Lady Peacock, after whom it was named.

It is a dazzling seat by any standard, over six feet high from the floor to the tip of the back which is covered with a sheet of gold and enameled and encrusted with precious stones, the majority emeralds and rubies. Glorious to behold and surely uncomfortable to sit in. There are crowns, not so much to adorn one's head as to bow it under the weight of precious stones and egg-sized pearls. Many people have seen the Koh-i-Nur diamond, the Mountain of Light in the crown of Great Britain in the Tower of London. Forget that paltry bicycle lamp. In the vault of the Bank Markazi in Tehran blazes the Daria-i-Nur, the Sea of Light. Both stones belonged to the first Mogul Emperor of India, and the nomenclature is not all that imaginative. In the diamond world they are truly a mountain and a sea in size. The Daria-i-Nur, pale pink in color, is table cut, an inch and a half long, one inch wide and three eighths of an inch thick. Weight 182 carats. It is mounted in golden filigree and surmounted by the Lion and Sun set with 457 diamonds and four rubies.

The more muscular Shahs have been known to wear it as an armlet, a brooch, or an aigrette. A modest ornament that one might more easily support is a flexible gold girdle buckled by a huge oval emerald weighing one hundred seventy-five and a half carats. For Queens' crowns a diadem solid with diamonds literally the size of rocks and necklaces and pins galore.

Nor is the treasure all adornment. Not many people would think of ordering a globe two feet in diameter composed of emeralds, rubies, and sapphires and supported on a stand entirely encrusted with diamonds and rubies but Nasser-ed-din-Shah did and it was completed in 1869.

Another trinket that practically no one would be averse to owning, is a generously proportioned snuff box made of deep green blazing emeralds and diamonds.

Besides these set pieces there are dishes piled with rubies, emeralds, and diamonds. There are bowls made of turquoise and rubies and caskets from which spill ropes of pearls looking for all the world like loops of spaghetti. There are bottles and candlesticks of enamel and jewels of incredible workmanship and an unexpected and piquant object, a pink silk umbrella with diamond ribs.

Twice while we were viewing the collection the alarm went off and the great steel gates started to close. It goes off pretty frequently. Not that anyone would be likely to attempt to rifle the stupendous booty, even those undefeatable geniuses trained on television's *Mission Impossible* and similar power fantasies, would find the going rugged but if anybody so much as brushes against a case unintentionally the alarm sounds and the gates swing in to imprison the offender. This fabulous treasure is of course not only for fun. It is the backing of the country's currency and infinitely more appealing than Fort Knox.

INDIA   NEPAL   HONG KONG   TOKYO

Always some countries appeal to our imaginations more than others and India for many people is such a one. Depending to large extent on our reading, we think of Maharajas and jeweled elephants, of the fearful heat of the plains and the cool hills where the families of civil servants go in summer. We think of curries and the Vale of Kashmir, of saris and turbaned retinues and tea gardens, of the kaleidoscopic aspects presented for our perusal by Rudyard Kipling and E. M. Forster and Rumer Godden and all the others who have written of the teeming continent and the average reader's normal reaction is, Gee, I'd like to go there sometime.

Norton and I felt we wanted to go too, plus which, if you are circumnavigating the globe, it's likely to be on your way in any event. Of course in India as everywhere else there is the seamy side and because the fabric of the nation is so enormous the seams are long and rough and they are manifold. If you want to go you brace yourself for the desperate poverty you can not avoid seeing.

From Tehran to New Delhi we took one of those delightful flights that pick you up at eleven-thirty at night and set you down in an unknown world at four-thirty in the morning. It is a long drive in the gloom from the New Delhi airport to the hotel but, informed by our taxi driver, we appreciated that at one point we were passing Embassy Row. For a reason unknown to me I had thought the famed American embassy designed by Mr. Edward Durrell Stone was oval in shape. It is not, it is rectangular.

Once arrived at the Oberoi Continental we fell into bed, awakening a few hours later in a comfortable room that overlooked a large free form swimming pool and a lush golf course. Everywhere were trees and greenery, a refreshing change from arid Iran.

A large part of the morning was spent on the telephone trying to get in touch with Naresh Johri, a young Indian woman working with the Ford Foundation. Charles McVicker, a mutual friend in New York, had written her about our arrival.

The fact that nearly everyone in the public services in India speaks English should not delude the visitor into thinking that means he can communicate. They speak the language but somewhere along the line the meaning slips a cog, our ears are frequently unaccustomed to the accent, and the result can be unexpected. In the end however I did reach Mrs. Johri. Having lived and worked for sometime in Washington, D.C. her accent had the ring of home. She invited us to dine with her and her husband that night, adding laughingly, "We shall take you to a good tough Indian restaurant."

Our next endeavor was the American Express Company. Closed for the day. I thought, Oh dear Lord, it's going to be Iran all over again, an eternal religious holiday. But the closure was out of respect for the death of General Eisenhower. If it had to happen, from the Indian point of view it happened at a fortuitous moment, since for them it was a bank holiday. We tried to mail a letter but the post office was closed. Then we went to a liquor shop. When you get your Indian visa you also apply for a permit enabling you to buy liquor all over the country but we learned our first morning that there are days when it doesn't work.

We entered a shop, smiled at the man and presented our permit. He smiled at us and shook his head. "Dry day."

"But I thought Tuesday was dry day. This is Monday."

"Tuesdays and holidays. Today is a holiday."

Just when people have the opportunity to enjoy a bit of schnapps. There is no difficulty about getting a drink in the hotels but the prices are altitudious: one Scotch and soda, $2.

Despite the liquor tariff we enjoyed the Oberoi Continental and liked its remarkably able Swiss manager, Mr. George de Kiss. I do not know that he personally supervised the planting but the pool area and surrounding grounds are well laid out with spacious terraced lawns, trees called neem trees and beautiful rose beds, in full bloom on the first of April. Although as soon as the intense heat arrives I imagine it must overpower them. The best season for India would appear to be October through mid-April. The hotel's public rooms are full of fresh flowers from the gardens; roses, snapdragons and pinks.

We were enjoying them as we waited for a visit from Mr. Daljet Singh another friend of mutual New York friends Jane Grant and Bill Harris. He presently arrived very dapper in white short-sleeved suit glittering with cleanliness and a mulberry-colored turban. He had a handsome aquiline profile and a silky black beard moulded to his face by an elastic band worn under his turban and passing under his chin. He was an agreeable cosmopolitan type and we were pleased when he accepted our invitation to lunch with us at the hotel and even more so when he asked us to dine the next evening with him and his family.

Our afternoon was devoted to sightseeing and a bit of business. Dr. Brown, the secure one who had been so sure a letter from the Gyalmo of Sikkim would be waiting for us in New Delhi, had to admit defeat. Letters from New York, yes. Letters from Paris, yes. Nothing from Gangtok. However, helpful Mr. de Kiss had already told us that we should go to the Ministry of External Affairs where in all probability a visa could be arranged and we went off to see how matters stood.

While the British were in India they built. Afflicted by the megalomania of the Romans in Baalbek, they built big if not beautiful. Great avenues, enormously broad, enormously long, lead to enormous red stone government buildings, abodes of the awe-inspiring British Raj.

It is true that history is repetitious and that generations and countries never learn from the mistakes of other countries and generations. Today it is the United States of America who has so obviously been appointed by the Almighty to enlighten the rest of benighted mankind as to the ways it should follow, to lead it with a kind but firm hand along the paths of righteousness. This determined paternalism is the concomitant of power and wealth and success.

It is interesting to read Professor J. H. Plumb's account of the British in India when heads were the size nature intended, before they swelled to bloated balloons and before conscience and common sense dwindled under the pressure of power and limitless wealth.

In his England in the Eighteenth Century Mr. Plumb tells us that when William Pitt's grandfather Thomas Pitt was Governor of Madras in 1697 "there were fewer than fifteen hundred English in the whole of India, including wives, children, soldiers and seamen waiting for their ships . . . Trade and trade only was their business and there was a genuine self-interested attempt to make themselves agreeable to the Indians. They adopted Indian habits in food and dress, and frequently married Indian women, sending their children back to England or keeping them in India according to the lightness of their skin. They showed deep respect for Indian authority and an intelligent curiosity about customs and habits so alien to their own, but throughout their relationship with the native population, there was a refreshing absence of moral vanity . . . they were wholly free from the sense that manifest destiny had called them to rule the native people."

History marched on.

In the 1760s when members of the British House of Commons, intensely envious of the wealth not only of Robert Clive but of many other Englishmen who made vast fortunes in India, feeling a belated twinge of morality bestirred itself to demand, " "What right had these nabobs to extort such riches from the simple peasantry of India?' They were satisfied by Clive's outburst: 'By God, Mr. Chairman, at this moment I stand amazed at my own moderation!' "

The Englishman in India considered it his destiny and his alone to supply good government to his animal brothers and he was of course implemented and encouraged in his attitude by the missionaries and chaplins who came rushing in to convert the heathens to the only true God.

Mr. Plumb does add that in the early years of the nineteenth century "There was better government, greater security of persons and property than India had known for a century. Ignorant as it was of native ways and native customs the British Raj was more just and less extortionate than its native counterpart. But the spiritual price India had to pay for these improvements was intolerably heavy and one of the minor miracles of history is that the Indian Mutiny did not happen sooner and with greater effect."

More popularly known as the Sepoy Rebellion it happened in 1857. It failed largely through lack of organization but it did result in the transfer of power from the East India Company directly to the British Parliament.

In 1947, with 106,000,000 people voting, Jawaharlal Nehru was elected first Prime Minister of the new republic of India. Today the native government sits in the enormous buildings of the retired British.

In one of them is the Ministry of External Affairs where we negotiated with a Mr. Rava who when he saw our letter from the Gyalmo seemed to feel that matters could be expedited. "Which will help," he said, "because usually it takes six weeks."

"We would appreciate that," we said, "because we haven't got six weeks."

We filled out the forms and went for a drive, uncharacteristically without a guide. Guides are by no means infallible and what is worse they are frequently lazy, one may well miss a real treasure if the guide isn't in the mood to lead one to it, but by and large they know more about a place than a first-time visitor and can at least enlighten him to the extent of arousing his curiosity which he can satisfy through another visit, questioning and study.

We did go to see and later learned something about the Red Fort the great palace of the Mogul emperors. This vast structure begun in 1639 by Shajahan, whom we will be meeting again, is a group of palaces, audience halls and army barracks. The red sandstone walls seem to stretch for miles, actually the length is three thousand feet and on the river side, although the Jumna has now changed its course and runs farther to the east, is sixty feet high and nearly twice as high on the land side.

While much beautiful marble work and the pietra dura panels —those charming pictures made of inset pieces of colored marble and stone—still remain, the opulence of many of the great Indian palaces has vanished and the red sandstone walls without facings and without the frescoes that once so blithely adorned them have a certain bleakness.

I try to evoke for the reader what I myself have seen, the impression made on an amateur viewer by a specific building, but I am aware that I *am* an amateur and that my descriptions are lacking in professional architectural terms. That this is an out and out loss to the reader, unless of course he is an architect, I am less willing to acknowledge. I have some books—the beautiful *Splendors of the East* is one of them—and in these professional accounts of the temples and palaces of India are phrases like ". . . three arcades, nine bays wide with engrailed arches supported by elegant pillars, the pillars being double on the outer faces . . . In the back wall is a marble baldachino . . . standing on a square plinth . . . with a curvilinear roof" . . . Later on we learn that there is a single-storied building ". . . with massive square piers supporting engrailed arches very deep in the soffit. . . ." I don't say that this isn't the way to do it, I just say that I am not up to it and I hope the reader will bear with me and from what I do write be able to form for himself an impression which while perhaps hazy is not too grossly inaccurate. Ready team? Let's go!

Within the walls of the Red Fort is an ornate building—that's the one with the soffit—where the original Peacock Throne used to stand. It was carried off to Persia by Nadir Shah in 1739 and there broken up, parts of it probably going into the Peacock Throne currently on view in Tehran.

Outside the monumental walls I engaged in petty traffic buying from street hawkers two or three of those collapsible bead-dotted interlinked brass rings, flexible toys that may be made to assume various shapes and that have the fascination of all tricky, trifling puzzles. They cost a rupee each, about thirteen cents, and three or four years before in Paris, one of them had given me a nasty turn.

My old friend Drue Parsons had taken me to call on a couple who were good friends of hers. Madame had on the coffee table one of the Indian biblots. I had never seen them and when I said I thought it amusing she insisted I take it. I refused saying "Of course not, I wouldn't dream of it," and that ended the conversation. We were shown around the apartment and a little later Drue and I left. Out in the street I opened my bag to get a handkerchief and there, lying on top of it was the puzzle toy. I must have looked like a death's head because she asked in some alarm, "What's the matter?"

"My God," I said, "I'm a kleptomaniac! How did this get here?" My dear friend whom I could cheerfully have garroted broke into a guffaw. "We put it there, you dope, when you were looking around the apartment. Ellie wanted you to have it so we popped it in your bag." At the Red Fort I remembered the Paris nonsense.

We went on to Jami Masjid, the largest mosque in India, but we would have had to wait for twenty-five minutes before being allowed in and as we were tired from our late flight of the night before we walked away, going instead into the Ivory Mart, an atelier across the road where they make embroidered evening bags and ornaments carved from ivory. The work is done by hand, mostly by old men and they are wonderfully skillful but it is wearisome to think of the marvelous prehistoric beasts poached and snared and killed so their splendid tusks may be turned into little boxes and curving figures and strings of animals crossing bridges; gimcrackery briefly the rage then locked away in closets as dust catchers. The handbags are pretty and useful and sell for ten and twelve dollars.

As we were about to drive away a boy came up to the car holding out for our inspection a naked baby who couldn't have been more than four or five weeks old. It had tiny skinny arms and legs and a bloated belly. I shoved a handful of rupees at the child and turned away.

"That's what he does it for," Norton said.

"All right, but what are we supposed to do? Watch a baby starve to death?"

The poverty of India is frightful and so of course is the cause of it, the birth rate. The Pope of Rome should visit that country, it would give him quite a jolt. As are all sane governments and organizations, the government of India is trying to control it—everywhere are posters exhorting family planning, showing a mother, father, two children and no more but humanity is slow to learn the facts of death.

A little farther on we were accosted by an old fortuneteller. Old but muscular who grabbed hold of my hand and wouldn't let go. Like the reluctantly held wedding guest of the Ancient Mariner I had perforce to listen. He warned me against a woman whose name began with M and assured me I would live to be ninety-one and die without illness. That sounded encouraging until it occurred to me he might have a plane crash in mind. He then thrust a tiny piece of folded paper into my hand and told me to pick a number below five. I picked three, unfolded the paper and there it was. It was a good trick and coupled with the prophecy of a long healthy life was worth the five rupees he demanded and which the doctor grumblingly doled out. A gentlemen with two snakes also popped into our path but we shooed him off, we had had enough of those in Marrakech.

That evening about seven-thirty Madan Johri picked us up and drove us to his house for cocktails. He was a dark singularly handsome young man, a commander in the Indian navy and he and Naresh live in a government house, simple but comfortable with a big walled garden where their eight-month-old daughter can roll about with the family pet, a beautiful police dog.

The abstract paintings on the walls were, we learned, the avocation of Madan who spends every minute snatched from the bounding main slaving happily at his easel.

Our sari-clad hostess greeted us with their baby in her arms and we presented the young lady with the handsome silver cup Charles McVicker, our mutual New York friend, had entrusted to our care and which had by then traveled halfway around the world with us.

After a couple of bracing gin and bitters the baby was turned over to an ancient Chinese amah and we departed for the "good tough Indian restaurant" Naresh had mentioned over the telephone.

It proved to be out of doors in a big courtyard and its name was Moti Mahal or Pearl Palace. The pièce de résistance was Tandoori chicken. Tandoori might be fancied by those who swallow flaming swords but less callused palates would in my opinion do well to steer clear of it. It is bright red in color encased, or so it tasted, in a shellac of cayenne pepper and searing curry. If one is to survive, the vital accompaniment is cold beer but this was India and there wasn't any. The chicken was followed by roast lamb which calmed things down a bit and then another chicken dish, this one on the bland side. I think. But it may have been that my taste buds were numb.

When our hosts asked us after dinner if we would like to visit the kitchen Norton and I said yes, being curious to see the source of such ignescent fare.

A long metal hood projected from the wall and under it the sweating cooks sat cross-legged in their shorts and undershirts. The ovens were sunk into the ground and long spits on which were impaled the red chickens and pieces of lamb were hooked over railings and when their time came were dipped into the pits to cook. Chapatti, the unleavened bread, is kneaded and slapped into flat round pancakes and dropped into the ashes to cook. It is very good.

We returned to the hotel after dinner and Naresh and Madan came up to the roof garden with us and we drank coffee and sat chatting in the soft air under the stars.

Another evening they took us to call on friends of theirs, Mr. and Mrs. Pahdahri. We had drinks in the cool garden and then they asked us to look at the house. It was new, spacious, and modern in design with terraces on the upper floor where they said they slept in hot weather.

There were three children, a girl, a boy and a brand new baby brother. Attractive Mr. and Mrs. Pahdahri were not heeding the government billboards. We met the baby's nurse who joined her hands together in the greeting of the Orient and our hostess told us that she ran her considerable establishment with only one servant. Of course there was the nurse and Naresh explained later that in all Indian households there is a sweeper—I suppose what we could call a cleaning woman or man—and a gardener but *that* is so well known that it never occurs to anybody to mention them.

Service in the backward slow-poke countries is so much more pleasant than in progressive, speedy America.

Most of the Travelers Tips will be found at the back of this book but one I mention here because it is apposite. In a city where you know no living soul, how *can* you be disturbed? You can be, so hang that Do Not Disturb sign on your door and instruct the operator if you do not wish to receive any calls. Having neglected to do this, we were awakened by a shrill peal at an unholy hour. I lifted the receiver. "Good morning ma'am I am your guide from American Express."

"You're early," I grumbled, "you were supposed to be here at nine-thirty."

"Yes ma'am. Good morning."

Reluctantly we order breakfast, reluctantly we rise. Three times the creature for whom I have now developed a holy hatred phones from the lobby. We go down to meet what we had anticipated, a crashing bore. The doctor indeed is so put off that he announces firmly that I may do as I like but that *he* is going to lie around the swimming pool getting the sun and relaxing. He does so and the guide having me alone in his power announces that we will first see the monuments, then shop. I announce just as firmly that we will shop and *then* see the monuments which is how it came to pass.

Following a suggestion of Naresh Johri I went to call on Mr. Bhagat Singh. To find him one goes behind the mosque and behind the Ivory Mart, through a short narrow alley and up a flight of stone stairs to a loft packed with brasses and copper and wood carvings. Metal to the left, wood to the right. On the right I fell in love with two carvings, one a long rectangle with trees and goddesses, another a female figure of pale fruit wood. I think both of them, and they were delights, could have been had for a reasonable price including shipping.

Before ordering them however I consulted the management of the Oberoi Continental and Naresh. They both said the only thing they could have said. "We think the man will send them to you, we believe he will but obviously we can't guarantee it." And the hotel added, "We advise all our guests against having anything sent." Who likes to lose money? The upshot was we did not order them and I think we were wrong. Shops in hotels seem more reliable for the reason that they are concessioners dependent on the good will of the hotel and the customer has a better than equal chance of receiving his purchases or of recouping his money. On the other hand there is no reason to assume that one not connected with a hotel is any the less honest. That is a matter on which the traveler must make up his own mind but my suggestion to anybody going to New Delhi is at least to visit the shop of Mr. Singh. He has some extremely nice things.

Leaving his crowded eyrie we went off to the Cottage Industries Emporium, a well-organized shopping center selling engaging trinkets, lovely stuffs, handbags, costume jewelry, flexible necklaces of beautifully colored enamel and seed pearls that are charming and reasonable in price—about $20 and more handsome old wood carvings.

When we left the Emporium, having missed it the day before, we returned to the mosque. It is huge but I thought of no great interest. The enormous courtyard is surrounded by an arcade but there too the tiles have been removed, the frescoes have faded. We took off our shoes and walked around in our stocking feet, a dirty procedure but one I was distracted from by my guide suddenly sparkling into life on the subject of the Indian government. "Sucking the blood of the poor," he cried unexpectedly. "England sucked the blood of the poor too but we thought that when our own people would be in power it would all be different." It was a cry from the heart and it was moving.

Understandably Indians feel even more bitterly about corruption or indolence or impotence with their own people at the helm than they did when they could blame everything on the British. Once *they* were out everything was going to be different. They forgot about human nature and staggering problems. My man went on, "No matter how good or able or hard-working I may be I can get nowhere unless I have relations in high places." That might or might not have been so, I had no knowledge of the situation, I could not tell, but I believed him when he said he received the equivalent of $1.50 a day. A chauffeur, he added, got $30 a month. No wonder they drive a tourist crazy with their incessant demand for tips. "In the States," he said, "workers have cars and transistor radios. We have nothing. The only way to change it is revolution. Communism, that's what India needs." It is not hard to see why he felt as he did although I murmured that I did not think it a system one should deliberately court. "Communism is not all it's cracked up to be. Few governments are so indifferent to the comfort and desires of their people as they are. Governments are only composed of men and women you know. Russians are corrupt too."

"But in Russia if someone is corrupt they hang him!" He said it with real relish and I could see a whole ballet of bureaucrats dancing on air.

Returning to the hotel we found a message from Mr. Rava our personal bureaucrat of the day before. Our visas for Sikkim and exit permits from India were validated and we had only to pick them up. *Much* less than six weeks. Now however we confronted the contrariness of human nature. We can go but do we want to?

While Norton was on his way to the Ministry of External Affairs to get the papers I fell into conversation with a widely traveled American official living in New Delhi. "Do you," said he to me, "do you *know* Hopie?"

"No, we do not. We have not had the privilege."

"Well," said he, "she's a dear but she's vague, Hopie is, very vague, and if you haven't heard from her again, and if she and His Highness aren't going to be there, you may well arrive in Gangtok and nobody at the palace will have the foggiest as to who you are or what you want. Plus which it's quite a trip."

"You mean long?"

"Long and hard. I know you're going to Katmandu. From there you'll have to fly to Calcutta or maybe Darjeeling will be all right but then you must fly to Bagdogra, end of the line. From Bagdogra into Gangtok is seventy miles in a jeep and the roads are pretty well washed out."

My voice sounded squeaky. "Oh," I said.

"You'll be seeing Katmandu and Gangtok isn't all that different. It's up to you and your husband of course but my advice is, Think it over."

We thought. It would have meant rescheduling our time in Hong Kong and Tokyo by four or five days at least. If their Highnesses weren't going to be in Gangtok undeniably the gilt would be off the gingerbread. We still had much that we wanted to see and do so we chickened out.

In the end we did hear from the Gyalmo again but she had sent her letter to Marrakech long after we had left there and we finally received it in New York two weeks after our return home.

That conversation with our American official friend was frustrating in more ways than one.

I had been struggling over the telephone trying to send a cable to the American Ambassador in Katmandu, the sister-in-law of my friend Isabel Bunker whom we had run into in Marrakech but Her Excellency, my American official told me, was in Washington with her husband Ellsworth Bunker. They had flown home from their respective posts, she from Nepal, he from Vietnam for the Eisenhower funeral and were snatching a few days together from their diplomatic jobs. "It's too bad," added my informant, "because she has a lovely house you'd enjoy seeing." Not a good day.

Mr. Daljit Singh came to fetch us, this time turquoise turban topped, to drive us to dinner and the evening was considerably more perky. On the way to his house we told him our intended journey to Sikkim had aborted and he told us an experience of his.

We gathered that his business interests were manifold and included the Coca-Cola concession in New Delhi and a contracting firm as well as assorted factories. One day he was in his office in his furniture factory when the foreman came in and said there were two young ladies outside asking to see him. "They're not bad-looking either," added the foreman with a knowledgeable wink. Mr. Singh was not a man to let a hint go unheeded. "Show them in," he said.

The ladies entered and indeed they were most personable and

notably soft spoken, especially the one who seemed interested in placing an order.

"Do you," she asked in almost inaudible tones, "make Hollywood beds? Those very big broad ones?"

Involuntarily lowering his voice to match hers, leaning forward and feeling like a fool as he did so, Mr. Singh murmured, "Yes, we do. Would you like one?"

"No," she whispered back, "I would like twelve."

"Twelve!" It was practically a shout. Softly, softly, mouse paws on velvet came the next question, "Could you deliver them in about a month's time?"

Mouthing the words Mr. Singh implied that he could. The young lady thanked him, rose and followed by her companion took her leave. She passed through the door but on the threshold the companion stopped and came back into the room. "I will give you the address," she said. "You know who that is, don't you?" Virtually in pantomime Mr. Singh said he did not. "That," she said, "is Hope Cooke Namgyal, the Gyalmo of Sikkim."

She has aroused our curiosity and Norton and I greatly hope we may someday meet the lady for we feel we have a long way to go. So far all we know is that once in New Delhi she ordered twelve beds in a whisper. Still waters run deep.

The Singh house was a spacious dwelling—we learned from our hostess that she and her husband have six children and ten bedrooms—and although there was no wood-burning fireplace Mr. Singh must manufacture mantelpieces in his factory for one or two of them were placed against the white walls of the living room. Maybe they intended to install real chimneys for I understand that in winter the New Delhi temperature can drop below forty degrees.

There were several people there when we arrived all of whom with one exception appeared to be family and relations. The exception was the Chief of Staff designate of the Indian army. He himself was an Indian but extremely British in speech and manner. Indeed aside from Mr. Singh's elderly mother everyone in the party was speaking English. It made me think of *War and Peace* and all the Russian aristocracy eschewing their native tongue for French before the Napoleonic invasion.

The men were in Western clothes although they wore turbans and the women were in saris. Nearly everybody drank Coca-Cola or fruit juice but whiskey was passed and I was relieved that two or three of the men besides my dear husband seemed to enjoy it.

After half an hour or so there was a general exodus as most of the group were going on to a wedding reception. On a bookcase I noticed a picture of a bride, one of the Singh daughters, a very pretty girl swathed in a diaphanous veil of soft pink with a ring in her nose. Some brides wear them, some do not, it is a matter of choice and actually we saw several Indian women, not brides, with small wire loops in their noses. We pierce our ears, why not a nostril?

Dinner was served buffet fashion under the very bright light popular in Asia. The unaccustomed highly spiced foods somewhat dislocated my innards but the dessert, delicious pistachio ice cream, was soothing.

When it came time to leave both Mr. and Mrs. Singh accompanied us back to the hotel and Mrs. Singh told us happily that one of their daughters was home on a visit with her month-old baby, their first grandchild. She is married to an American and lives in Schenectady, a somewhat different world from New Delhi.

Approaching the Oberoi Continental we passed the great rosy tomb of the Mogul Emperor Humayun with its façade and superstructure of arches, kiosks and a central dome built for him by his wife in 1565. It is one of the "sights" of the city but when I had asked to see it my guide of the morning said sternly that the office had given him instructions I was to be taken around the old part of Delhi and the tomb is in the new. The travel agencies make these arbitrary distinctions for economic reasons: two cities, two tours, two fees. I feel the traveler should have the right to state what he wants to see and if he wants to weave back and forth and is willing to pay the rate he should be able to do so.

About ten miles from Delhi the Qutab Minar, a superb victory tower dating from the thirteenth century, rises 238 feet into the sky; a shaft of convex fluted red sandstone ringed at intervals with ornate carved balconies from where the muezzin once called the faithful to prayer. He now sits downstairs and does it over a loudspeaker or probably if tired rolls a tape.

The New Delhi airport offers a very pleasant service that one could wish duplicated elsewhere. If you are leaving on one of these trying early-morning flights waiters come up and offer you hot tea, a real support when going through the endless formalities of tickets and luggage and passport validation that do so much to take the joy out of travel.

In our flight to Udaipur we landed for breakfast at Jaipur. Dr. Brown said grandly that he did not care to sit at the long general table where all the passengers were gathering, that he preferred to take nothing. I am a plebeian type and sat down. Minutes later, sniffing the good smells, seeing that the food was fresh and hot he swallowed his pride along with bacon, eggs, and coffee.

Another half hour brought us to Udaipur. Although skeptical by nature I too occasionally succumb to the wiles of advertising. My dear one is Madison Avenue's pigeon. It is by no means his professional attitude but in the non-medical world he thinks that if something is advertised it's probably good. My own tendency is to believe it has no value at all but where Udaipur was concerned we saw eye to eye and what our four eyes saw were photographs of the Lake Palace Hotel and we yearned to go there.

From the airport we shared a taxi with a very nice American couple, the Otis Gettles of New Jersey. He travels almost yearly in India, his wife less often. They had been to Kashmir, lived on one of the houseboats and loved it. The price seemed almost too good to be true, $10 a day. We had been dissuaded from going by those who had said that in the mountains early April would be too cold but the Gettles seemed to think that mid-April to mid-May would be perfect; good weather and not yet too crowded. Early autumn, however, is perhaps the best season of all.

When we arrived at the ferry landing and got out of the taxi we looked across the water at our hotel floating on its shimmering reflection like a fairy palace, its gleaming white-marble walls delicately shaded by feathery trees rising from the courtyards. It looked just like the photographs in the advertisements. We made the brief crossing not drawn by swans as would have been appropriate but chugging in a sturdy put-put.

Once inside romance begins to wane. Some of the suites still have considerable magnificence and all the rooms are spacious but they do not yet have enough money for restoration and repairs. The place is pretty shabby and the food to my way of thinking almost inedible. Norton disagrees with this saying I am too harsh. Maybe he is right but good it wasn't. However it is only fair to say that I had begun feeling ill in New Delhi and throughout the rest of the trip my appetite was so peckish that I arrived home looking about as voluptuous as a knife blade.

Still there were compensations. If the air-conditioning unit in our room was hysterical—laboring, rattling, banging, given to sporadic convulsions—and if there was no light in the bathroom our windows overlooked Lake Pichola, and we could enjoy charming painted and scalloped archways, lacey marble and white plaster galleries, enclosed courtyards abloom with frangipani and jacaranda trees.

The gardens and palace cover four acres, the walls rising straight from the water as they do in Venice. The palace was originally built by Maharana Jagat Singh in 1754 and succumbing to my weakness for local guide books I learned that "Walls represent mosaics and ancient paintings and a luxury equip of beautiful fountains baths reservoirs furnitures. Columns etc, win it a mellow adore of visitors."

In the first week of April it was hot in Udaipur much more so than it had been in New Delhi, for the city is farther south and although there was a pool in the garden it was for décor rather than swimming. The water of the lake itself looked dubious but in the afternoon when we went for a boat ride we stopped off at Jag Mandir, a neighboring island palace where they were building a large swimming pool and we understood there was to be a restaurant and casino as well. The island was inhabited by a wizened guardian and three or four children played with a tethered deer who had two sets of little horns.

As the boat drew away we saw a marvelous sight: flights of small green parakeets winging their way over the lake. Thousands at a time they flew in waves across the sunset to nest in the island trees for the night. On the mainland the white City Palace gleamed in the light of early evening, a mammoth wedding cake of dreams.

That night a dance performance took place in one of the hotel courtyards for the entertainment of the guests.

The backdrop was a carved marble screen topped by a gallery of slender columns and a little tower with a cupola top and the air was embalmed with the scent of honeysuckle.

The Indian music was strange to our ears and although a brief description in English was given before each dance the plots and rigidly stylized movements seemed very similar. The costumes were the stars of the evening. They were in the lovely singing colors of India: raspberry and hot shocking pink, flaming orange and gold and every shade of amethyst, plum, and mulberry. The next day we saw a woman walking in a sari of white cotton printed with a delicate and exquisite design of autumn leaves.

We had gone over to the mainland to visit the City Palace and on the landing stage we met an Englishman, a Mr. Davenport in charge of the sprucing up of Jag Mandir. He highly recommended the City Palace and the Temple of Jagdish. We went to them

both. Both are exuberant and splendid buildings. The palace, set
on a ridge, overlooks the lake and the brown barren hills beyond.

Built by the Maharana Udai Singh one of the Rajputs, those
members of a Hindu tribe noted for their militancy as well as
their opulent tastes, it is rich with carvings and mosaics. Marble,
alabaster, stucco and grill work combine to form the most elegant
and luxurious of dwellings. One gets lost in the never-ending
courtyards, is amused by the jaunty frescoes of elephants and
gods and gazes with curiosity upon the eight arches where in the
days when they were still doing it the Maharanas were weighed
in gold, silver and jewels which were then distributed among the
poor. Not that the rulers cared about them per se but the pious
act would ward off evil spirits.

In an upper story of a wing of the palace are three charming
small rooms decorated with closely spaced murals depicting the
daily life of the sixteenth century. Peeking through the crack in a
door we saw appliquéd against the wall a great gleaming brass
sun designed in the form of a human face. In times past it was
traditional not to eat before seeing the sun so on cloudy days the
palace personnel having no relish for empty stomachs licked tradition by gazing upon their man-made substitute.

Wandering up the road one comes to the nearby Jagdish Temple built in 1651. With its steps, deep myriad carvings and coned
shaped towers it is remarkably reminiscent of Ankor Tom and
Ankor Wat in Cambodia, those fabulous temples and palaces
built by the Kmers in the tenth and twelfth centuries.

Our next stop restored us to modernity. More or less. It was
a liquor store where we were able to buy bottles of cold beer.

Carrying them with us we got into the carriage we had hired
at the landing stage and drove out to a pretty park, the Garden
of Fountains, where there is a great round pool filled with
lotus flowers guarded by four white marble elephants spraying
water from their trunks. From another pond surrounded by raspberry pink walls rises a small white marble pavilion. It would not
appear to serve any particular purpose but it is decorative.

Since we were leaving that afternoon for Jaipur, after lunch Norton suggested we go early to the airport ahead of a fairly large American tour that had bivouacked overnight at the Lake Palace.

At the airport we had a reasonably long wait and I was longing for a cold tart lemonade but there was only the stepped-up sugar-content Coke of the East or the ubiquitous bottled orange syrup. That is the Western travelers bane; no alternative to warm fluids usually so sticky they barely flow.

Our scheduled departure time was 5:25. At 5:45 the airport manager announced over the loudspeaker that they had encountered a mechanical difficulty and the pilot refused to take off. He sounded offended as though the pilot was being capricious and unreasonable but although my heart sank and my stomach turned over once more I respected a professional's judgment and blessed him for his caution. Later an American who had come down from Agra on the plane told us he agreed. "I didn't care at all for the sound of things as we were about to land here," he said.

The trouble with many American travelers I have learned is that we are naïve. One of the passengers addressed the manager. "But why not just phone Delhi and ask them to send another plane?" The hitch in that approach is twofold. One is you don't "just phone" in that part of the world. Phoning is a full-time serious occupation requiring experience, guile, and infinite patience. The second difficulty is that in most Asian countries such offhand suggestions cause the inhabitants to lose face. In our own case the man was obliged to explain that it would be dark before a plane could get to us and to admit that the airport was not equipped for night flights.

"Nonsense," exclaimed the American. "If he leaves Delhi now, say within half an hour even, he still has two hours of daylight. We're all here, we'll be ready to pop aboard the minute he arrives and pop right off again."

The local man loses face even further. It is painful for him to say it but he must. "You see, sir, we do not have another plane."

Air India is a large organization. The government goes all out competing with other international lines and I believe they do it successfully but the result is that domestic flights are limited. The pilots and the planes are good but there are not many of them.

We considered renting a car and driving to Jaipur. A couple of young Indians who wanted to go too said they would share the expense but the distance is 250 miles and there was no car.

Further to intensify our woes we were told that in all likelihood there would be no rooms back at the Lake Palace as a large Belgian tour had moved in as we moved out.

In despair and in a hot jouncing bus we drove the long road back to Udaipur, diverted sporadically by a herd of camels and troops of black-faced monkeys.

As we drew near the hotel we began invoking Brahma, Vishnu, and Siva. The trinity was merciful for despite the feared Belgians we got our old room back again and although the delirious air conditioner had given up entirely with a good ceiling fan and cross ventilation we were not too badly off.

The next morning dawned hot and beautiful and to give ourselves a sense of security we hovered near the crew of the stranded Jaipur plane who also had spent the night at the Lake Palace. The pilot, a lean intelligent-looking man who inspired confidence, told us the engineer had arrived at eight-thirty. It was then nine and he expected to hear from him about ten. We learned there was nothing the matter with the engine, the trouble was a precision instrument. "Inverters," the doctor tossed at me over his shoulder. Of course, what else?

With my eyes revolving in my head like marbles as I watched the plane crew's every move, we sat in the big lobby opening on the lake talking with Mr. Davenport who had come in to oversee some work that was being done in the hotel gardens as well as at Jag Mandir.

He told us he had lived in India for forty years and we learned he had been with the United Nations as India's representative of agriculture and manpower. India, it appears, is now sinking 100,-000 wells a year and their next goal is 400,000. Twenty thousand tractors are in yearly use and they need twenty thousand more. He felt that progress while slow was steady. "Educated young people are going back to the farms but the terrible hurdle is still the birth rate. The population, you see, increases by one million babies a month."

"But all those ads for family planning, two children, no more . . . and the birth control information that we understand is widely disseminated . . . has that no effect?"

Mr. Davenport sighed. "I'm afraid it will take at least forty or fifty years for the propaganda and education really to take effect."

Let us hope that long before that is not already too late. Indian life expectancy used to be twenty-six years. It has now risen to thirty-two and naturally one hopes it will go higher quickly but the brute fact is that the early death rate acted as a kind of balance wheel. With improved health care and prolonged life if birth control is not practiced, and with determination, the results for India will be catastrophic. They will not be good for the rest of the world either.

We went on to speak of the chasm between the upper and lower classes of India in both rank and income and Mr. Davenport said that the maharajas were no longer bleeding the poor as they once had. He indicated the lobby where we were sitting. "As you see, even they are now turning their palaces into hotels. No, the current villains are the grocery store money lenders. Sharks who take away a whole harvest and dole out subsistence livings in exchange. A peasant borrows a hundred dollars and through the years pays over a thousand in interest. Belatedly the government is beginning to clamp down on the system to some extent."

About a quarter to eleven the pilot, whom I had been watching like that reluctant pot, came to a boil. He gave the signal and we took off for the airport. The plane took off for Jaipur where we landed a roughish fifty minutes later.

In Jaipur we sojourned in another palace, this one the Rambagh. Built in the mid-nineteenth century the Rambagh must be the largest hotel on earth. It is certainly the dirtiest. At first sight, from the outside, one is awed by its mammoth proportions. "What have I done," thinks the traveler, "to merit such splendor?" He soon finds out. He is doing penance for every sin he has ever committed. Beer and Coke bottles defile the lawns, several square miles of carpet cover the floors all of it filthy and threadbare. Near our room an alcove where the servants sat was spattered with syrupy drinks and ankle-deep in watermelon seeds. An honest American—he must have been deranged—volunteered to the management the information that his child had spilled Coca-Cola on the floor. The management charged him eleven dollars for damage yet that particular stain among thousands was indiscernible.

True, the rooms are large, fresh flowers are set about and the servants when not involved with syrup and watermelon seeds give good service. With the collapse of the one at the Lake Palace of Udaipur still in mind we were pleased to see we had a functioning air conditioner until a large piece of cardboard that had been set above it fell down revealing a window without a pane. The dining room was huge, cavernous and shrouded in gloom. On a far vaster scale not unlike the dining rooms of some of the old and crushingly respectable hotels of London, where families up from the provinces come to spend the season. Eating there was like eating in a nightmare and the food was nightmare food; put on the stove at six in the morning, I should imagine, and boiled throughout the day, then smothered in curry and brought to the table.

I am not thinking of hotels in some of the small towns of the United States and Canada which really do not rank as hotels but more as enclosures one enters for the night so as not to sleep in the streets, but among professional establishments catering to

62. The delightful tomb of Itmad-ud-daula, the grandfather of
Arjumand Banu

63. Pietra Dura detail of Itmad-ud-daula's tomb. Wine carafes
and drinking cups, the signature of the happy architect

64.   Durbar Square, Katmandu, Nepal

65.   Carved window frames and market platform Katmandu

66. Temple of Krishna Mandir, Durbar Square, Patan. Three miles from Katmandu

67. Tusahity, the Royal Bath, Patan

68. Terminal Building, Meghauli, Nepal. From here one may ride by elephant or jeep to Tiger Tops

69. Round dining pavilion and bedroom tree house at Tiger Tops

70. Elephants and the Rapti River. Tiger Tops

71. The Order of the Bath. Wash day at Tiger Tops

72. "At your service, sir."
     Three of the five Tiger Top
     elephants

73. Buddhanath Stupa. Big
     Brother is watching you

74. The Square of Bhatgaon. The gentleman enthroned on his
     pillar is King Bhupatindra Malla

75. Crowd on Nyatapola Temple steps waiting to see the float righted

76. One of Pam Am's great birds. The touchdown at Rangoon

77. Our elegant and irrepressible Wally Kwok

78. Hong Kong Harbor

79.   One of the huge refugee Resettlement Blocks, Hong Kong

80.   The National Gymnasium of Tokyo designed by Kenzo Tange

81.   Interior of National Gymnasium

world travelers the Rambagh Palace ranks high on the list of the ten worst.

We had arranged for a guide and car in the afternoon and around three-thirty set out passing through one of the eight gates to the old part of town. Jaipur is often referred to as the pink city because, we had been told, the buildings are made of sandstone. That is true but a more pragmatic reason is that many of them are painted pink, perhaps to keep in the spirit of the thing. There are some remarkably lovely buildings including one of two stories with many arches and columns topped by a small pavilion and the airy pillared kiosks or cupolas so characteristic of architecture in that part of India.

The main street, two and a half miles long, is an extraordinarily broad thoroughfare called Jauhrai Bazaar and that is what it is, the Street of the Jewelers. Jaipur is famous for its jewels. It is a great gem-cutting center and from all over the world stones are sent there to be appraised, cut, polished, and set.

Traffic was light; a few cars, a few buses, hundreds of bicycles and the patient ill-fed bullocks. The broad road is bordered with carved, grilled and picturesque pink houses that have both gaiety and noble proportions. Unfortunately they are marred by tin roofs and ramshackle little shops propped up against them.

Our destination was the Amber Fort and palace and that is its color but in this instance not the reason for its name. The village in which it is situated is called Amber.

Jaipur named after its founder Jaisingh—pur means city—is the capital of the state of Rajasthan and the palace was built by Mogul emperors who occupied it from 1526 to 1750. A wall surrounding it and climbing up and down the mountainside is eleven miles in circumference. A high stone platform stands at the foot of the drive leading up to the palace and from it we mounted a handsome elephant with a flat howdah on his back. His face and trunk were painted with a charming design of leaves and foliage and a pink and blue flowered calico edged with fringe was draped over his stately bulk. The mahout sat on his neck and Norton, our guide, and I shared the howdah, our legs dangling down.

As we wound up the cobbled driveway a musician walked beside us playing a long-necked stringed instrument called a ravanhatta. He played a quirky little melody plaintive and gay. It was a journey into another world and back into time and we looked down from our lofty swaying perch into a pretty patterned garden behind an old wall where schoolgirls in blue pinafores ran and chattered like birds in flight.

Arrived at the top, we dismounted in a large square at that time torn up and disheveled for they were planning to put in flower beds and more trees. Those already there were the ashoka tree a variety we had never seen before. Shaped like the cypress they were deciduous with narrow pendulous green leaves. The great problem in growing things is water for that part of India is sadly arid. The animals were eating dust, it was all there was.

Amber Palace, like the others, is built around a series of courtyards and some of the apartments are charming. There are mirrored shenanigans rather like those of Naranjestan in Isfahan but they fall short of the former's delicious euphoria. Bits of convex mirror are inserted in plaster lace work and the upper parts of walls are cut out in vase shapes, long narrow necks and full bottoms, filled in with what appears to be colored mica. It is a curious conceit but pretty and lighthearted.

We had intended visiting an adjoining temple but reconsidered on being told no leather was allowed through the portals. My husband and I are old feet at removing our shoes but it would have entailed leaving behind not only my handbag but the belt of Norton's trousers. "The hell with it," said the sophisticated man about the world. "I'm not going to drop my pants just to see one more temple."

We had ridden up in splendor but we descended shanks' mare passing on our way pitiably thin dogs nosing in the dirt. When I commented on their condition our guide laughed. "In India people are hungry, why worry about animals?"

"That's largely people's own fault," I snapped, "it's not necessary to breed the way Indians do."

The doctor squeezed my arm. "Take it easy," he muttered, "the poor guy hasn't had a chance. Why *would* he have any understanding or compassion?"

Just as one is thinking one cannot endure India another minute one finds oneself living in a fairy tale. Along came two camels drawing a flat cart on which were perched a dozen laughing children followed by their mothers on foot veiled in gauzy saris of lemon and orange over shell pink and raspberry. Behind them lumbered a painted elephant bearing two small boys on his back.

Returning to the hotel we found two friends of the Uhrys whom we had met at the Villa Taylor in Marrakech, Dr. and Mrs. Robert Heileg. They had come to see us but also Dr. Heileg was attending a Rotary meeting held in one of the enormous halls of the enormous Rambagh Palace. He asked Norton if he wouldn't like to go along but to my surprise my doctor refused. Since the speaker was to discuss Russia and China I thought he might have found it interesting but I have noticed that very often husbands do not fit into the preconceived grooves wives may have arranged for them.

Mrs. Heileg took me back into town to a jeweler she considered to be one of the best and although his authentic wares were beyond me I did buy for $16 a sparkling pretty necklace of imitation emeralds and rubies. She also very kindly invited me to her house for tea but my interior miseries had undermined my stamina and I was too exhausted to go.

I had found that the safest thing to eat was soft-boiled eggs. Usually they are fresh and demoniac cooks cannot invade the shell. We breakfasted on them the next morning and before leaving for the airport and our flight to Agra, Norton priced film at a shop in the hotel. No matter how bulky or heavy it may be it is more economical to tote your own. Duty is high in India and for a roll of thirty-six exposures of Kodachrome which at home costs $4.50 one must pay $11.

The Jaipur-Agra flight takes forty minutes and there the hotel is a different story. The Clark Shiraz is good. Clean, comfortable, well run, and with very decent food.

We lunched in the Mogul Room on the fifth floor. It is rather exotically decorated, there is a pleasant bar and we wondered why so attractive a place did not draw more people. Later the reason dawned on us in all its simple purity. The ground floor dining room is American plan, the Mogul Room is extra. The ground floor also has good shops, the specialty being inlaid marble boxes, ashtrays, plates, and small animals. They will pack and ship.

While on an unaccustomed binge of praise I would like to recommend the Clark Shiraz travel agent. He was agreeable and efficient and his name was Shyam Agarwal. One may get in touch with him at the hotel or his address is 179 Shazadimandi Gwalior Road, Agra, India.

Thanks to him we were provided with a car and guide and that afternoon drove to the deserted skeleton city of Fatehpur Sikri some twenty-four miles from Agra. Its history is as extraordinary as it was brief. Begun in 1568 or '69 by the Emperor Akbar, the son of Humayan of the great New Delhi tomb, it was for seventeen years the seat of the brilliant and opulent court of the Mogul empire.

At the end of that time in 1585 the emperor, his wives, his ministers, his servants, his eight hundred concubines, one hundred elephants, thousands of horses, carriages, and tame deer departed for Lahore and the city was left to its slow and quiet death under the hot sky. The beautiful and fanciful buildings that had rung with life and laughter and discussion, for Akbar was one of the most enlightened of rulers, fell silent except for the pattering of jackals' feet, their night time howling and the day time shrieks of peacocks across the echoing sun-struck courtyards.

The story goes that Akbar built the city out of gratitude. At the age of twenty-seven although he had sired many children none had survived infancy. He longed for a son and urged Salim Chisti, a holy man of Sikri renowned for miraculous powers, to grant his wish. Chisti assured him that his wife Jodh Bai would soon conceive and that the child would be a boy. This is indeed what happened and overjoyed the young father named him Salim after the saint and built Fatehpur as a thank offering. It is sad to relate that Salim, later the Emperor Jahangir, rebelled against his father causing him a great deal of unhappiness and bringing down his gray hairs in sorrow to the grave.

Before the melancholy denouement however Akbar proved himself a wise and immensely successful administrator, one whose name is still revered in India. He was a humane man who abolished the barbaric Bramanical custom of trial by ordeal and the burning of widows against their will. He established schools, he was singularly just in his collection of taxes and he became known as the Guardian of Mankind, a title which he may have been influential in bestowing on himself, since the slogan of his personal religion, one he invented, might be translated either as God is Great or Akbar is God. The people who genuinely admired and loved him probably embraced it readily enough but unlike Mary Baker Eddy's the emperor's contribution did not last.

Fatehpur Sikri is walled on three sides and in the old days a large lake that has since drained away bounded the fourth.

It is said that the court left the city due to a shortage of water and that is true but there were more pressing reasons of state; political upheavals along the northwest frontier, dictating to a great extent the choice of Lahore as a residence.

Palaces, audience chambers, the tomb of Salim Chisti and the mosque are spaced widely apart in the great open courtyards making full allowance for fine perspectives and vistas.

One of the most curious buildings is the Panch Mahal, an open five-storied pavilion, the stories diminishing as they rise each supported on a series of square cut columns. Although here and there a few frescoes remain the over-all impression is one of deep red sandstone and elaborate carving rather than color. Dominating the hill on which Fatehpur is built and reached by a flight of broad shallow steps is a high gate with a huge domed archway, the entrance to the mosque.

On a level below the great squares stands a tower from which it is assumed the women of the court watched the elephant fights in the arena below.

The pavement of one of the squares is laid out like an enormous pachisi board and the emperor used to play on it using the prettiest girls from the harem as counters.

It is difficult to see a harem without thinking of the thwarted lives of the women incarcerated there. They were prisons for the innocent and helpless for it was the rare family that could or would refuse an emperor's request for its daughter. Healthy young women, some undoubtedly of potential intelligence, were doomed to inactivity. There they were trapped and there they remained until they died. Due to sheer force of numbers they could not hope individually to experience companionship or sexual intercourse with their masters more than a stringently limited number of times throughout their lives. The rivalry, the jockeying for favor for themselves and their children, if any, must have been cutthroat. Frustrated, bored, impotent to change their lots, it is not surprising if homosexuality of the most passionate kind developed among them.

Our guide had told us that the emperor's favorite wife, Jodh Bai—maybe the wives got a better break than the ladies of the harem—owned an elephant to whom she was much attached and when he died she had him buried beneath the tower overlooking the arena. It is nice to know that once in India someone loved an animal even if it was over four hundred years ago.

Driving away from Fatehpur Sikri we passed on the road a small black bear being tormented by children and forced to dance in the broiling sun. I asked the guide if I gave them money would they give him a little peace and get him some food and water. The man looked at me with incredulous amusement. "You *care* about animals," he said. This caused an explosion to which quite naturally he reacted with anger. Our guides felt toward me the same hostility for defending the animals that I felt toward them for abusing them.

By early evening we decided we had waited long enough to see the great raison d'être, the pièce de résistance, the goal of every traveler to Agra, the Taj Mahal. We drove over from the hotel to the big parking lot outside of what appears to be a building in its own right but is in fact the red sandstone white marble-inlaid gateway to the gardens of the Taj.

One passes through it to view one of the architectural splendors of the world. There are as many opinions and almost as many written descriptions of the Taj as there are people who see it but the structure itself, enhanced by the passing of three centuries as much as by the romance inherent in its construction, stands today, a fable incarnate.

In his monograph on the subject Mr. J. Burton Page is enlightening. He explains that the name of the monument is a corruption. "The lady buried there was Arjumand Bano known as Mumtaz-i Mahal or 'Chosen of the Palace' but the local population knows no difference between Z's and J's and from their 'Mumtaj' the name as we now know it has been formed. 'Taj' however means 'jewel'—a happy coincidence but nothing more."

There are of course those to whom it does not appeal and Mr. J. Burton Page tells us that as knowledgeable and distinguished a critic as the late Aldous Huxley observed, and I must say it does sound snippy, that its elegance is "of a very dry and negative kind . . . the product not of intellectual restraint imposed upon an exuberant fancy but an actual deficiency of fancy, a poverty of imagination. One is struck at once by the lack of variety in the architectural form of which it is composed."

With Mr. Huxley I do not agree. There are arches, rectangles, domes, minarets, carvings, inlays, portals, plinths . . . what did Mr. Huxley want? The kitchen stove as well? Many will lean more to the opinion of an American, Mr. Bayard Taylor who wrote in 1853 that "It is a thing of perfect beauty and of absolute finish in every detail, it might pass for the work of genii

who knew naught of the weaknesses and ills with which mankind
are beset." While perhaps not going so far as to agree with the
genii theory it may well strike the viewer as the summation of a
deep emotion, the manifestation of a special time and world and
way of thought, a serene absolute.

The famous classic view of the symmetrically divided garden,
the parterres, cypress trees and long canal leading to the central
unit with its arches and shimmering dome and guardian minarets
at the four corners of the marble platform on which it stands, is
the one that meets the eye. Circling it however the sides and the
rear elevation overlooking the Jumna River are almost as impressive. In sandstone buildings flanking the tomb on either side lie
buried maids of honor and the favorite lady-in-waiting of the
Queen.

For many years elaborate arcane discussions have raged over
who was responsible for the architecture, who for the décor.
According to the Encyclopaedia Britannica Isa of Turkey was the
chief architect. According to J. Burton Page there is no proof at
all, at least before the nineteenth century, that such a person
ever existed. The pietra dura and the superb marble carvings of
flowers and leaves have been attributed to both Vereneo, an
Italian goldsmith, and to the French jeweler, Austin de Bordeaus.
Outraged shrieks of "It isn't so, it isn't so" reverberate around
a student's ears and really it doesn't matter, the important thing
is that they exist. Just to list the names of the materials used in
the over-all composition of the building is pure pleasure. Glistening marble of course but also turquoise, lapis lazuli, jasper, mala-
chite, onyx, coral, amethyst, chalcedony, cornelian and, a name I
never knew belonged to a stone, heliotrope.

This wealth came from all over Asia, some purchased, some
gifts, for news of the romantic enterprise spread over the Eastern
Hemisphere and everywhere monarchs and art patrons wished
to be able to say they had contributed to it.

The Taj was begun in 1632 and with as many as twenty thousand men involved in the building was completed twenty years later, a unique monument to love.

Shah Jahan and his wife must have known each other all their lives for they were born in the same year, 1592, and grew up in the same court and were married in 1612. In accordance with custom Shah Jahan had other wives, in this case probably acquired for political rather than sexual reasons, for the devotion between him and Mumtaz-i Mahal was profound. She accompanied her husband everywhere and when he came to the throne in 1627 she shared with him the responsibilities of state. She was a woman of intelligence and compassion using her influence to obtain mercy and concessions for political prisoners. In either 1629 or 1631, again authorities differ, she accompanied her husband when he set out from Agra to crush a rebellion in a neighboring province and died in Burhanpur giving birth to their fourteenth child, a daughter.

Shah Jahan's grief over her loss was overwhelming. Although still a young man his hair turned quite gray and for many weeks he saw no one nor would he transact any business. He contemplated retiring and dividing the empire among his sons. He ordered the entire court to dress in white, the deepest mourning of India, and the wearing of jewels, the use of perfumes or the enjoyment of luxury of any kind was strictly prohibited and every Friday there were solemn services at the Begum's grave.

For six months her body lay at Burhanpur and was then transferred to Agra where it remained buried in a garden until the tomb was ready to receive it.

Great married love affairs are few. Elizabeth Barrett and Robert Browning perhaps, Mr. Justice Holmes and his wife. In Egypt, Nefertiti and Akhenaton, until he started marrying their own daughters and having children by them and, one greatly hopes, Shah Jahan and Mumtaz-i Mahal.

There would seem to be no doubt that love spurred the Emperor to create great beauty at great expense but apparently Arjumand Bano had expressed herself as not averse to luxurious

memorials. After all opulence was their element. Shah Jahan
founded the city of Delhi—it is still known as Shahjahanabad—
built the Red Fort and ordered the Peacock Throne. When it
came to a tomb for the woman he adored he was hardly likely
to skimp.

Indeed he was planning a similar one for himself to be built
of black marble, a shadow contrast to the Taj. Situated across the
river it would be joined to his wife's by an exquisite bridge.
What with one thing and another this project never materialized.
The chief hindrance was his son Aurangzeb who demolished three
of his brothers in violent and unattractive ways and usurped his
father's throne while the Emperor still lived. He imprisoned him
in Agra Fort where he remained until his death in 1666, his
faithful companion to the end his eldest and favorite daughter,
Jahanara. Shah Jahan himself had been largely responsible for
the design of the apartments in which he was subsequently confined. They were large and lovely but he was a prisoner just the
same.

On his father's death, which he did all he could short of patri-
cide to bring about, Aurangzeb had him buried beside his wife.
Although distinctly unpleasant Aurangzeb was not a fool. He was
a good and efficient administrator who considered it quite unnecessary to repeat the enormous expense that had been involved
in the creation of the Taj. Since his parents had been so devoted
he said, it was only fitting they should lie side by side in death.

The bodies of Shah Jahan and Mumtaz-i Mahal rest in an underground crypt but the two sarcophagi are on the ground floor,
his slightly higher than hers, surrounded by an octagonal exquisitely carved marble screen six feet high.

Originally the Queen's cenotaph was covered by a pall of pearls.
It was stolen and a gold railing thickly encrusted with jewels
which enclosed it was removed for fear of further theft. If it
was Aurangzeb's idea to erect the screen in its place he had the
wit to pick an artist to design it.

The tombs or cenotaphs are covered with delicate and beautiful floral designs of pietra dura and the day we were there they

were strewn with nosegays of fresh nasturtiums. On the Emperor's tomb reposes a slim oval box that was used to hold pens. On that of his lady a flat tablet or slate symbolizes the creed that man makes his imprint on the soul and mind of woman. It makes the Muslim male feel secure.

We spent quite a while at the Taj and after an interlude for rest and dinner returned, as every right-thinking traveler must, to view it by moonlight. Seated on a bench in the shadow of the imposing gate we waited for the moon to rise high enough over the wall to shine on the gleaming dome, a mysterious and ethereal sight. Although many people were walking about, talking in hushed voices, the tomb itself seemed aloof, untouched and very still. Like a great opalescent pearl it shimmered against the night sky. Walking toward it I turned to look back at the huge gate; dark, massive, solid, and earthbound. The Taj Mahal seemed to float.

Around half-past eleven as we were leaving our guide urged us to stop a moment within the gate to look at a magnificent example of Arabic calligraphy over the doorway. It is beautiful and also curious, an extraordinary example of perspective for the texts rise for eighty feet yet appear to be of uniform size from top to bottom.

As we stood there a light was switched on, we gazed for perhaps half a minute the light was switched off and we started to go. "No no," cried the guide, "the light man, the light man." For the hundredth time that day Norton reached into his pocket. "If I am asked my profession," he said grimly, "I shall say Tipper." It is true that in India the eternal "Gim'mes" are exasperating. You cannot move without a hand outstretched under your nose. If tips are the only income or the major part of the income of attendants at public monuments such insistence is understandable, but if that is so it is an unfortunate way for a government to run its tourist industry.

Wishing to see as much of the superlative Taj as possible we went next day to visit it in morning sunlight. There is nothing

the matter with it then either. From what may be termed the
zenith in its category we betook ourselves to a less grandiose but
highly engaging mausoleum, the tomb of Mirza Ghias Beg, otherwise known as Itmad-ud-Daula. It was built by his daughter, the
Empress Nurjahan, who loved her father dearly. It is of marble,
the Empress having been dissuaded from her original conceit, one
of silver, by the argument that it would be a horrendous head-
ache for all concerned were it to be kept free of tarnish and such
other blights as weather might impose. What she, and incidentally
her old man, got instead is a small airy lace-like gem. Her mother
is also buried there as are other members of the immediate family
in four corner rooms opening off the central apartment. In
death the Mirza Ghias Begs reminded me of the Daljet Singh
dinner party in Delhi: members of the clan in close corporation
assembled.

On the walls of the pavilion are charming designs in mosaic
and inlaid marble the most amusing of the latter being carafes
and wine cups, the architect having been as distinguished for his
toss pot capacity as for his elegant designs and the tools of his
pleasure were his signature.

From this delightful final resting place we went to the large and
rugged but also elegant Agra Fort. It too was built by Sheh
Jahan and parts of it are still used by the Indian army. A long
sloping ramp paved with flagstones up which elephants used to
haul cannon leads into it.

The exterior is all very businesslike. Within the walls it is imaginative and rococo adorned with beautifully carved galleries,
columns and terraces. The grill work is intricate and lovely especially in the apartments used by Shah Jahan and his daughter
during their incarceration and the walls and ceilings were at one
time brightly painted. The glowing frescoes as a background for
the pinks and crimsons, gold and green and mulberry of Indian
court dress must have been an exhilarating sight.

Our eyes still dazzled with bygone brilliance, the picnic lunch
boxes we picked up at the Clark Shiraz Hotel to stay us on our

drive back to New Delhi, seemed distinctly prosaic. Even Norton, not as gluttonous for history and color and ye olden times in general as I am, sensed the contrast. "Twentieth century stinks," he muttered picking up the cardboard boxes.

We had been driving for perhaps half an hour when the air conditioner in the car broke down. Despite my frequent impugnment of it I will say that in India in April that particular development of the twentieth century is to be cherished. We suggested stopping at once to see if there was any remedy we might effect but the driver insisted in going on. "Just little more, just little more." Since he was at the wheel and we were not we continued in considerable discomfort until we reached a big tree beside the road. Here he announced we would stop. As we did so a snake charmer with a large cobra draped around his neck and an assistant with a fiddle immediately popped out of the shade. Hot as it was I wound up the window with a shudder.

"Come on," said Norton. "Come on, let's go." The air conditioner was indubitably on the blink but we were both convinced that the snake charmer and his pal were friends of the driver and that since we were in difficulty anyway he felt we might as well stop at that tree so his chums could pick up a bit of baksheesh from his American fares.

We returned to the Oberoi Continental, spent our last night in New Delhi and left early the next morning for Katmandu.

Driving to the airport in the early morning we passed a string of race horses being exercised, each led by a turbaned trainer. They stepped proudly, the sun shining on their gleaming coats. They were beautiful creatures and it was a beautiful sight.

The airport less so. All through the East the airports are grim examples of the results of overbreeding. Porters swarmed on us from every direction fighting for our bags, and tips must be divided between so many that they half starve. Were there fewer of them each, obviously, would fare much better.

We went through passport and customs formality with little

difficulty, muttered as usual when paying the departure tax, in India fifteen rupees or about $1.95 per person, and were somewhat restored to good humor by the hot tea thoughtfully brought by the airport waiters and by our purchase of duty free Scotch and gin, $4.75 for both bottles.

Waiting in the lounge for our plane to be called—I think we have spent a brief lifetime waiting in airports—we eyed our fellow passengers, especially three hippies, two male one female, bound for Hippy Heaven, Katmandu. Their only visible luggage was a guitar and in the early morning though the air was still chilly the girl, her lank blond hair falling over her shoulders was barefoot and attired in nothing more cozy than a bra and a cotton sarong.

Our flight, about two hours, was on India Central and as we began to let down over Nepal I looked eagerly out the window. The country was hilly and fertile, the farmhouses of adobe brick high and thin. Touching down at the Katmandu airport we revised our opinion of Indian porters. If they were like swarming hornets the Nepalese were ravening beasts; snarling at each other, clawing, kicking, scratching to get at our bags. The airport itself was small, filthy, flyridden and noisy but they were in the process of construction and there is no question that by now things are a great deal better. At least architecturally. I don't know about the porters.

Battling our way out to the road we were picked up by a taxi driver and an enterprising lad named Lal. He was a sweet-faced intelligent kid, all the children seemed to be sweet and intelligent, and his English was understandable. After a couple of hundred yards our taxi lay down and died and we had to pile out but Lal helped us to find another. He was, he assured us, a guide.

Driving to the hotel we explained that we would like to use him but that we understood a guide had already been engaged by the travel agency, however we would let him know. "Do you have a phone?" I asked. "Where we can get in touch with you?"

"No phone, no phone," he cried and his anguish was evident.

"Never mind, you come to the hotel and we'll see what we can do."

Our original intention had been to go to the Royal, the old hotel of Katmandu that figured so prominently in *The Mountain Is Young,* that other novel by Han Suyin, author of *A Many Splendored Thing* but we had been dissuaded. "I think," said our informant, "you will be better off at the Soaltee."

The Soaltee while no great shakes is perfectly feasible except for the food which, with the exception of breakfast, was lethal although in fairness it should be recorded that one day we were served a very decent mushroom and tomato omelet.

Pluses are a nice swimming pool, two tennis courts and a lovely fragrant hedge of sweet peas dew spangled in the early morning. An Englishwoman, Mrs. Rodell, acted as hostess. She organized a tour for the afternoon and confirmed for us our reservations at Tiger Tops, a junket we had been looking forward to for a long time.

The headwaiter who presided over our lunch was a pleasant chap and instructive. He said that Katmandu has a great tourist potential, which it has, but that it is not yet equipped to cope with the unanticipated influx of travelers—the country has only been opened to outsiders since 1951—and he groaned over the hippies. "They don't come to this hotel," he said, "they have a special place where they stay. Their visas are short lived like everyone else's"—ours were for two weeks—"yet they stay five, six, seven months." I had no desire to put up at the hippie pad but I was curious to see it. My desire went unfullfilled.

As he was sweeping up the crumbs and apologizing for the poor service the headwaiter tipped over a small vase of flowers on the table. He mopped up amid profuse apologies but we said, "Never mind, no harm done, we'll move over to the next table." We settled down there and had just ordered coffee when a waiter passing with plates of dessert knocked over a small vase of flowers on the table. Norton and I gave up and canceled the coffee.

At another meal when we were muttering about the slow service the waiter was entirely in agreement. "I know, it's terrible," he cried happily. "But what can I do? I am only a cog, a cog in the machine." And what a machine! He glowed with joy. The men who built the lunar module doubtless felt the same.

I hope I may not be accused of dwelling unduly on the quality of the food we ate but the traveler must brace himself for the fact that from Beirut to Hong Kong, with a few exceptions, Asia is a gastronomic wasteland. The kitchens are disaster areas and their product sinister.

The Soaltee has a small orchestra that played at dinner and while it was not unpleasant we felt the management would have done better to put the money into a chef's wages. One trouble with the hotels of Katmandu is that with the exception of fresh vegetables every bit of food has to be brought in from Calcutta.

The pleasurable reaction of those who live there in discovering that their city has become a profitable magnet for tourists is adulterated by the grueling shortage of skilled help and the need to acquire virtually everything. The airport is their life line and its improvement and enlargement their priority.

It seemed to us that the emergence of the so-called Developing Nations into the nuclear age has a fascination that could not have been present at, say, the opening of the American West. That was wilderness, uncharted and largely uninhabited. To do what they did the pioneers required courage and vision certainly but in themselves and in their environment there was much that was crude, wild, greedy, and ignorant.

Countries such as Nepal or India, Indonesia or Arabia or some of the lands of South America while usually poor and technically backward have still an ancient civilization, an artistic and literary tradition. The collision or more hopefully the confluence of old and new is interesting to watch.

One service that was extremely good in Katmandu was that of The Third Eye Travel Bureau. They have an office in town and a desk at the Soaltee. Presiding over it is a charming, capable, and distinctly personable young Nepalese woman with thick shining dark hair and a softly rounded figure draped in a sari. Her name is Mrs. Munni Shah and the office address is Kantipath, Katmandu, Nepal.

She will arrange tours, a sojourn at Tiger Tops . . . whatever you wish. She is also honest, a quality not necessarily indigenous in travel agents. We were longing to see the Himalayan range and there is a place, Daman, a three- or four-hour drive from Katmandu, where apparently the view is spectacular. "Why don't we hire a car and go there?" we said but Mrs. Shah shook her head. "I would like to rent you a car but at this season you would see nothing, it is too hazy." We were in early April. "Come back in October or November, any of your winter months, then the air is clear and lovely. Also you should go to Darjeeling in India where you have a marvelous view of Mount Everest." We made a note.

Actually Katmandu lies in that region of Nepal known as the Inner Himalaya at an altitude of 4500 feet. The temperature is equable ranging from an average of 50° in January to 78 in July, with June, July, August and September being the monsoon season. To the north is the Great Himalaya where it is bitterly cold and to the south the Terai or tropical region, a land of rivers and lush growth, all this in a country roughly the size of Florida. Katmandu itself is in the same latitude as Tampa.

Since we couldn't see it all we decided to concentrate on what was at hand and to that end drove the couple of miles into town where we left the car and climbed a steep staircase built against a hillside. From the top, standing in the roadway we looked down onto the shallow Bagmati River where naked men and boys were bathing and where low stone platforms on which the Napalese burn their dead jut into the water. We were sorry not to witness so time-honored, wide-spread and sanitary a custom but there was no funeral while we were there. Sacred monkeys gamboled along the stone coping of the road and a small band of ragged youthful musicians danced and jigged to their own accompaniment. Across the river was the Pasupatinath Temple with its two-tiered golden roof, the most sacred Hindu temple in Nepal, probably founded in the fifth or sixth century A.D. It is a fascinating structure but entrance is forbidden to non-Hindus. Katmandu is a textured city: its fabric is rich and thick and intricate, abounding in ancient stone shrines, pagoda roofs and heavy carved wood lattice work, framing doors and windows.

The square on top of the hill, Hanuman Dhoka, is a dirty colorful area crowded with conical carved towers, pagodas and demons, a kind of cross between Ankor Wat and the Palace complex of Bangkok although without the gold and glitter of the Thai capital. Rotting garbage and animal droppings covered the ground. A good many people were wandering about and on the floor of a small littered temple, bald-headed priests in saffron robes sat on the floor praying.

Hoping that in their orisons all our sins would be remembered we went on to visit the refugee camp. When China invaded their country about ten thousand Tibetans fled south to Nepal and about a thousand are settled in the Katmandu community. They are scarcely settled in luxury but they are considerably better off than the Palestinian refugees in Lebanon. A school has been organized for the children and in big sheds the adults work at carding and weaving carpets and woolen goods and making heavy silver jewelry. Their products are sold in a cooperative shop and when ordered by foreigners they may be shipped out of the country and the proceeds are divided among the Tibetans.

Adjoining Katmandu the ancient Newar city of Patan is an outdoor museum. It is also called Lalitpur, City of Beauty. Its Durbar Square, much larger than the first one we had seen, is a rich jumble of pagodas, temples, stone beasts and monsters, and a deep elaborately carved sunken stone bath, a tiny dunking pool used by royalty in the old days. The temples, they are dwellings as well, built around small courtyards, are dull blood red in color with balconies and window frames of dark intricately carved wood.

It is customary to pick a ten-year-old girl to be the goddess of the temples, a position she holds until her first menstrual period when she is replaced by another innocent. "Would you like to see her?" asked our guide. Since it is not every day one sees a living goddess we said we would indeed if so exalted a being would present herself to foreign strangers. The guide passed this on to a small boy who stood watching us with wide-eyed curiosity. The moppet departed on the double and sure enough in three or four minutes the goddess obligingly appeared at an upper window. She was a pretty child in a long tight-sleeved red silk dress with what looked to be a pearl dangling on her forehead from a little round cap. We joined our hands together in greeting but her Exaltedness regarded us indifferently and in another moment withdrew from the window.

We gave a rupee to the conjurer and returned to the square, an area teeming with life. The royal palace fronts on it and the market place is a raised stone platform in the center piled high with tomatoes and onions, garlic and beans and beets. Cows wandered about and the tiger-striped taxis, gray and black tigers, honked their way through the congested streets. The flag of Nepal fluttering over the lively scene has none of your conventional stripes and bars and bands but is a scarlet double burgee with two round white faces, the upper the moon, the lower the sun.

Before returning to the hotel we stopped off at the American embassy to deliver to her sister-in-law the letter our friend Isabel Bunker had given us in Marrakech. Regretfully we learned that the ambassador had not yet returned from her trip home for Eisenhower's funeral and a reunion with her husband, our ambassador to Vietnam. There was, said a member of her staff, a very *slight* chance she might get back before we left Katmandu but our luck ran out and we did not have the pleasure of meeting her. We were, however, impressed by the American embassy. No side. It looked like the offices of a small middle-class business firm, one that was modestly solvent but was spending no money on fripperies or hanky-panky.

Back at the hotel it was we who indulged in a bit of financial hanky-panky in the Traditional Crafts Shop of Saga Rana. We bought a small jewel-encrusted rooster and a mouse. The jewels were fake but the beasties had personality. The doctor ordered a warm Tibetan wool jacket and then my eye lighted on the erotica, two hand-carved panels of painted wood highly entertaining and innocent. On one of them a white bull is mounting a brown cow—how *now* brown cow? and on the lower half of the other two small brown saddled horses are at play, very trim and businesslike. Above them a lady and gentleman duplicate their activity. Everybody, human and animal, is extremely neat, the lady blandly resting on one elbow, the gentleman with not a hair of his gray mustache out of place. They are comical and gay and obscenity does not enter into it.

Nepal is renowned for the erotic carvings on the struts, which braced against the walls of the temples support the overhanging eaves, and yet they are singularly inoffensive. They interpret the facts of sex in a forthright if somewhat athletic fashion. To indulge in such curving and bending and legs cavorting at right angles, two partners would have to be in the pink of condition. It's probably all that mountain air. The Nepalese philosophy is that God made men and women and in order to get more men and women certain actions are necessary. Most adults engage in them, it is to be hoped with joy, so why be squeamish? Having been reared on the native art in all likelihood the adolescents of Nepal are remarkably clean minded. What is dirty or shameful about sex?

It rained in the night and the next morning we woke to relatively haze free skies. It was my birthday and Norton gave me a huge lovely smoky topaz cunningly acquired without my knowledge while we were in Udaipur. "But *when* did you get it? We were together all the time." He looked smug. "Oh no we weren't. Remember that time you went to the bank?" I remembered. I had gone to cash a traveler's check the day we visited the City Palace but the process took forever and while waiting in the carriage Norton had had the driver whip up the horses and they had gone to a jewelry shop he had been told about. The result was the impressive glowing chunk I held in my hand.

I left it in the hotel safe when we went to catch the small plane for Tiger Tops. On the way to the airport we passed the market going full blast. Produce had been brought in during the night and all the vegetables and fruit looked fresh and appetizing. The mayhem takes place in the kitchens.

Tiger Tops, patterned to some extent after Tree Tops in Kenya, is a tree hotel in a game reserve, Nepal's National Park and Wild Life Sanctuary, a tract of one thousand square miles of jungle and bush about seventy-five miles southwest of Katmandu. The flight via Royal Nepal airlines takes thirty-five minutes.

Try to get a seat on the right of the plane, because from that side, in clear weather, you *should* be able to see the Himalayan range. One touches down on the Meghauli landing strip where the terminal building is a pitched roof of brush mounted on poles, perfectly adequate since all that is needed is a bit of shade.

Guests who had spent the previous night at the lodge and who were taking our plane back to Katmandu began arriving in an assortment of jeeps but unfortunately another one meant for our party had a broken axel so we had to hang around for about an hour waiting for transportation. It finally arrived in the person of Bob Murphy, one of the two Americans who run Tiger Tops, driving a Land-Rover. We hopped in and bumped off through heavy jungle growth and coarse grass crossing sandy beds and the shallow Rapti River where we moseyed along the banks hoping for crocodiles. We did see part of the back of one somnolent specimen but it could not in honesty count as an exhilarating treat.

The considerable number of domestic cattle browsing along our way invoked Bob Murphy's justified wrath. They are strictly forbidden in the game reserves because they eat the high grass so necessary for rhino life. From time to time in order to call a temporary halt to the ravagement Bob shoots a cow. This throws the natives into an uproar but does persuade them to obey their own government's ruling for a week or two.

Having been to Tree Tops and Secret Valley in Kenya* Norton and I were eagerly looking forward to Tiger Tops. It is modeled after them but while simple is perhaps a little grander. Texas money. It is however done with taste and in harmony with its surroundings.

The rooms, about twenty feet above the ground, built on stilts and the branches of trees, are reached by rough hewn solid steps. They are more than adequate in size and are comfortable and attractive. The walls are bamboo, the ceilings thatch and three exposures insure ample ventilation. There were oil lamps, yellow linen curtains and slip covers and bedspreads of brown and yellow plaid.

Each room has its own bath—shower, basin, and toilet. Appreciating the sophistication we hoped the game viewing would live up to it.

Leaving our overnight bags—clothing is simple, slacks and safari boots or the equivalent for men and women—we went down to the dining hall, a very large circular structure with a stone floor, a central fireplace, a bar at one side, and tables scattered in the ample remaining space.

The guests numbered, I should say, about twenty and we all agreed that the first order of business was cold beer. It was a pleasant companionable group, one of the nicest couples being Mr. and Mrs. Julian Kelly of Savannah, Georgia. Madam K. was attractively endowed with bright brown eyes and short crisp white hair.

Norton and I considered ourselves adventurous but the Kellys were more so for they were going on to Afghanistan and Swat making their way eventually to Marrakech. They knew Rom Landau who had guided us so knowledgeably through the souks

---

* I wrote about these trips in, respectively, *Elephants Arrive At Half-Past Five* and *The Varied Airs of Spring*.

and tombs of the Saadian kings and we suggested they might enjoy staying with Boul de Breteuil. When they said it sounded like a good idea I promised to write her.

While waiting for lunch to be served we watched five of the camp elephants disporting themselves in the river. They have their own built in shower systems but not content with that their agile keepers clambered up their trunks and over their huge bulks as they lolled on their sides in the shallow water spraying and scrubbing and hosing them down. The elephants were ecstatic. They enjoy water as much as seals and otters and polar bears.

The game drive was to begin at three-thirty, one group starting out in Land-Rovers and later meeting up with the elephants and changing over so everyone would have the fun of the elephant ride. We asked to start in the car reserving our elephant until later. It is usually the better way because toward sunset as the air cools more animals are likely to be about and visible.

After having been out an hour we met up with the other team, five amiable docile beasts who knelt down on all fours while their riders dismounted and we newcomers climbed aboard. Norton and I drew Flower Lei Goddess and had her broad back to ourselves. The Kellys were on another and an enterprising young couple en route from Calcutta to London by bus shared a third with a large lady schoolteacher. Other guests mounted a fourth and the fifth carried his mahout and the head guide. Our own chauffeur sat on our elephant's head his small brown feet guiding him by pushing and caressing his ears. He also carried a long sharp-hooked stick which I cared nothing at all about but I am happy to say it was never brought into play on our outing.

From the clearing where we had mounted we moved out into the tall grass, some of the old brakes waving high over our heads. And from on an elephant's back the altitude is already not negligible. One quickly adopts to the gently rolling motion and to the quiet broken only by bird song and one's vehicle tearing up fresh grass.

We saw two gaur, largest of wild cattle, two small wild boar,

a wild peacock, and two deer. That is to say everybody else saw
two deer. I saw one and some waving grass. There were also six
imposing rhino. Viewing rhino from the back of an elephant is
a good way to see them but being so shortsighted they are suspicious of moving bulk and having testy tempers, I couldn't
help wondering what would happen if, alarmed, one of them
turned peevish and charged. Later Bob Murphy told us that occasionally they do. Once he was on an elephant when actual
contact was made but aside from grunting and trumpeting no
harm ensued.

The slight fillip of danger or what the tenderfoot thinks of as
danger makes the ride exciting. Most of the time all was peaceable
and the evening light on the grass and the river glowed luminous
and lovely.

At one moment our boy threw his stick at a buffalo to goad
him into a bit of action. He trotted off and our elephant moved
slowly over to where he had been, picked the stick up in his
trunk and handed it—if that is the word—up to his rider. Observing this courteous service and considering the domestic help
situation in New York the traveler is given food for thought.

One cannot say that at Tiger Tops the wild game is as plenti-
ful and as varied as that of East Africa, but riding the elephants
is a special pleasure, wandering about unmechanized is unusual
and stimulating. Also there is always the hope of a tiger. Not on
the afternoon rides, that is not when they appear, but the night
holds tantalizing promise that is sometimes fulfilled.

About six-thirty we returned to camp, tired out. Our contribution had been passive enough, we only sat, but an adventure
as novel as that can be fatiguing.

After a rest and cocktails we dined and with the dessert arrived
a large rectangular birthday cake with one tactful candle. Norton
and Bob Murphy had had a clandestine meeting with the cook
and this was the result. Everyone broke into cheers and sang
"Happy Birthday." I had a lump in my throat and was about to

cut into the handsome affair and pass around the pieces when word came that tiger was on the kill.

I don't like to have to relate it but what they do is to tether a live bullock in the tiger's domain which almost invariably attracts him. It is not so much that the animal is killed, all predators live on other game, but that the poor beast has no chance. The gazelle or zebra or wildebeest *can* escape his hunter, the bullock is domed.

I cannot pretend however that any sympathy interfered with our eager rush to climb into the jeeps and drive to where the tiger had been spotted. As we were hurriedly organizing ourselves Bob Murphy admonished us that we were not to speak a *word,* we were in effect *not to breathe.* Total silence was requisite. I kept wondering why our voices would disturb the tiger if the sound of the jeeps would not. I soon had the answer.

We drove, yes, but only a few hundred yards then the cars stopped. We got out and walking as quietly as possible, following in single file the flashlight beams playing on the jungle path we came to a blind, a stockade of logs. Small squares cut into them at intervals served as windows and a couple of rough benches stood under them. We knelt or sat on the benches and peered out. There, perhaps seventy-five yards away from us, at the foot of an incline lighted by a couple of powerful electric torches held by Bob and one of the camp boys, a magnificent tiger was enjoying his dinner.

He was a big animal, Bob said later nearly ten feet long and weighing about three hundred and fifty pounds—and he was superb. His black striped coat was a deep rich golden orange and when once or twice, suspicious of an imagined sound, he turned his head our way his white muzzle was stained crimson with blood.

I do not know whether or not William Blake ever saw a tiger. If he did it was in all likelihood in a zoo for he never went to Asia but it was impossible to gaze upon that beautiful creature and not recall the evocative cadences learned in childhood:

Tiger, tiger, burning bright, in the forests of the night,
What immortal hand or eye could frame thy fearful symmetry?

The strangest part of the scene was the silence. Although
there were fifteen or twenty of us we had been well indoctrinated.
There was no whisper, scarcely a breath nor was there any
sound from the tiger.

We could see him, his chest raised up on the carcass of the bullock, his claws tearing at its flesh but we could hear nothing.
We watched him for about twenty minutes and until we return to
Nepal, which we want to do, I never expect to see a sight to rival
him. A tiger in a zoo is no longer the same species.

We went back to the lodge and the birthday cake and a discussion of tiger lore. Bob Murphy said he had seen a male kill
two of his own cubs out of a litter of four. When we queried so
unparental an act Bob said it was because he wanted the female
to stop nursing and come into heat again which is what happened.
The male sex is very self-centered.

Murphy and the managing director, John Coapman, who was
not there when we were, are working hard to make their lodge
even more successful than it is. They need more deer, they need
more game of all sorts and fortunately the King of Nepal has
ordered that the sanctuary be maintained. But while working
and building a clientele the Tiger Top people wait to see what
happens, for the King has had three coronaries. Were he to die
all kinds of political bickering and power plays would ensue and
it is perhaps too much to hope that Nepalese politicians would
be more sensitive to the vital importance of wildlife and the
conservation of their nation's ecology than are their American
counterparts.

We did not see King Mahendra and his Queen but we saw
several photographs of them. They seemed very serious and
earnest and they had both left their glasses on. It was rather
touching but perhaps they felt it was more honest that way. I
was disillusioned to learn that so sincere a chap dissolved an

elected Parliament in 1960, jailed the prime minister and suspended the fundamental rights guaranteed by the constitution.

The country is now ruled directly by the King with a council of ministers who function under his chairmanship and with army officers in the key departments of government.

For whoever rules the job is not easy. Despite its small size, five hundred miles from east to west and less than half that from north to south and its small population, approximately nine and a half million, Nepal is infinitely complex and varied. A government must cope with assorted tribes, religions, political beliefs, nearly universal illiteracy, a tottering economy and population densities varying from practically no one on the slopes of the Himalayas to 47,783 persons per square mile in urban Katmandu.

For those interested in that part of the world I suggest *The Himalayan Kingdoms,* a Van Nostrand Searchlight book written by Pradyumna P. Karan of the University of Kentucky and William M. Jenkins, Jr. of Western Kentucky State College. It is succinct and extremely informative.

Our overnight trip to Tiger Tops came to about $150 for two including airfare, room, board, bar bill, elephant ride and tiger viewing. The season runs from October 1 to June 15.

If making reservations one may write directly to:

Tiger Tops (P) Ltd.

P.O. Box 242, Katmandu, Nepal.

For those who enjoy long-distance telephoning and to whom cost is a bagatelle the number is Katmandu 12706.

Or you may also write to:

Tiger Tops (P) Ltd.

1112 Vaughn Building

Dallas, Texas 75201 U.S.A.

I do not know what the capital P in parentheses stands for.

When leaving the lodge one may have a last go on an elephant if he so desires and ride to the airstrip or take the sissy's way, a Land-Rover. Returning to Katmandu we touched down at Pokhara. Their airport is a strip and a windsock and the terminal is even nicer than that of Meghauli: a huge tree under which the traveler awaits his plane. On landing we were immediately surrounded by a crowd of Tibetan children including a pretty girl of ten or twelve and two enchanting small boys who spoke astonishingly good English. We were asked if we were near Mount Everest and one of them pointed proudly in the direction of some haze and clouds assuring us it was right there. We were misinformed but we *were* near Annapurna and when the clouds parted momentarily we had a glimpse of a majestic snow-covered slope. We would have preferred the peak but when it comes to mountains and famed volcanoes we are humble, having learned long ago that one settles for such snippets as deign to present themselves through the shrouding mists.

In the afternoon we strolled through the grounds of Pasupatinath Temple that we had previously seen from across the river. Desperately poor cripples may live in the temple grounds where as our guide said, "Their lodging and fooding is given them by the government." They are indeed pitiable but the constant unrelenting begging accompanied by self pitying nasal whining does not touch the heart. One could easily pauper oneself in India in self-defense. Even the babies beg. I waved at a three- or four-month-old infant in its mother's arms and promptly a tiny hand shot out.

One of the most curious features of the Katmandu Valley are the stupas, shrines peculiar to that part of the world. Built up on platforms they are huge white plaster-covered brick domes on which are set high step-pyramid towers topped by a gold umbrella shaped pavilion or kiosk. On the four sides of the base of the pyramid two big painted eyes gaze out over the four points of the compass. Strings of brightly colored prayer flags like ships burgees stretch from the summit down to poles driven into the ground. The pyramid tower steps represent the way to heaven and the eyes are the eyes of Buddha, supposedly symbolic of peace and prosperity, but one can also get a distinct Big Brother Is Watching You feeling.

Tibet and Nepal have always been allies and religious companions and it has been the Tibetans who have kept the great stupas in repair. One must hope with D. L. Snellgrove, the distinguished authority on Nepal, that despite their troubles with China they will be able to continue to do so.

It was prayer time and from the base of the stupa we looked down into the road where under a white awning stretched from the side of a house a group of monks and women were praying aloud. From a window across the street came the sound of more prayers.

Inspired by so much holiness we went into a temple and were rewarded for the purity of our hearts for it was a delight. Reasonably clean, this one, and brightly painted, with three goddesses, one deep bright blue, one blazing red and one a striking Kelly green, each damsel standing on one foot the other leg crooked at a sharp rakish angle. The beamed ceiling was alive with fierce tigers and a ferocious Pekinese with a green mane and green feathers on his legs.

We felt that was a *good* religion and passed through alleys thronged with worshippers and shaven headed priests, male and female, draped in yellow and dark red robes, some carrying black umbrellas against the sun, to visit a couple of other temples. These were so dirty they were hard to distinguish from junk shops. The floors were littered with priests' soiled robes and frayed prayer rugs.

In the unpaved streets dogs as hungry as those of India rooted in the dust for scraps of food or, mercifully, slept in such patches of shade as they could find. The lot of much of the populace is little better and yet aside from the beggars the Nepalese are a beguiling people. They smile a great deal, they are friendly and intelligent and theirs is a world of color. A group of schoolgirls ran past us wearing turquoise pants and skirts, white scarves fluttered around their necks and they had pink flowers in their hair.

A good deal of building is going on in Katmandu and they were planning to pave the streets and will doubtless introduce sanitation and by banishing disease create a serious population problem.

Since our original plan had been to stay at the Royal Hotel we stopped by to see if there was any mail and went up to the Yak and Yeti bar for a beer. It is or was a well-known rendezvous and I believe used to ring with bonhomie and cheer but the old days have gone. It appeared to us that the hotel was falling into desuetude but possibly we were simply there at the wrong time of day.

In the afternoon we drove nine miles to Bhatgaon, the third city forming, along with Katmandu and Patan, the valley trinity. It is an extraordinary spot and its Durbar Square is remarkably rich in temples and carvings, erotic and non.

Although the city itself was founded in A.D. 889 none of the buildings one sees today is earlier than the fifteen century. One of them has been transformed into a museum housing a collection of Nepalese and Tibetan paintings mostly of gods and demons. The best ones unfortunately are hung above a moulding and as the lighting is virtually nonexistent it is difficult to see them. The outdoor splendors are more rewarding, especially the dark heavy beautiful lattice work on the fifty-five windows of the old royal palace and the Golden Gate, a magnificently carved doorway considered one of the finest pieces of art in the country. Through it one enters another museum where there are some interesting wood carvings.

The Great Goddess, a perculiarly hideous creature with short fat little arms juts from the upper arch but she and the façade of the building are surmounted by a roof topped in turn by lyrical figures, the royal insignia; elephants, umbrellas, flags, centaur-like creatures, all sorts of gaiety, beautifully sculpted in metal.

The Nepalese have always been superb craftsmen and it is sad that theirs is a dying skill.

Another renowned building in the square is the Nyatapola Temple, a rare five-tiered pagoda dating from 1708. The building itself stands high on five terraces, each adorned with stone figures. The first is furnished with two men, the one above with two elephants ten times stronger than men, the one above that with two lions, ten times stronger than elephants, the next with two griffins, although I personally doubt that they are ten times stronger than lions, and above them two gods Baghini and Singhini who must indubitably be stronger than griffins.

The day we were there a crowd had inundated the square; I should think two thousand people, possibly more. They milled around and flowed up the temple terraces and were packed tight on the steps. The reason for all the excitement was a huge overturned float that had been constructed for a festival that was to take place the following week. Top heavy, it had keeled over the night before and now a truck and crane had arrived and an effort was about to be made to right it. We wanted to see it for I am sure the exuberant crowd would have cheered wildly but we were closely packed and having no idea how much time a victorious maneuver might require, we squeezed our way through the mob to wander about a less densely populated part of town.

A charming little boy, for once not a beggar, joined us. He spoke good English and had a few words of French and Italian. He must have had an able teacher but then, as I say, one is immediately struck by the intelligence of the Nepalese.

The next morning we left early for the airport, a wise procedure for getting out of the country is an involved process requiring forms and documents and long unexplained waits and again the porters swarmed over us, snatching our bags, snarling and screaming at each other. They reminded me of nothing so much as the hyenas and vultures we had seen on a carcass in East Africa.

Once one succeeds in sorting out from the pack those who have really rendered service with the luggage and tips them they calm down and are so sweet and helpful that unworthily one thinks, Oh God, they're only doing it for another tip.

The flight from Tribhuban Airport, it is named after the late king, the father of the present King Mahendra, to the DumDum Airport of Calcutta is an hour and forty minutes. Driving away from it one understands the well-worn phrase "the teeming millions of India." They coursed through the streets of the enormous city, a solid river of humanity, almost all of them clothed in dirty white garments with the exception of the schoolgirls who were in clean white blouses and skirts with red bows on their shining pigtails.

Bullocks and buses, bicycles, taxis, and rickshaws thronged the boulevards. Curbside markets, no matter how poor and dilapidated, still exert a fascination and we passed a five-story house, its façade adorned with balconies and beautiful carvings and grill work. It must once have belonged to a very rich man in what would have been at the time an elegant quarter of the city.

As we drew up at the Grand Oberoi Hotel my heart sank. It was right on the street, old Chowringhee Road current Jawaharlal Nehru Road, in the dirtiest and noisest section of the city. We asked for a quiet room and the receptionist obligingly changed our first reservation, which had apparently been considered grander since it overlooked the broad brawling avenue, and we heard him tell a bell boy to move the flowers to our new quarters. They never materialized but having trekked to our room we could understand why. The Oberoi Grand is another of the vast caravanseries of Asia and from one place to another is a five-mile hike. We walked forever, climbed a flight of stairs, passed through an enormous gallery where we looked down over the railing into a gigantic well that was the dining room but not being air conditioned it was not in use. A small girl with an amah in attendance was crouched on the floor looking down too. Perhaps she was hoping for a gay dinner party. Only a part of the hotel was air conditioned and heavy double doors separated heaven from hell. Passing through them into coolness we reached an elevator and were raised to the fourth floor and our hideously furnished suite. There were signs all over the hotel saying PLEASE DO NOT TIP IT IS NOT EXPECTED but the personnel had not read them.

As I opened our bathroom door I leaped back with a shriek. A large lizard startled the daylights out of me. I say to myself that I am not afraid of lizards but I am not keen on being cooped in a small enclosure with a large one. We summoned two bell boys and eventually he disappeared although I think they had only chased him down an open drain in the corner and during our night's stay we kept an upturned wastebasket over it.

It was too early for dinner so we decided to go out and ramble about a bit although getting back to the front door must have consumed a good fifteen minutes. Even so the Oberoi Grand is not as big as the Rambagh Palace of Udaipur.

The streets near the hotel bristled with homebound crowds and again the beggars swarmed like locusts; whining children, nattering adults. One man didn't beg but contented himself with accompanying and harassing us. He fell into step beside us and we couldn't shake him off.

"Where you from?" he asked. "California?"

"No."

"Where? New York?"

"It's none of your business where. Please leave us alone."

"Come see market, market down street. Come, I show you."

"Please go away. We are not interested in seeing the market." Actually we were but not in his company. We deliberately passed it by, finally succeeded in shedding him and then returned to view it on our own. We were not tempted by the wares but were interested to see four bookshops in one short street and we watched for a few minutes the men who were doing a brisk business selling freshly squeezed orange and pineapple juice from electric blenders. Finally the beggars swarmed so badly—they were like clouds of insects—that although we didn't particularly want to we went back into the hotel for sanctuary.

We dined in our room and the authentic mulligatawny soup and the local beckti fish were very good. Having to arise at four-thirty to make the Hong Kong plane we left a call with the operator and went to bed and to sleep. At twelve-thirty the phone rang. It was Pan Am telling us the morning flight would be delayed half an hour. A thoughtful service but we would have preferred not to have been wakened. I then ring the operator and ask him to change our call from four-thirty to five and having already ordered tea and toast for the earlier hour, stick a note in the door asking the waiter please to return at five. With some difficulty we finally get back to sleep. At four-thirty there is a knock on the door. Tea and toast. The phone rings. "Four-thirty," says the operator, "time to get up." Norton says, "What the hell." We get up, breakfast and dress. At five the phone rings again. "Five o'clock, time to get up."

"Thanks. We know." Surprisingly no second breakfast arrives. We made the long trek down to the front door followed by a train of porters, our bags on their heads looking like an old-time safari.

While waiting for the airport bus we strolled along the street in front of the hotel. Not half a block away I counted eighteen men asleep on the pavement. A few had rags or newspapers under them, most had nothing. It seemed utter destitution yet in the climate of India it is perhaps preferable to sleeping in sweltering hovels made of mud bricks or flattened tin cans.

When the bus came we got in and as we waited for it to pull away from the door beggars crowded around holding up their hands to the windows. A quite beautiful boy looked at me with dark mournful eyes. "Money, money," he murmured softly. I looked at him without emotion and as the bus pulled away he and the others were left behind. The begging is habitual, it grates on the nerves yet the poverty is overwhelming.

On the way to the airport we passed through the slum district of Calcutta. Along the streets the sleepers outside the Oberoi Grand were multiplied a hundred fold. It was 6 A.M. The city was beginning to waken and, marginal though it was, a way of life was obviously organized. Narrow alleys between the building served as filthy but convenient latrines and from pumps set at intervals along the curb what looked to be clean water gushed abundantly. A few people had tooth brushes and were washing their teeth and booths were set up where one could get tea and the wherewithal for breakfast. It was poor, public, endurable.

To us it was very sad yet it did not induce the same crushing sense of despair nor the outrage we had felt on seeing in the early morning thousands of Africans outside Johannesburg pouring from the wretched hovels that were their homes on their way to work in the white controlled mines. This was probably because in India their woes though real are not imposed by a dominant race. They are indigenous and in part their own doing caused primarily by relentless breeding, vast unproductive areas inducing national poverty and by a government not yet capable of the gigantic task of effective reform.

To try to judge Calcutta from an overnight stay is as presumptuous as it would be to assess any other great city with an equal lack of knowledge. This I do not mean to do and what I put down is simply our own impression and experience. To us, thirteen-day visitors, the great ancient country seemed composed of equal parts heartbreak, exasperation and beauty.

Nearing the airport we left behind the awakening poor and passed canals abloom with water hyacinths. I thought them very pretty. "Don't say that to a southern farmer," Norton said, "they pass their lives fighting them. Indians must too." Trees along the road were circled by walls of open brick work and the good doctor's theory which I surmise to be correct was that they were to protect the leaves from being eaten by cattle.

The Katmandu airport had been a dirty bedlam but for reasons that were understandable. Calcutta is a huge modern city and its airport is a scandal; dirty and ill-equipped. Having cleared formali-

ties one must walk in the blazing sun to a departure lounge
where it is impossible to get even a drink of water.

However, while waiting for our plane to be called we had one
lucky break, we met a delightful American couple whom we had
glimpsed the evening before at the hotel. They were David and
Mary Lou Martin from Saudi Arabia and their three youngsters:
two small boys and Miss Elizabeth aged three.

He was a schoolteacher involved with Aramco and they were
interested to hear we had been in Jidda, Riyadh, and Dhahran.
"How did it come about?" They asked, "Who sponsored you?"
We explained about Sheikh Kamal Adham, Mr. Olayan and company. "If you ever want to come again," they said, "let us know,
we'll be happy to put in a good word."

David Martin was a musician and would sometimes go to Jidda
from Dhahran to tune pianos for the diplomatic corps, native
Arabian tuners not being in heavy supply. When we observed that
we had been favorably impressed by Ambassador Eilts, Mary Lou
said sadly, "Yes but he is not musical."

They seemed to us intelligent parents in action. When small
Elizabeth let out a scream of frustration seeing her mother put
something she wanted in her handbag, instead of the immortal
" 'Shut up!' she explained" which I fear would have been my own
reaction Mary Lou said calmly "Well now let's see what we've
got in here that's interesting," and she pulled out an emery board.
Within seconds the moppet was contentedly filing away at her
minute nails. One of the boys was naughty. Mary Lou said,
"That's too bad. I had something nice planned for your birthday
in Hong Kong. Now I guess we can't go through with it." A
mantle of pure-holy-altar-boy descended on the miscreant.

With so much progressive and permissive lack of education going on it's refreshing to see parents who are smarter than their
children, and who discipline them both gently and effectively.

The Martins were on their annual holiday and when I said how
lucky the youngsters were to travel so extensively Mrs. Martin
laughed a little ruefully. "But it works the other way too. Kids

who live as we do, in out of the way parts, get very blasé. When someone says, 'Where are you going on your vacation?' I've heard them say 'Oh around the world again I guess.' But where else *can* you go?"

The small fry were looking forward eagerly but not without apprehension to a visit with their grandparents in the States. Grandpa and Grandma, we gathered, were no-nonsense types.

When our flight was finally called the airline made good its famous slogan "Pan Am makes the going great." It was great to get out of hot dirty Calcutta into a cool clean spacious plane. To be served cold fresh fruit juice and later a good breakfast. Also we were able to succor a fellow creature who was suffering from La Tourista. Norton handed him six sun cholera capsules which he received like a devout Catholic ingesting the Host.

Although the actual flying time from Calcutta to Hong Kong is about four and a half hours we landed briefly in Rangoon and Bangkok where we were sorry to say goodbye to the Martins.

From Bangkok to Hong Kong the flight passes over Vietnam. Speeding through the sky with every comfort and convenience it was strange to realize that thirty-five thousand feet below us were blood and death and terror, guns and hunger and for reasons that no government on earth can justify or elucidate.

In Bangkok we had drawn a mixed bag. In a basket that was brought on board I had discovered the fruit of my dreams, mangusteen. It had been ten years since I had tasted one, when we had visited Thailand in 1959. They have a thin dark brittle shell, they are sectioned like tangerines with the white translucent flesh of lichen nuts. Their flavor is unique and delicious yet they never seem to be imported into Europe or the United States.

The other cargo that had come aboard was less appetizing; a thin Chinese with ugly yellow buck teeth weighted down with guns. He entered immediately into a spirited conversation recounting his prowess in the hunt. He was returning from Nepal where, guess what? He had shot a magnificent tiger.

"Do you know," I said, "that that magnificence is in short

supply? What makes you think you have any right to help exterminate it?"

He laughed comfortably. "No, no that's not the way to look at it. I myself am a conservationist but I've wanted a tiger for a long time."

Someday it will be refreshing to meet a hunter who skips the conservationist gag and states the simple truth. "I love to kill." Diogenes himself would feel rewarded.

His act might have been less galling had the hunter himself been a fine specimen but remembering the one we had seen at Tiger Tops it was bitter to think that so superb an animal had been destroyed by this puny ugly runt thirsting for self-aggrandizement.

Norton and I had enjoyed Hong Kong when we were there in 1959 and were happy to be going back again. Our pleasure began at the airport. It was *clean* and the personnel friendly and efficient. The air unfortunately was heavy with fog and rain yet we had been lucky for we learned that the plane before us, unable to land, had had to fly on to Taiwan.

Driving to the hotel through the gloomy evening I shivered and thought how cold Hong Kong was compared to India. When we got out I realized that the car was air conditioned with the control knob turned up to glacial. I suppose the driver had been warned about the American mania for manipulating the temperature but a sense of proportion is helpful.

The Mandarin is one of the best hotels we stayed in. It does not radiate charm and coziness being a large and frankly commercial enterprise but it is admirably run by its English manager Tony Ross who personally radiates a great deal of charm. The rooms are comfortable, the food both European and Chinese very good, the service excellent and the infrequent lapses entertaining. When one morning I pointed out to Chan, our room boy, that the shoes outside our door that had been left to be polished did not belong to us he laughed delightedly. "I unnestan'. Long loom.

Long ownel," and gathering them against his chest he trotted off to what we hoped would prove to be the right room and the right owner.

From our balcony we could see the harbor and two great high-rise buildings nearby from which floated the Union Jack and the red banners of Communist China. The road bordering the harbor might have been the East River Drive in New York.

We found that in ten years much of the charm and color of Hong Kong had vanished before the onslaught of Progress but the city is prosperous and like the rest of the world the Chinese seem quite willing to sacrifice picturesqueness for financial gain. Some of the back streets still retain their character and there are junks and sampans in the harbor but Modernity, Western style, is the order of the day.

Awaiting us at the hotel were flowers and bottles of liquor from our old friends Julie and Wally Kwok. We telephoned them and Wally invited us to take a cruise around the harbor the next morning. "But I'll call you," he said. "The weather may not be good and you may want to change your minds."

He was prophetic about the weather. In fact the week we were in Hong Kong we rarely saw the sun. It rained that night and the next morning was overcast and humid but Wally was as good as his word. He called and laid Hong Kong at our feet.

"Ilka, you say you're not feeling too well. Our Chinese herbalists are very good doctors, you know. They only look at your lower eyelids and your fingernails and take your pulse and cure you. Shall I send one around?" Dubious as to the reception he would likely get from Dr. Brown I bowed out as gracefully as I could from the ministrations of the local medicine man.

"Well then, I know a masseur, an excellent masseur. Would you like to have him come over?" I have women friends who luxuriate in massage. Speaking for myself if I am going to have that much body contact I prefer a lover, this includes husbands acting as such. Still he was trying and I didn't like to seem ungracious. "Just not now, thank you, Wally. Maybe another time."

"Well now, let's see . . . Oh I know! Have I ever taken you to the naughty house with the mirrors in the ceiling?"

"Wally, listen dear, I really don't want to go to a Chinese brothel in the morning. Let's save something to look forward to. I'd *much* rather go on the cruise. You can ask Norton but I think he'd rather do the cruise too."

"Good, good," said Wally, his ebullience quite undampened. "That's what we'll do. I'll pick you up in half an hour."

While we were standing on the dock chatting with some friends he had introduced us to, an old Chinese woman leading a small child by the hand joined our group. She seemed so bright and interested in the conversation I thought possibly the child was the daughter of friends of the Kwoks and the old woman the amah who often saw them at the house. Not at all. The old lady was a beggar and when Wally slipped her a few coins, with a courteous little bow and merry smile, she and the child drifted away. A beggar yes, but with dash. Her style very different from the nagging Indians.

Over on the Kowloon side of the water long lines of people were waiting for trains to take them out to the cemeteries. It was the festival of Ching Ming, the Sweeping of the Graves, and corresponds to our Memorial Day.

Although I did not know it the first time we were there, I have since learned that the name Kowloon is an anglicized version of a Cantonese word meaning "nine dragons" and the city is called that because, to the imaginative, the hills behind it resemble a series of dragons. Hong Kong means Place of Sweet Lagoons.

When our party was assembled we went on board. To our regret, being allergic to choppy water Julie had begged off, but there were a couple of pretty English girls who worked in European offices, Mr. and Mrs. Boggs of the Parker Pen Company which does a large business in the Orient, and the Nick Healeys of Garden City, New York. The Healeys were intelligent thoughtful people much concerned with overpopulation and the vital need for birth control if civilization is to survive. They spoke so feelingly on the subject, saying how they had loved dear old Pope John and excoriating the present incumbent, that it came as a shock to learn they were Catholics with six children, some still unmarried, and already seven grandchildren. I thought ruefully, the world's oldest story: Do as I say, not as I do.

Although we had drawn a mean drizzling day the harbor was still fascinating. From a good many boats the scarlet flags of Peking whipped in the breeze, and not just one flag but seven, eight, and nine. This surfeit of patriotism was because Communist China was celebrating its ninth anniversary and boats and flags were in the British Crown Colony of Hong Kong, because England has long recognized Red China, a ploy to which we are averse. You may not like them but it seems unrealistic not to acknowledge the existence of 650,000,000 people.

Speaking for ourselves we hope the United States and China will soon reach an accommodation for it is a country we long to visit. The art, the architecture, the food, the physical beauty of much of the land and the people who are just people and not politicians, all of these we want to see and know. In Hong Kong of course one is on the threshold for the border is only twenty-five miles to the north of the New Territories, that area leased by Britain in 1898. In 1997 the lease runs out. What happens then is hard to say although many people assume it will be renewed but much will depend on the world situation at that time.

Our cruise took us to the village of Aberdeen with its great congregation of junks and sampans and two floating restaurants. Our preference was the Tai Pak although the neighboring Sea Palace has its own staunch supporters.

The Tai Pak is a gay affair, a great big houseboat painted scarlet and green with a pagoda roof, fluttering burgees and grill work balconies. Since we were already in a boat we had only to pull along side to disembark but if you go to Aberdeen by car as you step out you will be assailed by countless small cockle shells sculled by women and children competing for your trade. You can go with them for a very small fee or the restaurant's own launch will ferry you over in a couple of minutes free of charge.

The Tai Pak seafood is superb. But a word of caution! If possible go, the first time at least, with a Chinese friend who will order for you and insist that everything be freshly cooked. Some days later Norton and I returned on our own and were sadly let down by the steam table luncheon that is dished up to tourists during the week. Also should you be allergic to fish do not go at all for that is what there is to eat. Not being allergic we devoured prawns, lobster, crabs, abalone, scallops with green vegetables, snappers, fried oysters, grouper and noodles of inconceivable delicacy. That's right, we gorged. It is embarrassing to relate that that evening we dined in the grill room of the Mandarin on onion soup, minute steak and a bottle of Beaujolais and enjoyed it very much.

The next day we went to call on Mr. Austin Lee of Pan Am in an office building that would be at home on Park Avenue in New York; escalators to the first floor and then confusing banks of elevators. Mr. Lee had not come in yet but he had a pleasant and efficient Chinese receptionist. I wondered again as I so often do in New York how people endure working all day in enclosed areas in artificial light and artificial air with never a glance out the window to look at the sunshine or watch the rain.

When a few minutes had passed and Mr. Lee had not arrived we decided to return another time and took the Star Ferry over to Kowloon. I dearly love the Star Ferry and hope very much that the projected tunnel under the harbor long discussed and now, after sixty-six years of negotiation, actually to be constructed, will not force the retirement of the gallant little fleet: the Silver Star, the North Star, the Morning and Evening Stars and many, many more. For cars the tunnel will indisputably be more convenient but I would not think it could eliminate pedestrian travel. After all the two cities combined, number nearly 4,000,000 people. According to the newspapers the Ferry Syndicate was offered shares in the new venture but for reasons of its own turned them down.

Our goal on the Kowloon side was Charlotte Horstmann. We had heard of her on our first visit to Hong Kong and we had met her the previous summer when she was staying with her daughter and son-in-law who had a house near ours in the country although they live in Tokyo. It must have been a heart-warming interlude as for the first time in many years she had her three children around her at one time: the Tokyo daughter, with her two young sons, another daughter from South America with her new baby and a son who was about to go to Vietnam.

Mrs. Horstmann herself has lived a large part of her life in the Orient and in her shop has gathered together treasures from the entire East. Two that we found irresistible were a female figure of carved wood washed with softest oyster white and pale watery green holding a bird to her belly and a sturdy wood elephant with carved crimson trappings. Norton fell in love with it and since his birthday was nearly upon us the only sensible thing to do was to buy it.

Although our mouths watered we restrained ourselves from buying fourteen magnificent panels from a Hindu temple that had recently come into the shop. We refrained for a couple of fairly practical reasons. We had no place to put them and no money with which to pay for them. They were, however, very lovely; about mid-nineteenth century, painted on cloth, a sort of calico, they depicted strange slender figures, male and female with long disdainful noses and dark almond eyes, in exquisite diaphanous garments edged with gold, wandering through a green wood engaged in legato dancing and amorous pastimes.

Mrs. Horstmann and her partner were hoping to sell the series to a single purchaser, a national institution perhaps such as a museum or Mr. Stanley Marcus of Dallas.

It was after we left the Horstmann gallery that I committed a sin and was justly punished. In a nearby shoe shop I saw a handsome black lizard handbag and a lizard skin large enough to make a pair of shoes. In New York I do not buy such items. As a conservationist I disapprove of them and my disapproval is easily maintained since usually they are beyond my means. In Hong Kong the price of articles made of lizard is, in comparison, extremely reasonable. It is really marvelous how easily we sell ourselves a bill of goods. I made to myself the most spurious excuse of all; the animal's dead anyway. So he is but as long as customers keep buying skins and feathers and ivory, shopkeepers will keep ordering them and hunters and poachers will keep killing animals. There is nothing like inventory that doesn't move off the shelves to turn merchants into conservationists.

Knowing all this I still bought the bag and ordered a pair of shoes to match and I got my comeuppance. They were the most uncomfortable pair of shoes I have ever owned. To have worn them would have been to cripple myself and the handbag while elegant was far too small. Carting about glasses and notebooks, a wallet, cosmetics and keys, my marbles, fish hooks and bits of string I am a woman who needs space. A dinky bag is not my bag. That one for the most part languished in a bureau drawer and for all the pleasure or service I got from my moral lapse I might as well have torn up my money. The lizard was revenged.

After ordering the shoes and bag and before my conscience began pricking me too acutely—it went into high gear when they were delivered and didn't work—feeling a little empty we stopped in for lunch at the Peninsula Hotel. It is on the Kowloon side and Norton and I had stayed there in 1959 and although more than happy at the Mandarin we wanted to pay a visit for auld lang syne.

We found that the enormous lobby has been renovated and is now a palace of cream and gold. One of the pleasant old customs however still remains, it is also practiced at the Mandarin, and that is the paging of guests who are called to the telephone. No names are shouted above the muted clinking of tea cups and glasses. Instead bell boys pass around carrying a slate attached to a long stick. The name of the callee is written thereon, a small bell rings and at night the board lights up like a minute marquee. Every guest a star!

Later in the afternoon we took tea in Princes Arcade. The building is connected to the Mandarin Hotel by what may well be termed a Bridge of Sighs of Longing for its is lined with glorious and tempting shops with prices which, compared to home, make you think they are giving you the merchandise and the well-known slogan states an impregnable truth "You go broke saving money in Hong Kong."

I realize I have written a good deal about shops and temples and palaces and virtually nothing of night life which, as a rule, a traveler expects and wants to sample but I have two or three excuses. In many places where we were there was none and in Hong Kong where high jinks are available it rained so heavily on most evenings that leaving the hotel, finding cabs and cabarets that might have been recommended became a real chore. The third reason was me. I'm afraid India had got to me and I felt ill most of the time with little strength or ambition for nightclubbing. Pills and drugs and incantations ranging from aspirin to the arcane made no difference. My trouble was exhaustion. More than once Norton had the telephone in his hand about to make reservations on a plane home but I would not admit defeat. That ill, I insisted, I was not and here I still am, in the pink, so I was right.

However I did feel sorry for my fellow. He had been room bound long enough so one evening when he seemed restless I urged him to call Wally, who, I knew, would be delighted, and go out on the town. "Go have some fun, darling. How about that brothel with the mirrors in the ceiling? I've never seen one, you can tell me all about it." The great healer looked pained and turned down the suggestion and my feeling of guilt for keeping him from the flesh pots was somewhat assuaged when he got into bed and fell asleep the minute his head touched the pillow.

He and Wally did go off one day with two or three business-

men but I understand it was a stag luncheon with no girls popping
from pies. I lunched with Charlotte Horstmann and two or three
other women she had invited at the Crystal Palace. In case the
name conjures up something like Naranjestan, the gay and glittering folly of Shiraz or a ghostly glimmer of the pride of Victoria
and Albert the reader must disabuse himself.

Hong Kong's Crystal Palace in Cameron Road, Kowloon, just
opposite Benny's shoe shop, is in a small unimposing building, one
flight up. It is one of those little nothing places, unadorned and
with only the most utilitarian tables and chairs. Course after
course served to us was each a triumph of skill, imagination and
the highest expression of culinary art. I do not doubt that the
knowledge and guiding spirit of our hostess had a great deal
to do with the marvels set before us and possibly foreigners un-
accompanied might not fare so well, but if you have a Chinese
friend or a long time inhabitant who enjoys eating, cajole and
hound him into taking you to the Crystal Palace. Since we haven't
got all day to pique your taste buds I shall mention only tender
succulent chicken steamed in lotus leaves and duck livers sliced
paper thin and stewed in the residue of Chinese wine.

There were five of us; Charlotte Horstmann, an exuberant
young English woman married to a German, who is the New York
correspondent for *Der Stern,* an extremely attractive and beautifully dressed Chinese, myself and the American wife of one of
the senior correspondents of the New York *Times.*

Like the famed newspaper for which he worked the correspondent's lady had it all at her fingertips. She didn't have to tell
it all but we knew it was all there and she told quite a lot.

She was an authority on antique silver jewelry, on the art
treasures in the museum of Tai Pei and as each dish was set on
the table she announced which province in mainland China it
derived from.

Charlotte said the rumor was that the Communist government
was beginning to sell off some of the fabulous jewels it had confiscated and she knew of a jade necklace that was being offered

for $250,000. She herself owns a pair of pendant earrings and a ring of brilliant emerald green jade. They are very beautiful and although my ignorance of it is great I enjoy looking at fine jade but were I the Mesdames Ford, Rockefeller, Onassis, Duke, and Hutton rolled into one I would not pay $250,000 for a string of beads. Pearls possibly but they would have to be huge glowing globes which really are better placed on the generously upholstered chests of British female royalty.

That day we were relatively sociable, lunching with friends and having a cocktail with Tony Ross, manager of the Mandarin and a few people he had invited. We were in one of the top floor lounges and the light was so bright I could not see the face of a woman standing against a window. "How do you do," I said. "My name is Ilka Chase."

"I know your name is Ilka Chase," she said drily, "my name is Barbara Parsons." Barbara! She and her husband David Parsons, the head of Public Relations at Pan American, are old friends and she was on a whirlwind tour with Max Hampton the press representative for the Intercontinental Hotels which are allied with the airline and of which the Mandarin is one.

At dinner we met up with Mr. Austin Lee whom we had missed the day before. He looked young to be a Power in so far flung an enterprise as Pan American World Airways but nevertheless he was and his background was almost as international as the line he served. He considered himself Chinese but he could easily pass for a Westerner and he told us that one grandparent was Scottish and another Persian. His ancestors traveled a good deal too.

The Communist rulers of China are not characters to whom I warm but rarely have I met a normal Chinese person whom I did not like, exclusive of the tiger hunter and his normality was debatable.

A most delightful member of her race is Miss Kai Yin Lo assistant to Tony Ross and a friend of the Kwoks. One evening when we were dining with them Wally picked us up and we stopped off at her house for cocktails. She lived in a tiny flat over her parents' garage that she had furnished with gaiety and imagination. Any American girl with a similar background would have felt cozily at home. She, the Kwoks, Norton, and I lunched together one day and she proved to be a formidably well-educated young woman who had gone to school in England where for the first few weeks she anticipated dying of starvation. She sat for exams at Oxford and worked for three years in the reading room of the British Museum. Happily her brains and ability have not defeminized her. She is pretty, she has charm and she is fun to be with.

At luncheon Wally, undeterred by his lack of success the first day in selling us the herb doctor or a brothel, was still determined we should skim the cream of Hong Kong. He knew all about a special hairdresser, all his women friends were crazy about him. "You must go, dear Ilka, I will make you a present of his shampoo and set."

"Dear Wally, you are more than generous and I appreciate the offer but no matter how I may look because of the constant rain, I had my hair done yesterday."

"Oh. Well then"—this one was pitched to Norton—"how about trying a little snake spleen? The effects are extraordinary. A couple of hours after you take it the hairs on the back of your neck rise and curious hallucinations begin."

"How do they get the snake's spleen?"

"That part is fascinating. They hold the snake by the head, feel down its length for the spleen"—graphic gesture illustrating procedure—"when they find it, with a short sharp knife they *flick* it out."

I must have looked both distressed and disgusted for he hastened to reassure me. "It doesn't hurt the snake."

"It doesn't?"

"No."

"What happens to it afterward?"

"It's sold to the restaurants for snake soup."

"Oh, so it does kill it?"

"Of course it kills it, it just doesn't hurt."

The snake having flunked the course our chum next suggested a visit to a dance hall where we would meet the Chinese counterpart of the Japanese geisha girls. Norton laughed and shook his head.

"Well then how about a Chinese chiropodist?" I felt we were being uncooperative and sensing desperation I agreed to the suggestion. A chiropodist I reasoned would be preferable to a brothel or the snake spleen. Wally looked very happy. Success at last! "He uses no scissors you understand, just knives."

I swallowed. "I'm sure he's very skillful," I said. He came the next day and lived up to his billing. I even let him persuade me into having a massage, he did both jobs, and was glad I had. I append his name, address and telephone number should any Hong Kong bound reader be interested.

Lim Kin Chung

Marsh Road

Kam Kwok Mansion, 7th floor, Flat 12

Telephone 722474   730747

We had declined Wally's offer of the dance hall and geisha girls but his ebullience remained undimmed. After our return to New York we received a letter from him. "Believe it or not," he wrote, "but I have given up golf, hiking, and jogging for dancing. I take a lesson a week from a Martha Graham graduate. My repertoire at the end of six months consists of a naughty hula, a sissy hula, two warrior dances (supposed to be my best) some modern movements and, most enjoyable of all, some Japanese go-go. I practice one hour daily as soon as I wake up. Sweat like a horse. I enclose herewith a recorded snapshot showing me in one of my warrior dances."

For the reader's delectation the snap is here reproduced in black and white. What verve! What style! What elegance! Dear irrepressible Wally.

If Hong Kong does not lead the list of great shopping centers it certainly ranks very high and there are those who will contend it is peerless. All the merchandise of the world seems to be available and at prices possible for thousands of people. Every traveler naturally has his favorites but four shops that we consider outstandingly good I list below.

Charlotte Horstmann, 104 Ocean Terminal Building. She has moved from her original location to the Kowloon side, right at the ferry landing. The art objects and furniture she handles are of first quality.

Trio, in the Peninsula Court Building just behind the hotel, a reliable jeweler, sane in his prices. We had him mount the topaz Norton had given me for my birthday. Even in Hong Kong a fine jewel is not cheap but women "just looking" will see some beautiful objects and those who *can* shop in those brackets will consider they have got a bargain.

George Chen, also in the Peninsula Court. This excellent tailor for men also has a good woman's department.

Elsie Tu, 121 Chatham Road, one flight up. Miss Tu has a large and varied selection of sweaters and handbags at reasonable prices. She has a catalogue one may write for and she as well as all the other places will ship overseas.

A shopping district that exerts great magnetism, although less swank than the names listed above, is Upper Lascar Row, the famed Cat Street known and loved by all travelers to Hong Kong. In 1959 I had spent many happy mildly pauperizing hours browsing through it and one afternoon Julie and I decided the moment had come to pay a return visit. To get there one must drive up Hollywood Road, park the car near an old temple and walk down a flight of steps to a short street crowded with hurrying porters and strolling shoppers. Since our first trip I had often thought of Cat Street with affection and nostalgia but sentimental journeys are tricky. It is still there but I am older and perhaps less greedy. "Which of us has changed, Julie?" Julie smiled. "Maybe both of you a little, dear Ilka. However it is true that things are not what they used to be. Prices have gone up a great deal."

That was so. The good things were costly and there were few amusing or inexpensive trifles. It was the next day when Norton and I were wandering there by ourselves that we saw an object we both fell in love with. A cat, a small dark gray creature who although made of porcelain looked as though he had fur. He was an admirably modeled feline, I should say more curious than beautiful, but he had magnetism and we decided it would be a mistake to pass up the cat of Cat Street. We brought him home and our friends who are cat fanciers keep needling us in subtle ways hoping, I suspect, that we may be persuaded to give him up but we are standing firm. The best behaved and most loving friend will be remembered in our wills.

We returned to the hotel in a taxi of which there are now any number. By American standards they are cheap and tipping is not expected. There are still a few rickshaws and although I do not know it for a fact I should not be surprised if some of them are owned by the taxi companies and kept on for the tourist trade. The rickshaw men looked to be better fed than when we had last seen them and indeed if the prices they charge are any criterion they should be portly.

When we were there before Norton never would ride in a rickshaw, he felt it to be demeaning but I used occasionally to take them when returning tired from a bout of shopping. This time when debarking by myself from the ferry I succumbed to the ardent solicitation of a rickshaw man and explained as best I could that I wanted to go to Pedder Street which is not far from the terminal. We got there in jig time, less than five minutes, and when the man demanded his fee I nearly dropped in my tracks: forty Hong Kong dollars about $6.60 American. If I was angry he was more so. He looked at me, his eyes blazing. It made me sick to see him, panting, sweating, hating me. In the end I gave him thirty Hong Kong dollars and with a look of outrage he vanished into the crowd. So all right, I said to myself, you've given $5 to charity. I burned at being robbed and I understood why all the time we were there we saw only one Chinese riding a rickshaw. No fools they.

If rickshaw transportation is dwindling so are other customs less open to legitimate criticism. The pigtail fell into desuetude long ago but the cheong sam—those dresses with high stiff little collars and a slit almost to the hip bone on one side—have nearly vanished too and the mini skirt is as much a part of the passing scene as it is in the West.

In the back streets and among the working classes one still sees women wearing black trousers and blue or black jackets hurrying by with laden baskets dangling from a yoke over their shoulders. Babies are still carried in slings on their mothers' backs, small heads bobbing sleepily and if one follows Queen's Road he will still see perpendicular signs and buses covered with decorative Chinese characters and may still climb the narrow steep step streets lined with booths where food and buttons, stationery and jade are sold and where the family cat with a collar around its neck is tethered to a post or the leg of a stool. The family dogs look relatively well fed and despite the jokes—containing here and there a grain of truth—the Chinese do not eat them.

With the exception of the rickshaw man the Chinese whom we met casually—merchants, the hotel staff, airport personnel—all were affable and cooperative. Many Americans who live in Hong Kong and whose bailiwick, either for business or recreation is the Orient, are distressed by the foreign policy of the United States.

To a man they consider Vietnam a fearful mistake. As one of them said to us (at this time the Vietcong leader was still alive), "Ho Chi Min is a Communist, yes, but he hates the Chinese. The best thing we could have done would have been to encourage him to grow strong and to unite North and South Vietnam. He would have been a staunch bulwark against China. The Vietnamese don't want them in there, they don't want any foreigners in their country; not the Chinese, not the French, not the Americans."

"Except those who are lining their pockets," Norton said.

Our friend shrugged. "Graft is universal but those who want the best for their country aren't that way." And he went on to say, "It's hard for Americans, for any Westerner, to appreciate what 'face' means to these people. China feels she has lost face because she is not allowed in the United Nations. Also the United States' attitude that Chiang Kai-shek means anything to mainland China any more is nonsense. If Mao and Chou En-lai were to die tomorrow he would *never* get back."

On the subject of face another friend said, "Take my secretary for instance. If she makes a mistake typing a letter I never say so. I say, 'Yvonne, I obviously made a mistake in dictating, will you be good enough to retype this.' I know she's wrong, she knows she's wrong, she knows that I know that she knows but to come right out with it would be to lose face with other members of the staff. She would feel obliged to leave and I would be out a good secretary."

I'm not sure that I myself could tolerate so much pourparleying and palaver and beating about the bush, it seems a frightful waste of time. It also seems a little inhuman not to be able to say, "Good Lord what a fool I am! I did make the mistake, sorry, I'll do it over." But perhaps an Oriental employee feels that a frank admission of error would jeopardize his job. I dare say it's a matter of degree. A Westerner who might readily acknowledge a minor slip might go to great lengths to wiggle out of having a major bungle laid at his door.

Our own Chinese friends we thought singularly forthright. Certainly they were hospitable and it was with pleasure that we went to see the apartment Wally and Julie had moved into since our last visit. It was furnished with simplicity and sophistication, qualities frequently lacking in Eastern décor. They had a superb Japanese screen, a boat scene with figures dressed in the mode of A.D. 1000 approximately the period of that enchanting diary of Japanese life, *The Pillow Book of Sei Shonagon*. There were other lovely pieces, some beautiful sculpture and from a balcony one overlooked Hong Kong. The view was more or less a repetition of the one they had had from their old apartment on the Peak. Their Pekinese looked much the same too but this one's name was Chippy.

"In *The Carthaginian Rose*," Julie said, "you mentioned his predecessor. *He* was a watch dog. This one . . . someone arrives at the door and it's 'Come in, come in, this way to the family silver.'"

On another evening we drove out to Sassoon Road to dine with Dr. and Mrs. Ernest To to whom we had been given a letter of introduction by a mutual friend in New York.

Dr. To, an eminent radiologist, was about seventy. His wife, Minna, a good deal younger was half Chinese and half Austrian and she confided to us that she was expecting a friend, an Austrian with whom she had gone to school, and had not seen in forty years. "I suppose I'll recognize her though," she said laughing, "the only other couple coming is Chinese but what on earth are we going to talk about?"

I myself had had a bit of trouble recognizing Mrs. To. When we arrived Dr. To was at the door to greet us, followed by a pleasant-looking Chinese woman in black trousers and white jacket. She seemed so cordial, so pleased we were there that, although I had misgivings because of her costume, possibly she *might* be our hostess so I responded enthusiastically. Moments later Mrs. To arrived, elegant in hostess gown and pearls. Ah well, better to greet the maid than ignore the mistress.

The Chinese couple next put in an appearance and when the Austrians arrived we *all* recognized them. Though they had little English and we less German we sampled the hors d'oeuvres with international relish. Delicate pastry tidbits and something of nearly black jelly-like substance eaten with paper-thin slices of fresh ginger. These it turned out were the famous ancient eggs of legend and they were delicious.

The next morning we left Hong Kong. We had been there for six full days which I feel is the very least one should spend. Our previous visit had lasted nearly two weeks. Although it seemed to us not quite what it had been from the point of view of color and Oriental flavor, I suppose the impact is never again so fresh as the first time, it is still a magical city with much to see and savor. And if you're ordering clothes . . . well one *has* to stay long enough to have them made after all. Chinese tailors are quick but with more time the fit is better. Then there are the shops, the restaurants, the beaches, the endlessly fascinating life of the harbor and, one hopes, friends. Oh yes, at *least* a week.

There are also fascinating and on occasion heartwarming little dividends. When we were there a dear man, Mr. Victor Steiner, the managing director of Gulf Fisheries one day saw in the market a giant turtle who had been placed helpless on its back so that it could not turn over. It was captive and covered with grease. Watching it gulping for air Mr. Steiner saw tears slipping from its eyes. "I felt it was looking at me, crying for help." Not one to relish the suffering of a fellow creature Mr. Steiner asked his Chinese manager, Mr. Chan, what he could do about it. Mr. Chan's reaction was, not much. "It would cost you several thousand dollars to buy it," he said. This gave Mr. Steiner pause but he was a businessman and he approached the fisherman who held the turtle in thrall.

"Five hundred dollars," said the fisherman. One must remember these are Hong Kong dollars. Even so. About $83 U.S.

"But," said Mr. Steiner, "I don't want to buy it to sell it myself and make a profit, I only want to release it."

The fisherman looked at the helpless weeping turtle. "All right, forty dollars," and as Mr. Steiner was pulling the money from his pocket swept by compassion the man cried, "No! Twenty dollars." The deal was closed, the turtle was placed aboard one of Mr. Steiner's trawlers and returned to the open sea.

As usual the morning of our departure from Hong Kong we had to rise at dawn. Our breakfast appeared promptly at six-fifteen and at the Mandarin you do not have to call the bell captain. It's a little like being a job applicant. "Don't call us we'll call you," only the Mandarin does. "Are you ready to have us send for

your luggage, Madam?" A little army arrived and there was much
hustling about and opening and shutting of drawers to make sure
nothing had been overlooked. I would just as soon they had
waited until we had gone before they found the pornographic
paperbacks so thoughtfully left behind by Dr. Brown. His curiosity and amusement had been aroused by the literature on sale
in the lobby of the Hotel Phonecia in Beirut. "I think I'll make a
little collection," he said and along our route he was on the lookout for ever more lurid jackets and titles. Some of them he maintained were not at all badly written. By Hong Kong however he
had become jaded and tossed them into the scrap basket. "The
room boys will enjoy them."

"I can't think," I said, "they'll get much of a thrill. What can
they understand?"

"They'll get the gist," said the doctor. "Look at those glorious
covers, nothing but breasts and bottoms."

For reasons unknown to us, unless it be that Mr. Tony Ross is
a man of uncommon generosity and thoughtfulness, we were
swept off to the airport free of charge in a glistening Rolls-Royce.
Sitting in it waiting for the luggage to be stowed in the rear I
glanced out the window. Not six feet away a Chinese squatted
on his haunches between the shafts of his rickshaw. I smiled. His
expression was sardonic.

Norton and I had been in Japan before on the same trip that
had taken us to Hong Kong and while we had loved Kyoto and
the portions of the countryside we had seen we had not been too
keen on Tokyo. Still, wishing to break the long trip from Hong
Kong to New York we had decided to stop over for two or three
days.

The Pan Am flight takes about three hours and a half and the
Japanese shore line, deeply indented with bays and coves and in-
lets and jutting irregular peninsulas is provocative. The drive from
the airport to the city is long and the road has all the bucolic
charm of the Long Island Expressway at the rush hour.

Our room at the Hotel Hilton was a garden, thanks to Japanese acquaintances, and a little prodding of them by our friends Jane Grant and Bill Harris in New York, a couple who have traveled a great deal themselves and have no intention of letting their friends arrive in foreign parts with no resident to turn to.

One such resident was Mr. Yamamoto who telephoned and said he would like to come to call on us. Since I didn't feel up to much Norton went down to see him alone and on returning pronounced him a fine chap. They had fallen to talking of the war and my husband had said that the task force of which he was a member had cruised very near the Japanese mainland and Mr. Yamamoto had said, "At that time I was in New Guinea." The tenor of the exchange had been cordial, "So sorry old boy, had I been here we could have got together."

Another person we were happy to encounter was Bri Johnston, Charlotte Horstmann's daughter whom we had met the summer before on Long Island. We went to lunch with her in her charming little house with a pretty garden quite near the hotel. Bri loved it but said that after many years they would probably be leaving Tokyo to live in Hong Kong. One reason was that the house was to be torn down to make way for an apartment building and the other was the expense of life in Japan. Quite simple apartments she said were renting for $1500 and $7500 a month. We paled. Food too is very high. A dinner for four or five people can come to $100 and even breakfast at the hotel was expensive. They add a 10 percent service charge which is to be expected but on top of that comes a government tax of 15 percent.

We were joined at luncheon by Linda Beech. Her ex-husband Keyes is a correspondent who has spent a great deal of time in Vietnam. They had entertained us the last time we were in Tokyo and we had liked them both immensely and were sad when we had learned of their divorce.

Linda is a big woman and she wore a black wool leather-trimmed mini skirt, black net stockings, and leather boots. With her pale platinum hair and lavender lips she was quite striking.

Luncheon was civilized and delicious. Spanish omelet, cold chicken, salad, white wine and strawberries with brown sugar and sour cream. Afterward we went off to the Shinjuku Gardens, a sort of Central Park of Tokyo. There was a large lake, stone lanterns, a pagoda and an enormous aviary. Best of all the double cherry trees were still blooming, exquisite clouds of pink against the blue sky.

The day was chilly but clear, a welcome change from the fog and rain of Hong Kong. Couples strolled about, took pictures of each other and their children and lay together on the grass. It was a perfect urban Sunday afternoon but unfortunately closing time is four-thirty and everyone must leave, a real hardship on a beautiful day. A few, a very few women wore kimonos, the rest were in Western clothes. One reason for their popularity is that they are less expensive than the native wear. A good kimono can cost a lot. Also they are confining and they are hot, good in cold weather but uncomfortable in warm.

There is no doubt however that they are delightfully picturesque to look at. Coming into the hotel one afternoon I ran into a wedding party. The guests were all in native dress and it was like a sunlit flight of butterflies. Waitresses and elevator girls in hotels wear kimonos, the management probably hoping that this small concession to tradition will create a Japanese atmosphere for the tourist but except for occasional pockets of parks and restaurants and maybe a few small shops, Tokyo today is a huge commercial westernized city. There are I believe thousands of night spots, some small and discreet, the majority brash, colorful, vulgar and deafening. We did not investigate.

We did go to see the National Gymnasium, an extraordinary structure designed by Kenzo Tange for the Olympic games in 1964. It seats 12,000 people and 4000 can be accommodated in the annex. It is remarkable for its vast roof upheld, not by beams or girders or columns, but hanging from a ridgepole suspended on cables that run into the ground. Despite its impersonal World of the Future aspect the great roof, like a free flowing wave, turns up at the corners in a distinctly Japanese fashion.

A Japanese fashion to which I capitulated with not even token defense was the wares of the shop called Hayashi Kimonos. It is under the elevated railroad near the Imperial Hotel in the International Arcade. The stock is enormous with every size, shape, color and price. The austere ones for men are especially handsome. The authentic old ones are beautiful, some expensive but some unexpectedly reasonable and most of the modern ones are at very possible prices. We bought several for presents including a few for children in which they are irresistible. If your wee ones have to be chastised do not put them in kimonos. One look at them and stern parental intentions melt like butter on the stove.

Takashimaya, the great shopping landmark that now has branches in New York and other foreign cities, is of some interest but not exceptional. Most women however will probably want at least to wander through it so it is well to remember that it is closed on Mondays but open on Sundays.

We lunched one day at Ten-Ichi Tempura near the Ginza, Tokyo's Broadway. It is short on charm being a kind of businessman's lunch but you feel very authentic taking off your shoes on entering so as not to soil the tatami, sitting with your feet in a hole while a smiling old chef prepares fresh hot delicious tidbits. Japanese beer is very good and for a stomach in turmoil warm saki is soothing.

A steak restaurant to be recommended is Misono. I believe there is more than one Misono restaurant but this one is opposite the Tokyo Broadcasting Station. It was Bri who suggested it and remembering the unbelievably tender Kobe beef we had had before in Japan we willingly followed her advice. She had not misled us. Also it is pretty. One looks out the window into the little garden to see red lanterns like balloons bobbing in the breeze.

Afterward we dropped into the Pokan, a tiny bar the size of a dressing room where healthy girl singers with leather lungs used microphones to make themselves heard. My own eardrums are obviously an anachronism in today's world. They do not tolerate the roaring, shrieking and pounding that are now the indispensable means of communication.

A third excellent meal we owed to Mr. David Jones the director of the Tokyo Pan Am office. This short dark-haired dynamo and shrewd observer took us to the pork specialty place, Ton Katsu in the Ueno district of the city.

He enjoys his job and he enjoys Japan but he is candid in his appraisals and said he considered *Japan Unmasked* a book written by the Japanese ambassador to the Argentine to be a thoughtful and impartial commentary. The ambassador incidentally was called home for his trouble. Recalling some of his own experiences Mr. Jones observed that the Japs are always pulling poor mouth but that they are terribly tough in any business deal.

From his locker David Jones also pulled a pair of seats to the Takarazuka, the famous all-girl theatre of Tokyo. It has an all girl audience too. Norton and another American were the only men. It was as we remembered it; a huge stage, mindless entertainment and spectacularly brilliant.

Again the amplification was terribly loud and the choreography listless but the costumes were lovely, many of them adaptations of old provincial dress and wonderful in color. Our particular show was *A Sketch of Japan's Festivals.* Lanterns and dragons and monkeys, planting rice shoots and twirling parasols.

The program is helpful, giving you thumb-nail sketches of what is happening. "The impression of festivals of various regions of Japan, closed up and dramatized." "People worshipping a shrine followed by songs of festivals for a while?" "In sharp contrast to the dance of the previous scene which was of the feminine this one is of the masculine."

The cogent reason for our return visit to the Takarazuka however was not for the vaudeville of the first half of the afternoon but for the performance that took place after the intermission: the all-girl singing version of *Hamlet*. We reasoned that even Joseph

Papp, no slacker when it comes to taking liberties with the classics, was hardly likely to put on anything as tantalizing as that.

As the program states the production is "From the works of William Shakespeare in 20 scenes." The title role was played by the same young lady who had been the leading man in the Festival Sketches. She was tall and lean and beautifully costumed in black velvet, the trappings and the suits of woe relieved, rather unfortunately I felt, by modern white shoes.

The Prince of Denmark was referred to as Homelette which sounded like a Cockney describing his breakfast but let us not quibble, the production was sincere if unconventional and obviously cost a sum that might well have staggered Broadway.

The curtains parted on the battlements of Elsinore veiled by scrim, with ominous clouds rolling over them and shrouded gray figures wafting through columns and archways. It looked more like the heath of Macbeth but the general impression was indubitably one of mystery and foreboding and the ghost was a figure at once magnificent and eerie glittering in gold and silver armor enveloped in the clouds of steam that curled up around him.

With the hall of state scene the mood changed abruptly to one of splendor, the whole court blazing in gold and crimson costumes of the Renaissance.

Later on, getting the bad news from Dads about the poison in his ear, Homelette fell over backwards in a dead faint, very skillful bit of calisthenics, and on coming to sliced off the head of an unoffending flower with his sword and broke into song.

Ophelia when her turn came sang Hamlet's letter and when he appeared he was accompanied by villain music. She rose from the greensward and they did a little pas de deux. Very pretty.

Polonius was a big hit and there was a lot of him and we enjoyed the play within a play but as there had been no previous scene between Hamlet and the actors matters grew a little confused but nobody minded, and the Player King costumed like a demon was splendid as he poured the poison into Claudius's ear. The closet scene was crowded with gray witches and unidentifiable characters with tight helmets and long gauzy skirts and that, understandably, ended the first act. I am afraid our stamina gave out and as it was then nearly half past eight we did not wait for the second.

As though that were not treat enough the next day was Norton's birthday and Bri had thoughtfully arranged a little party.

The first time we had been to see her she had called for us. This time she was busy with preparations so the doorman of the hotel called her house, got directions from her maid, relayed them to the taxi driver who after a few false starts deposited us successfully at her doorstep. Two or three other friends were there including Linda Beech. We had champagne for the birthday boy and Bri gave him a beautiful book on Japanese gardens and Linda presented an amusing example of folk art: koke, small stones painted with faces, some serene some forbidding. They may be purchased in a shop called Shimuras.

We dined at Seryna a restaurant where they serve only crab but what crab! In honor of the occasion Bri had persuaded them to go far enough afield to include a cake and Norton and I agreed that we would long remember this year's birthdays, falling as they did in such exotic places.

As matters turned out he had two for the next day, homeward bound, we roared off into the sunrise crossing the international dateline en route, and he, good man, was born anew.

Travelers Tips

1 Keep your passports and vaccinations up to date. Who knows when opportunity may knock?

2 Make a list of people to call before leaving home. Man to take down, clean and store curtains. Also rugs. Man to repair furniture. Head off milk man. Stop papers. Car on dead storage. Suspend insurance. Etc.

3 Make a packing list starting at the top of your head descending to the soles of your feet; supplies for the care of the person. A systematic checkup at the start saves time and frustration later on.

4 Despite tags on the outside lay a paper or card with your name and next address on top of your clothes inside your suitcases. That way, should the tags get ripped off you still have a chance of getting your luggage.

5 Equip each member of the family of writing age with his own pen for filling out the countless forms dispensed by officials. Explain to the younger members that they are not to make jokes.

6 Find out from your travel agent who is his correspondent in foreign parts. Should any hitch occur it is good to know where to turn.

7 Cold statistic to remember. Travel always costs more than you anticipate. Unexpected contingencies arise. Be prepared.

8   Keep a little American money in small bills in your wallet. Use it sparingly as you probably pay more in dollars than you would in native currency but it is always negotiable in an emergency.

9   Register typewriters in your passport.

10   Re cameras: Register cameras in your passport.

In allotting your budget include cost of film and developing of same. It's a big item. Also make some allowance for postage which can balloon unexpectedly.

The native residents of many countries are shy birds reluctant to pose. If you can manage a Polaroid and make them the dazzling present of a picture of themselves they will more willingly let you get a permanent record with a conventional camera.

Even if a color fiend have some black and white film for late day shots.

A camel's hair or sable air brush to blow dust from the lens is an invaluable aid.

If you are going to places where you can have color film developed take along a hand viewer. Admiring your masterpieces is fun and a grand way to pass the time on long flights.

11   When coping with letters of introduction make a double list. On one side the people to whom you are sending the letter with a covering one of your own. On the other the name of the person who gave it to you.

This is especially important in Asia and Africa where names bear little relation to the sounds you are accustomed to and where telephonic communication is often faulty. The name of your mutual friend gives you a clue as to who they are should they phone you.

12   If you have difficulty sleeping on soft or sagging beds consider a lightweight folding board that fits in the bottom of your suitcase. It may be a nuisance, it can also be a lifesaver.

13   Take a small stiff nail brush. Invaluable for scrubbing collars and cuffs of drip-dry shirts.

14   Pack washcloths.

15 Carry creams and lotions in small containers rather than in one large one. Thus, as they get used up they can be discarded.

16 Take a couple of small bottles or flasks. Plastic are the lightest but they can affect the taste of liquor yet you will need something when the residue from a large bottle is too much to leave behind while not enough to make toting the parent bottle worthwhile.

17 There are bound to be slack moments, sometimes depressing ones. Have a few paperbacks handy including a hair-raising murder or two. They will tide you over the bad spots.

If you are game people cards and traveling chess and checker sets may be welcome in the evenings especially when the light is inadequate for reading. Needlepoint addicts will want a small piece of work in hand.

18 Take a flashlight. One you can set on a table for reading or writing is a good idea.

19 Pack a Do Not Disturb sign. Some hotels have them some do not, but English is spoken over a large portion of the globe and the message usually gets through.

20 Take matches. They are available but they are never where you are and you have to buy them. In Africa they are more precious than pearls.

21 Take hangers either inflatable or the folding kind. No hotel ever has enough.

22 Pack Scotch tape, labels, and a few manila envelopes. They are good for sending home scarves, handkerchiefs, postcards, catalogues, etc.

23 Pack a hobby when you go. Seeing the world is marvelous but if besides what may be termed the automatic sights . . . museums, palaces, churches and the countryside itself one has a special interest, enjoyment can be greatly enhanced. Schools, old carriages, boatyards, markets, musical instruments . . . It doesn't matter what. A hobby is fun.

24 Try to hold on to a sense of values. New impressions will

be flooding in on you and strangers will be giving you information you cannot always check. Common sense is as valuable on a journey as it is at home.

25 When traveling abroad if you see something you yearn for and can afford it at all, buy it. If you don't you'll regret it all your life.

26 When you get home you'll be tired and excited by being back. Try to keep twenty-four hours for readjustment. Forty-eight are better.

Special Travel Tips for the South Seas, Australia, New Zealand, and Africa can be found in two other of my books, *Second Spring and Two Potatoes* and *The Varied Airs of Spring.*